The Soap Opera Paradigm

The Soap Opera Paradigm

Television Programming and Corporate Priorities

James H. Wittebols

ROWMAN & LITTLEFIELD PUBLISHERS, INC.
Lanham • Boulder • New York • Toronto • Oxford

10742520013

ROWMAN & LITTLEFIELD PUBLISHERS, INC.

Published in the United States of America
by Rowman & Littlefield Publishers, Inc.
A wholly owned subsidiary of The Rowman & Littlefield Publishing Group, Inc.
4501 Forbes Boulevard, Suite 200, Lanham, MD 20706
www.rowmanlittlefield.com

PO Box 317, Oxford OX2 9RU, UK

British Library Cataloguing in Publication Information Available

Library of Congress Cataloging-in-Publication Data
Wittebols, James H.
  The soap opera paradigm : television programming and corporate priorities / James H. Wittebols.
    p. cm.
  Includes bibliographical references and index.
  ISBN 0-7425-2001-3 (cloth : alk. paper) — ISBN 0-7425-2002-1 (pbk. : alk. paper)
  1. Soap operas—United States—History and criticism. 2. Television broadcasting of news—United States. I. Title.
  PN1992.8.S4W57 2004
  791.45'6—dc22

                               2004003352

Printed in the United States of America

∞™ The paper used in this publication meets the minimum requirements of American National Standard for Information Sciences—Permanence of Paper for Printed Library Materials, ANSI/NISO Z39.48-1992.

Contents

Contents

Acknowledgments

In the course of this project, many individuals were helpful in creating this book. My colleague Brian Murphy has been a source of encouragement and helpful critique.

My students in the 2003 Senior Seminar course were helpful with the research in chapter 3—Rossi Carron, Adrianna Curcio, Amy Davidzik, Nick Dentice, Megan McNerney, Carrie Ward, and Wendy Zehder; and chapter 7—Eric Cotton, Bridget McErlane, and Sarah Piechuta. Kristina Costanzo helped conduct the reliability study for the data in chapter 5.

The resources and help from the Niagara University Library staff were crucial in securing some hard-to-find sources and books. The research in this book was also made possible by a Summer Research grant and an academic year grant from the Niagara University Research Council. Funds from the academic year grant were used to procure videotapes of network news from the Vanderbilt Television News Archive at Vanderbilt University, which led to the evolution of news study. Chapters 5 and 6 are based on that research.

A section of chapter 7 (pp. 133–42) is presented here in revised form with the permission of The Kent State University Press. It originally appeared in the Press's *Media Profit and Politics: Competing Priorities in an Open Society* (2003).

This project never would have been completed without the gracious and helpful assistance of Kathy Sydor. Her work helped to ensure the organization of the manuscript and the accuracy of the tables presented in chapter 5, and she helped build the extensive references for this book.

Finally, I would have never kept my wits about me if it weren't for Sandino, my canine companion. Long walks helped to clear my head, and his wonderful spirit helped maintain mine.

Though I am indebted to all these folks and others who were helpful over the last three years, if there are any errors in facts, the responsibility for the ideas and data presented here is mine alone.

Introduction

The last quarter century has seen a great deal of change in the way television and the mass media in general have evolved. Increasing concentration of ownership, enabled by deregulation of the broadcast media industries and the expansion of cable television to nearly every corner of the United States, has resulted in a shift of the mission of the television industry farther away from a public service orientation to an almost exclusive concern with garnering profit for a conglomerate parent company.

While this development has been decried by many analysts and critics of the media system in the United States, and many of these criticisms have dealt with the increasing lack of diversity in the media, analyses of how this lack has changed what appears on the television screen have largely concerned themselves with how the parent company's interests are promoted and/or protected by media producers. While it is important to know how, for example, Disney uses ABC programs to promote film and music products also owned by Disney or whether reporters at ABC News are allowed to explore stories that may cast a shadow on the Disney reputation, there are other dimensions of the relationship between concerns with profitable television and the programs produced to meet that goal.

This book is largely focused on how the shift from a public service orientation to a concern with the bottom line has affected the manner and mode of storytelling that occurs on television. Several questions are dealt with throughout the book: Is there a form of storytelling that corresponds or meshes with the primary concern of garnering profit for the larger media conglomerate? Are there ways of making television programs that are cheaper to produce yet effective at drawing large audiences for exposure to advertisements, the primary vehicle for producing profit? How does storytelling, especially in media environments defined as "news," affect the way the world is presented to audiences and what those audiences then think about the world they live in?

Fictional programs, news, other program genres, and even advertising all in one way or another tell a story. Storytelling is as old as human culture and reflects a society's values and mores. This book argues that a particular form of storytelling has increasingly overtaken other forms of storytelling on television over the last few decades, and that this storytelling form serves well the priorities of media conglomerates. The soap opera, or more largely, serial storytelling, has emerged as the dominant guide by which stories are told on television, regardless of whether we are looking at news, prime time programming, or the presentation of sporting contests. Though the serial form has been around since the invention of mass communication in the form of newspapers and books, soap operas came on the scene during the infancy of television's broadcasting parent, radio. This book looks at how the early decision making surrounding how to govern and use what was then a powerful new medium made soap opera storytelling a logical consequence. Soap operas are regarded as the commodity form of a private broadcasting system that won out over public service interests in the 1920s and early 1930s, thus ensuring that commercial interests and values would dominate American broadcasting for decades to come.

The logic on which this book is based can be summarized as follows:

1. The past fifteen years have seen unprecedented consolidation of media industries. The convergence of media and television industries under the larger umbrella of conglomeration has fully integrated television into the larger corporate structure. This development has moved television programming farther and farther from a public service orientation to a more narrow focus on corporate profitability and promotion of a consumer society.
2. Soap opera storytelling is regarded as the commodity form of television and is its most profitable genre. Stories in soap opera formats are organized in ways designed to develop and maintain audience interest.
3. The focus on profit has moved television operations to adopt characteristics of soaps as a way of developing large and loyal audiences. This orientation has transformed programming in just about all television genres—news and public affairs shows, sports programming, prime time programming, "reality" television—into ongoing soap operas.

While the rationale for the derivation of the five elements of soap opera storytelling that serve the needs of profitable accumulation is fully discussed in chapter 2, they are presented here in brief to provide an overview of how they manifest themselves in a variety of television genres.

Seriality: A soap's most distinguishing characteristic is its continuity from one program to the next. Suspension of stories until the next episode is a primary element in developing audience loyalty.

Real-time orientation: Soaps reflect an everyday world in which events flow as seamlessly as possible to create an air of realism. This is designed to give the audience a sense of immediacy. As they reflect the larger culture's calendar, they provide a parallel to the viewer's own world.

Seeming intimacy: This element fosters a sense of involvement or spectatorship for the audience without actually being there. Viewers can become a "fly on the wall" in the world of soaps, as soap storytelling brings viewers into the minds of the cast of characters inhabiting a soap community.

Story exposition: The manner in which stories are presented to audiences allows them to gain a sense of omniscience by grasping the overall set of relationships in the story. Through multiple perspectives on a story, the audience comes to feel a greater command of an issue or situation than do the characters in the soap world.

Characteristics of the soap stories: Three subelements help define the types of themes found in soap operas: conflict and/or chaos, good and evil characters, and generally presenting a materially comfortable upper-middle-class existence.

Examples from a number of television genres presented below are meant to show how these elements provide a guide for the programs to be analyzed here and serve to illustrate how soap opera storytelling has found its way into many other television program genres. These examples are elaborated throughout the chapters to follow.

Seriality is typified by suspension—mini-cliffhangers before ad breaks suspend a story line, and the cliffhanger at the end suspends the episode. The mini-cliffhangers in most prime time fictional programming are a classic device for keeping the audience from switching channels during ad breaks. Cliffhangers at the end of episodes are a way of building brand loyalty as viewers get teased in network promos throughout the week leading up to the next episode.

The rise of prime time soaps over the last two decades is the best example of how the soap as a daytime serial has moved into non-daytime programming. As discussed in chapter 8, the growth of prime time serials closely parallels the explosion in media mergers and consolidation. The rise in prime time serials in the mid-1980s is paralleled by a movement toward industry integration with larger corporate concerns. Other prime time shows, especially sitcoms, while not explicitly serial, also embody serial elements in terms of character and relationship developments.

News programs use teasers in much the same way as fictional programming—promoting the eleven o'clock news in the guise of news breaks. Often the complete story is known at the time of the tease but is not revealed by the anchor. During the newscast, ad breaks are used to tease upcoming items. Sports broadcasting can be seen as a never-ending series of episodes—the results of one game create implications for the next one (or next week's) to be broadcast. Seriality is also embodied in sports rivalries; what happened in the last contest is speculated to have a role in the next meeting.

The real-time orientation found in soaps is present in several other genres. News has a natural affinity for a real-time orientation. The emphasis on giving the viewers the sense of being there can be found in how local television news uses its capability for live remotes when there is no real rationale for doing so. Often, going out "live" to the reporter in the field during a news show occurs after the event being reported has long since finished. Sensational live coverage in local news (especially high-speed chases in large cities like Los Angeles) has allowed viewers to "look in" as authorities frequently fail to subdue a homicidal or suicidal individual. Sports events in themselves have a real-time orientation; commentary during the game helps bring shifting story lines, changes in momentum and score, and so on. The "narrated" element of live sports, the reality constructed by "expert analysis," provides a heightened sense of drama beyond the natural drama of the clock or score.

Soaps generate a sense of intimacy through interpersonal discourse and audience involvement in the show. The voyeuristic nature of "reality based" shows like *Cops* can be seen as exemplifying the devolution of public affairs programs. What many call the tabloidization of news can be attributed to the infusion of soap opera values and techniques in how news stories are covered and what kind of stories news programs now focus on. The last decade has brought a series of stories given wide play in "serious" network news environments that in earlier years would not have gotten much coverage. Personal tragedies offering looks into the lives of the often less-than-famous have become regular fare in television news. The Tonya Harding/Nancy Kerrigan skating scandal, the John and Lorena Bobbitt genital mutilation incident in the 1990s, and the Jon Benet Ramsey and Laci Peterson murder investigations more recently are just a few of the kinds of stories that have become prominent on television news. And of course the O. J. Simpson murder trial and the Clinton–Lewinsky scandal are in a class by themselves. Other, less-protracted sensational stories reflect numerous instances of mass voyeurism that squeeze out more serious issues in the news.

As an element of interpersonal talk about sports, sports call-in shows offer the opportunity to vilify players not doing well and project future "story lines" given the team's most recent performance. The flourishing of fantasy sports leagues allows fans to construct their ideal team and live and die with the consequences. In news, the growth of "journalist talk" shows and segments in shows can be seen as similar to the function of soap publications and websites offering a "behind the scenes" perspective that is supposed to help explain what's going on beneath the surface.

One of the more striking ways soap storytelling has influenced other kinds of television is in how stories are presented in news programs. A TV news story often serves to give viewers a sense of omniscience. Global crises now are covered by technological hops throughout the world. Multiple points of view are given by coverage rotating from the White House to the Pentagon to the State Department and perhaps to the United Nations or another country, similar to how soaps' redundant exposition of the latest plot twist enables surveying all characters' reactions.

Finally, the themes of storytelling in soaps dovetail with some of the basic priorities of news. The world of governance is similar to the soap world; conflict between parties or within parties is a prime ingredient of most political news stories. This orientation to news takes political news out of the policy arena and reframes politics as an interpersonal squabble. Tests of power and exchanges of threats are put in the context of the battle for the control of public opinion. Conflict and chaos are a big part of sports reporting as well, whether concerning on or off the field activities (contract disputes, strategic philosophies, interpersonal conflict, and criminal behavior). The emergence of twenty-four-hour sports news cable channels requires that time be filled with news, and contemporary television news is by definition focused on conflict and chaos.

Often the delineation and portrayal of the actors involved in the news reduce the personalities and issues to a stark good guy/bad guy orientation. Coverage of foreign affairs usually begins by identifying good guys and bad guys in ways that mostly follow the perspective of U.S. foreign policy. While not as clear in domestic politics, there is a general consensus that at least one strong challenger to the named "frontrunner" must emerge in the presidential primary season—this is necessary to give the primary season an edge of conflict and thus something to report. Television sports seems to thrive on an ever-rotating cast of good guys and bad guys. Outrageous behavior (on and off the field) and showing anger at the press are just two examples of how good guys and bad guys are labeled. Likewise, these scenarios can involve redemption as a player comes back from drug habits, has a religious conversion, or plays so well that the player's negative off-field lifestyle or behavior is overlooked.

Finally, the world of television is an affluent world, and when less-affluent elements are presented, it is through the perspective of an upper-middle-class worldview. This characteristic is so pervasive in television that it becomes a given—indeed, it is the rare deviation from this that is noteworthy. Stock market reports appear constantly on twenty-four-hour news services even though just less than half the households in the United States have any money directly in stocks or mutual funds. The world of sports is a world of rich celebrity. Rags-to-riches stories in sports are common and serve to project the idea that hard work gains rewards. The fictional world of prime time television is a solidly upper-middle-class world. While the characters in *Friends* may appear as regular folks in Manhattan, none of their work lives in the real world would afford the expansive living spaces they occupy on television.

The rest of this book puts more flesh on these skeletal ideas as it examines the history of the soap opera, the evolution of television as a commercial cultural force in American society, how television news has changed in the era of media conglomeration, and how the soap opera paradigm has influenced a whole host of program formats present in today's television world. This book argues that the emphasis on profit to the diminution of social and aesthetic values has had an effect on the creative process behind television programming and has resulted in a sameness to all television programs regardless of the particular genre.

The book's general theme is that television programming increasingly has been driven by the ongoing evolution of television as a vehicle for corporate profit (as opposed to a vehicle for education and artistic expression and enlightenment). The critical analysis of the political economy of the television industry's influence on programming, which is the focus of this book, provides for a better understanding of the values and priorities guiding the construction of new television programs and formats.

Part I of this book presents the full rationale for the soap opera paradigm in chapters 1 through 3. An overview of the history of television in terms of its full incorporation as an integral part of American capitalism is followed in chapter 2 by an examination of the soap opera phenomenon. It addresses the importance of the soap opera in the evolution of American network radio as well as a fuller explication of five soap opera elements that serve as the foundation for the soap opera paradigm. Chapter 3 details the World Wrestling Entertainment corporation's particular "genius" in using soap opera techniques to create a multiprogram, multiple revenue stream system of making money. For our purposes, it stands as a prototype for how the soap opera paradigm operates.

Part II deals with the world of television news and its evolution as the primary means by which most Americans inform themselves about the world beyond their everyday experience. Chapter 4 looks at the history of network television news. How news programs changed from 1970 to 2000 is the subject of chapter 5. Chapter 6 presents a case study analysis of how coverage of natural disasters has come to reflect the soap opera orientation. Chapter 7 analyzes the particular ways in which campaign reporting has taken on soap opera storytelling characteristics.

Part III deals with analyses of several other program genres. The growth of prime time soaps is the subject of chapter 8. Chapter 9 examines how the most unlikely reality TV show, *Boot Camp*, still ends up as a soap opera. Chapter 10 looks at how live sports and the proliferation of sports programming in cable television embody soap opera storytelling elements. The book concludes with a review of its findings and presents implications for where the television industry may be headed.

I

THE SOAP OPERA
PARADIGM AND THE
TELEVISION INDUSTRY

Broadcasting systems do not just pop up overnight or change with lightning zeal. They are the product of a struggle of competing forces and values, with identifiable winners and losers. The particular evolution of television in the United States is a story of continuing, effective pressure by private broadcasting interests, which have moved the medium away from promoting social and aesthetic values toward an almost exclusive identification with larger business concerns and the parent company's bottom line. As chapter 1 illustrates, a consistent campaign by private broadcasting interests resulted in a television industry that would move television programming from modest public interest requirements to an almost complete deregulation of the industry, with little concern for social values.

The early years of radio illustrate this clearly, as its initial orientation toward public service programming devoid of commercial messages in the mid-1920s quickly gave way to a commercial takeover once private broadcasting concerns had successfully prevailed in the public arena of representative government. This early success in determining the direction of broadcasting brought about the invention of the soap opera as a program genre meant to entertain homemaking wives during the day while also supplying numerous commercial messages for household products. Chapter 2 addresses the evolution of the soap opera genre and presents an analysis of the characteristics of soaps that make them so attractive for commercial purposes. Soap opera storytelling has become television's most profitable genre and as such has increasingly served to influence numerous other television genres.

Chapter 3's look at the world of televised wrestling via the evolution of World Wrestling Entertainment (WWE) provides a prototype example of how the soap opera paradigm functions at the program level. Readers are shown how, through a combination of story lines about wrestling and a multiplicity of revenue streams that are constantly promoted during WWE programming, soap opera storytelling serves the interests of garnering loyal audiences and solid profit margins. While the soap opera has been regarded by some as a uniquely "feminine" form of storytelling, chapter 3 illustrates that it works quite well for the young and primarily male audience drawn to the numerous WWE programs aired weekly.

In presenting the argument for the viability of the soap opera paradigm, part I provides a global look at why television has come to increasingly rely on soap opera storytelling in virtually all forms of programming. As such, it sets the stage for the rest of the book, which demonstrates how soap storytelling influences the world of news, dramatic, reality, and sports programming.

1

The Evolution of the
Television Industry

/ The evolution of television in the United States is, at its core, an example of how what was initially regarded as a public resource ended up as a system that increasingly serves private interests whose primary goal is profit, not public service./It is a story reaching back about eighty years, born in the debate over what purposes radio technology was to serve. The precedents established in that debate set the stage for how television would be organized and the values around which it would be focused.

The development of the soap opera during the radio era as a result of corporate interests winning that debate signaled the use of the medium to serve commercial interests as opposed to the larger public good. The term "soap opera" first emerged in the early days of radio as the private interests that prevailed in the debate sought ways to bring programming to American households throughout the day. This chapter looks at the long development of the commercial broadcasting system from its roots in radio to its full integration with larger media companies and links to the larger world of capitalism. Chapter 2 looks more specifically at the invention and evolution of soap opera storytelling.

The efforts of private interests to secure as much control over the airwaves as they could can be typified in several stages. The first stage consists of corporate interests seeking, through both policy making and distribution of broadcast licenses, to abrogate or limit the portion of the spectrum explicitly dedicated to the public interests of the day. Once the territory of radio was demarcated, the corporations comprising the radio industry then sought to define the degree to which radio would contribute to democratic governance and be required to fulfill the public service

values written into broadcast law./Well into the television era, broadcasting and later cable interests increasingly sought to curtail the government's role as a "traffic cop" of the industry. The final phase, encompass-
ing the last fifteen to twenty years, has seen industry interests
reconsolidate to close off new challenges to the corporate domination of
both wireless and wired forms of mass communication./The rest of this
chapter examines these trends as a way of mapping the structure of the
tele-vision industry's values over this time. The evolution of these values
provides markers for the development of the soap opera paradigm as it
has increasingly influenced the content of television from the 1980s onward.

THE EARLY DAYS OF RADIO:
WHO OWNS THE AIRWAVES?

Almost from the start, corporate influence over the development and
function of radio was enabled by a government seeking to ensure U.S.
preeminence over the airwaves on a global basis. The U.S. government facilitated the development of radio technology by organizing a monopoly
to secure patents for broadcast and reception. A U.S. government–
organized consortium of companies, eventually called the Radio Corporation of America (RCA), purchased the radio patents of the primary competition to U.S. interests, British Marconi. Corporate interests, in the form
of early global companies such as United Fruit, saw radio as an essential
factor in managing, rationalizing, and coordinating their numerous operations around the world. The U.S. military also saw radio as a significant
advance in managing an increasingly globally focused military projection
and saw radio signals as virtually invulnerable to attack in comparison to
the wired technology of the telegraph. After its exclusive use of radio in
World War I, the U.S. government was less able to argue for a state monopoly over the medium and began to accede to the demands of powerful corporate interests to loosen the reins on the military's control of radio.
The formation of RCA in 1919 (a joint effort of GE, Westinghouse, American Marconi, and later AT&T) was devised to buy the patents owned by
British Marconi to enable the domination of radio by U.S. corporate interests (Kellner 1990; McChesney 1993; McDonald 1990).

    This "foot in the door" enabled almost immediately the establishment
of commercial radio as AT&T led the way in developing "toll" broadcasting: leasing airtime to private interests and leasing telephone lines as a
means of putting together "networks" of stations. At this point, there was
general agreement that the airwaves were a public resource to be managed for the common good. In these early days, radio advertising as we

know it today was scarcely in existence. "Sponsorship" was signaled to audiences through a mere mention of the sponsor, with little "pitch" to listeners (Smulyan 1994). At this point, the public service values to which even politicians paid at least lip service seemed to dampen any explicit form of advertising. There was a strong representation of nonprofit and noncommercial interests seeking to use radio for educational, spiritual, and public interests. In 1925, 128 college radio stations and almost an equal number of other nonprofit stations were broadcasting. This meant corporate control of the airwaves was not a certain thing, and in many cases the ensuing debate over how to organize and use radio broadcasting required corporations to at least pay lip service to the public interest (McChesney 1993, 13–15).

By the mid-1920s the first commercial networks had been established. In 1926 NBC was created by RCA after buying AT&T's broadcasting interests, and the next year would see the establishment of CBS. NBC's two networks—red and blue—allowed it to establish its identity very quickly. The red network was composed of stations from larger cities, while the blue network was heard mostly in smaller cities. The proliferation of stations run by commercial, nonprofit, and even "amateur" radio operators led to signal interference among them and brought about legislation that created the Federal Radio Commission (FRC) in 1927 to serve as a traffic cop for distributing and regulating broadcast licenses. The FRC's requirement of higher technical standards for radio broadcasting put many educational stations out of business. Many of these stations were bought out by commercial interests and, although they promised to continue educational programming, they gradually diminished its role in the broadcast day (Sterling and Kitross 1990).

The establishment of the FRC by the U.S. government began the debate over the function and purpose of radio in the United States. The legislation creating the FRC stated that radio should serve the "public interest, convenience and necessity," the meaning of which would become a source of debate for many years. Until the revision of the FRC in the 1934 Federal Communications Act, a debate about what purposes radio should serve found commercial and noncommercial interests squaring off.

Ultimately, the debate over the role of the public interest in radio centered on pending legislation called the Hatfield–Wagner Amendment. This amendment would have required that 25 percent of broadcast licenses be allocated to noncommercial interests. Educational, labor, church, farming, and other civic interests wanted to ensure that this profound medium would go beyond the self-interest of commercial broadcasters and guarantee that part of the spectrum would serve the public good. Despite attempts to organize and coalesce these interests, Hatfield–Wagner was not passed, and the legislation creating the Federal

Communications Commission, passed in the same year, failed to contain specific language mandating a part of the spectrum for the nonprofit groups. Instead, the act merely required the Federal Communications Commission (FCC) to "study" the proposal for allocating a percentage of the spectrum to noncommercial interests (Kellner 1990; McChesney 1993).

By 1930, six hundred radio stations were reaching about 40 percent of American households, and radio was assuming an increasing importance in American life (Czistrom 1982). But its escapist fare and commercial underpinnings were alarming to those who believed it should serve higher purposes of education and enlightenment. The soap opera arrived on radio during this period. While the term "soap opera" was not coined until 1933, the prototype soap came on the air in 1929—*The Goldbergs*. These daytime programs were an attempt to extend the broadcast day and reach homemakers, who even during the Great Depression were making many purchasing decisions. Serial dramas during the day were fifteen minutes long from 1932 to 1933, and the frequency of each episode increased from three to five days per week during this period (Sterling and Kitross 1990). Use of the "commodity form" of storytelling accelerated when corporate concerns won the debate over radio through the 1934 FCC act. The process of creating soap operas and how they became mainstays of radio programming are discussed more fully in chapter 2.

Those groups representing public interests lost a battle not only with the commercial broadcasting interests of the day but with a whole set of industries being created to promote a consumer society. Early reluctance to do much advertising beyond mentioning sponsors quickly gave way to more open forms of advertising as corporate control was secured. Advertising-supported programming emerged on the commercial networks in 1928–1929. Dollars spent on radio advertising went from 2 percent of all advertising (across all media) in 1928 to 11 percent in 1932 (Sterling and Kitross 1990). Advertising agencies that promoted emerging national brand names were supplying radio networks with much of their advertising revenue. Many programs were themselves creations of advertising agencies and, as in the case of soaps (see chapter 2), established early forms of product placement in programming and endorsements by celebrities and actors in programs. Radio's emergence as a major medium during the Depression provided "cheap" entertainment by virtue of commercial sponsorship and was embraced by masses of people seeking respite from the daily grind of trying to make ends meet. Through the system of advertising and the development of the soap opera genre, the corporate media began to take on the character of what corporate media so amply display today.

Thus, by the mid-1930s the commercial imprint on radio broadcasting had been established and the debate over the use of the airwaves, while continuing to pay lip service to serving public needs, had been more or less won by corporate interests of GE, Westinghouse, and others. They won out over AT&T in the battle to dominate radio broadcasting when AT&T cast its lot with exclusive control over telephone lines. The NBC and CBS networks would establish dominance in radio, though a few other lesser networks established themselves over time.

NO SYNERGY DESIRED?
RADIO AND OTHER MEDIA OF THE TIMES

Though media today like to capitalize on opportunities to create synergy with cross-media programming and promotional schemes, this was not the case in the radio days. There was substantial resistance to radio from the other mass media of the day; the film studios in Hollywood and newspapers across the country were often hostile to radio. Many studios forbade the stars they had under contract from appearing on radio for fear that people would stay at home and listen to radio instead of going to the movies. And while newspapers were often investors or partners in local radio stations, they used these stations to promote their papers rather than to extend their news operations to the radio airwaves. Even the Associated Press agreed to provide news for free to radio stations and networks as long as those stations did not establish their own news-gathering departments (Hayward 1997; Czistrom 1982; Kellner 1990). This changed during World War II, when radio news and reporting emerged as a major vehicle for bringing news about the war to the American public. Radio reporters became household names who would later move on to television in the 1950s. In 1937, 850 hours of news was broadcast over radio. During the events in Europe leading to World War II, the total number of hours of news on radio jumped to 1,280 in 1938 and 3,450 in 1941 (Sterling and Kitross 1990, 178).

The initial animosity toward radio by the film studios and print media seems almost quaint today. Before long these interests recognized the synergism of media (using several media to cross-promote a media product within the corporate family) as providing a means to enrich the media corporation as a whole. The early days of radio provide the roots of so much corporate domination that it is difficult not to conclude that the media system of today is a logical result of the early regulatory debate and the establishment of radio in a clearly commercially dominated environment. An FCC survey in 1938 found that two-thirds of programs carried advertising (Sterling and Kitross 1990).

The decisions made in the 1920s and 1930s provided clear markers for how programs were constructed, how the popularity of programs would be measured, and most important, where the power of decision making would rest into the twenty-first century. The next section details what networks did with the power they gained in the early years of radio and how the regulatory structure established for radio was transferred to television. Once in control, the network system slowly chipped away at the regulatory structure to enable the emergence of an oligopolistic media system that would envelop all the media industries up to and including the emergence of cable television.

THE NETWORK SYSTEM SETTLES IN

By 1941 there were four national radio networks, NBC (blue and red) CBS, and Mutual Broadcasting, as well as twenty regional networks. Educational radio declined from around two hundred stations in the 1920s to about thirty-eight in 1936 and thirty-five in mid-1941 (Sterling and Kitross 1990).

From the 1930s onward, advertising's influence on radio grew immensely. Agencies not only began to fund a great deal of radio programming through the sponsorship of shows, they began to exert total control over the content of both evening and daytime programming. This was especially the case in the development of soaps in the 1930s and their control by ad agencies well into the television era in the 1950s and early 1960s. (See chapter 2.)

World War II brought about changes in radio beginning with the emergence of radio news operations as a serious enterprise. It wasn't until World War II that news became a regular feature on radio. As mentioned earlier, there was an implicit "no compete" clause between radio and newspapers (the primary source of news at that time) that prevented radio stations from developing their own news-gathering operations. But the instantaneous nature of the radio medium made it logical that the networks would develop news-gathering departments during the war, when millions of families had loved ones serving throughout the world. Radio served as the national glue of the war effort, selling war bonds, developing patriotic spirit through musical and dramatic productions, and using patriotic advertising to sell goods and produce positive images for companies associated with war production.

The radio networks cast these patriotic efforts as part of their public service obligations, and they were designed at least in part to keep the government at arm's length when it came to imposing more regulation on the industry. But the larger issue of broadcast monopolies that emerged during this period brought some concerns from government and public interest watchdogs. In 1941 the FCC carried out a "chain" broadcasting investigation that resulted in mandating that NBC sell off one of its two networks in 1943 (Kellner 1990). NBC sold off its blue network (the less-prestigious one that served smaller cities) to what would become ABC. It was purchased by Edward Noble, a wealthy conservative entrepreneur (Mazzocco 1994).

/World War II also delayed the development of television, which was largely invented and functional during this time. The three radio networks saw themselves as the natural heirs to the new technology of television. The "selling" of television in its infancy drew upon the same social values often cited when radio emerged as a mass medium. Paul Porter, FCC chair in the 1940s, saw TV as bringing the country together:/

/ [T]elevision's illuminating light will go far, we hope, to drive out ghosts that haunt the dark corners of our minds—ignorance, bigotry, fear. It will be able to inform, educate, and entertain an entire nation. . . . It can be democracy's handmaiden by bringing the whole picture of our political, social, economic and cultural life to the eyes of the nation. (McDonald 1990, 41)/

The FCC, which was supposed to serve as a brake on the influence of these corporations, made decisions over time that actually enabled their empire building. The development of FM radio is an example of this. FM radio would have expanded the number of radio outlets available in each community, potentially encouraging public interest groups to argue for more nonprofit stations. The FCC had initially encouraged the expansion as far back as the 1930s. But an FCC-mandated spectrum shift for FM in 1945 disrupted the emerging FM industry by making the sets purchased to receive FM unusable, setting back the development of FM to the late 1950s and early 1960s. This was beneficial to the AM radio networks, which fended off competition until they could absorb it.

Similarly, in 1948 the FCC consciously chose to inhibit the number of TV channels available by opting for the VHF over the UHF spectrum, which has room for substantially more channels. By 1960, only 7 percent of television sets were capable of receiving UHF channels, effectively maintaining the network monopoly in early television (McDonald 1990). Thus, as television emerged from the networks that dominated radio, they were already experienced at limiting competition and would continue to call on their government overseers to assist in this.

Into the 1970s, early cable systems and "pay" television were also blocked by the dominant networks. These early decisions secured the desires of the network system to keep the development of these technologies within the system they would control (Kellner 1990; Mosco 1979). Eventually these technologies were embraced by the corporations that had initially disdained using them, as they expanded into cross-media empires.

The growth of cable television presented challenges and possibilities to the networks. The broadcast television networks resisted cable while they were unconnected to the larger media system. As ABC, NBC, and CBS were scooped up by media corporations with interests in film, magazines. and other mass media, this resistance dropped as they began to buy into cable operations.

ABC USES SYNERGY TO CATCH UP

In the early 1950s a third television network, ABC, emerged and ultimately challenged CBS and NBC by using its political connections and reaching out to other media corporations to establish itself. ABC presents an interesting case study in using connections in industry and government to try to catch up to the two dominant networks. While NBC and CBS would eventually expand into other media holdings and relationships, ABC's limited number of affiliates, compared to the other two (40, ABC; 164, NBC; 113, CBS) made it a poor third sister in comparison. It chose to pursue relationships with other media companies early on. When it merged with Paramount Theater to avoid bankruptcy, ABC became the first network to produce programs in Hollywood.

By 1954 ABC had also signed on with Disney. The agreement resulted in the network having shares in the soon-to-be-built Disneyland in California and included the development of a number of one-hour series, access to six hundred films, and an eight-year agreement to purchase Disney programs for $40 million. In 1956 ABC also bought a 6 percent interest in News Corporation and bought TV stations in Central and South America, the Middle East, and Asia. The demise of the fourth network, Dumont, which was forced to sell its network to focus on manufacturing television sets, enabled ABC to become an even stronger third network (Mazzocco 1994).

ABC brought innovation to early television—50 percent of its schedule consisted of filmed shows while CBS and NBC were still producing many shows live. This would change quickly./By 1961, 83 percent of all prime time shows were on film. ABC had established an early form of synergy—revenues from TV helped stabilize the film studio, centralized TV production, and squeezed out pesky independent producers in the 1960s. Filmed productions were also more profitable—reruns, syndication, and exports to foreign countries brought a reuse of television programming with which live shows could not compete./By the 1960s live programs were down to one-third of all television programs, and the production center for television shifted from New York to Hollywood (McDonald 1990).

In a relatively short period of time, television was transforming itself into a cross-media linked industry. As Fred McDonald puts it:

\Nothing less than the rationalization of a new industry was occurring in the late 1950s. Standardization of product, reliance on familiar formulas, use of mass production techniques by the film studios and networks: national TV, like national culture, was emerging as an efficient, streamlined reality that existed to please the majority, a majority that in great part it had helped to create. Programmers were bringing regularity and controllability to their fare. No surprises here, with regularized genres, regularized plots and regularized characterization. Everything was being brought under control so advertisers could be enticed to spend billions of dollars in a safe and predictable medium. (McDonald 1990, 126)\

This served to fully rationalize television under the umbrella of market values. Again, McDonald puts it succinctly: "While Robert Sarnoff, the president of NBC could argue in 1956 that a network was constructed around three major service functions—to the public, to affiliated stations and to advertisers—it was increasingly obvious that making a profit and satisfying shareholders were prepossessing foci of industry management" (McDonald 1990, 123).\

It should not be surprising that the lords of TV would want to celebrate the version of American capitalism that enabled them to acquire such wealth and power. ABC in particular had a conservative bent, by virtue of its owner, Edward Noble. Not part of the long development of the broadcast regulatory structure from the 1920s, ABC had a different orientation from the beginning. Noble would see to it that his network espoused his political perspective. He brought in Fulton Sheen and Billy Graham to bring a religious perspective in line with his views. Graham, who got his big boost through Henry Luce's *Time* magazine, was brought on ABC to extol his anticommunist politics and fundamentalist Christianity. (This is in contrast to CBS's critique of Joseph McCarthy, also during this period.) But more significantly, ABC chose to focus its prime time lineup on the demographic slice of eighteen-to-forty-nine-year-olds with its crime/detective genres and Western programs such as *The Rifleman, The Untouchables,* and *77 Sunset Strip,* which brought a level of violence to TV programming unheard of in the 1950s.

ABC's political conservatism was also exemplified in its long-term relationship with the Federal Bureau of Investigation (FBI). ABC had developed *This Is Your FBI* for radio between 1945 and 1963 and later developed *The FBI* for television in the 1960s. The close relationship between the network and the agency was defined by Hoover's complete control over scripts. From 1965 to 1970, he collected royalty payments for his role in the show. In terms of news, the network disdained documentary projects and hired Walter Winchell and other conservative commentators to project Noble's politics (Mazzocco 1994). As the first network born because of the regulatory structure, ABC would become an arm of conservative politics that provided entertainment but little for public concerns. ABC's careful courting of key government agencies and individuals was a key in its survival as well, an ironic development given its antiregulatory and less than enthusiastic public service orientation.

FCC: ENSURING FAIRNESS AND DIVERSITY?

Meanwhile, the FCC attempted to combat such trends through a series of rulings and court cases that tried to instill a healthy debate of public issues in the broadcast media. The issue of how owners of broadcast media outlets used their ownership powers was a particular concern with respect to broadcasting, given the limited spectrum and space for channels. This is quite distinct from operating a newspaper or magazine, in which anyone can set up a publication and there are no limits on the number of publications that can be published. With radio, and later television, the limit on the number of stations any one entity could own was seen as a brake on the monopolization of a medium that could limit the breadth of debate on issues of general concern.

A number of FCC and U.S. Supreme Court rulings from the 1940s onward held up requirements for broadcast media to present all sides of a story. The first, a Supreme Court decision, affirmed a First Amendment right for people to receive information from a number of sources with a great deal of breadth in how they define and treat issues of a public concern. The second, an FCC decision that set up the Fairness Doctrine rule, was meant to make owners provide all points of view, not just those the owner agreed with. The third decision, commonly called the Red Lion case, was a court decision giving the right of reply to a one-sided report and affirming that the "needs and rights of viewers to diversity of views are more important than the rights of ownership" (Sterling and Kitross 1990).

In the late 1950s, with the rise of FM into a major source of radio programming, the FCC limited cross-country ownership rules for AM-FM-TV to 7-7-7. This meant that CBS (or any national broadcast service) could own only seven of each type of medium across the country (Sterling and Kitross 1990).

This was the regulatory structure set in place for the next thirty years, until the head of the FCC under Ronald Reagan, Mark Fowler, overturned most of these rulings and introduced a series of "reforms" enabling greater latitude in owning a number of radio and television stations and allowing owners to more closely direct the content of their channels toward their personal views (Kellner 1990).

Eventually opportunities for breadth and diversity were sought outside the privately owned networks. In 1952 the FCC allocated 250 channels for noncommercial TV, but the potential for public service television went untapped due to lack of money. In 1955 only two educational channels were on the air. By 1961 there were fifty-two noncommercial channels versus 527 commercial channels. National Educational Television was formed in 1963, and the Public Broadcasting System was created in 1969, twenty years after the arrival of commercial network television (McDonald 1990).

But the networks continued to consolidate as much ownership power as they could by using political connections. The rise of Capital Cities, which took ownership of ABC in the 1980s, provides a good example of how an established and politically connected company could take advantage of the regulatory structure to build up a broadcasting corporation.[1] Capital Cities was born in 1954 when Frank Smith purchased a failing UHF TV station and a 5,000-watt AM radio station in Albany, New York. Smith's corporate philosophy at Capital Cities was to operate "lean and mean." There were three aspects of his success: exploit the sales marketing potential out of failing stations, keep operating and labor costs low, and most significant, develop and nurture connections with the U.S. government that could further the company's interests. Smith had developed a reputation for buying unprofitable stations, and relied on fellow owners Lowell Thomas, Thomas Dewey, and William Casey to use their connections with government and industry to expand the company. Lowell Thomas had a reputation as a broadcaster with strong ties to the advertising industry. Thomas Dewey was a Republican stalwart, who ran for president in 1948 and was a part of the OSS transition to the CIA. William Casey, who would become CIA director in the Reagan administration, became an investor in 1954 and advised on tax matters; he was an expert at bending the law.

"Free marketers" all, these men often went to government to demand tax breaks and regulatory waivers to enable their expansion. Smith was not a broadcasting guru who believed in the importance of delivering quality entertainment and a breadth of views as a way to further the broadcast mandate to serve the public interest. He was a longtime advertising and public relations executive who brought a salesman's perspective to his enterprise. The company took an early lead in developing sensationalist local news broadcasts made up of crime, violence, and government waste and corruption. His aggressive style would lead him beyond the broadcasting industry and into other media industries; he expanded in 1968 to include publishing interests and moved aggressively into the emerging cable television market, owning fifty-four cable systems by 1984. But his main interest was in broadcasting, and he owned two hundred radio and television stations affiliated with ABC. He became interested in ABC, which Capital Cities would buy in 1985, around the time he got word through his connections that the FCC was going to expand television-AM-FM ownership from 7-7-7 to 12-12-12. This would help immensely in Capital Cities' purchase of ABC. This expansion was particularly important for the networks, as the strength of all three networks' profit margins rests in ownership of local stations; local stations under the network's ownership umbrella are a primary source of profits compared to other network divisions. This FCC ruling would be a boon for the networks.

/By the early 1960s the networks had amassed control over all aspects of production, and advertisers were beginning to look at demographic differences in what kinds of people were watching their programs. ABC's role in moving the industry in this direction cannot be overstated. Television programming shifted from innovation to predictability and convention. Profits doubled from $1.2 billion in 1962 to $2.5 billion in 1968. The networks owned or had proprietary rights to 67 percent of prime time shows, and the networks controlled syndication sales/As journalist David Karp put it: "TV is not an art form or a cultural channel, it is an advertising medium . . . people who watch television complain that their shows are lousy. They are not supposed to be any good. The are supposed to make money" (McDonald 1990, 152)/

An example of this trend can be seen in the drop in the number of news documentaries produced. Called "news features" (in the sense of "feature-length" films) in their early days (Frank 1991), networks produced them as part of their public service mandate. From a high of 447 in 1962, in 1968 only 251 news documentaries were produced and aired.

INDUSTRY EXPANSION, INDUSTRY CONSOLIDATION

/The 1960s saw the beginning of the third phase in the television industry's evolution: The networks were "going global" in a big way. They began to expand into nontelevision and nonmedia business acquisitions as well as continuing to consolidate power within television./Internationally, NBC was selling programs to eighty-two countries in 1968, but ABC was the most aggressive. It had created Worldvision enterprises for ABC International in 1959. By 1968 it was operating in sixteen Latin American countries and had extensive ties in the Middle East. Reselling programs that had already made money in the United States meant the networks could undercut production costs of locally produced shows. These exports also benefited the expansion and exporting of American consumer products via accompanying advertising. The J. Walter Thompson advertising agency is credited with breaking the British public television system through supporting the creation of ITV in 1955. By the end of the 1970s international sales totaled 20 percent of ABC's gross network revenues.

The moves by the network into nontelevision ventures in the 1960s and 1970s foretold the network mergers in the 1980s and 1990s, which would fully integrate television into the corporate landscape. CBS invested in the New York Yankees baseball team, Steinway pianos, and Creative Playthings toys and had interests in magazines and book publishing. NBC/RCA ventured into Hertz rental cars, real estate, and the computer business. ABC was a little less aggressive for a time due to the attempt by the multinational International Telephone and Telegraph to purchase it in 1965. The FCC submitted inquiries about the merger, and its concerns about ITT's ability to shape the news scared ITT off. But ABC did expand within the media industries, taking on publishing, music production, and the like.

Continued developments within the television industry resulted in a variety of changes that would ultimately consolidate the networks' power. But this did not happen without the FCC making some attempts to create a greater balance of power between the networks and their affiliated stations.

The major development in the 1970s concerned the "Financial Interest and Syndication Rules," or fin-syn, and the Prime Time Access Rule (PTAR), both of which were attempts to break the virtual network monopoly over prime time programming, which squeezed out independent production (McDonald 1990). When implemented in April 1970, PTAR limited networks to three hours per night of network-produced programming in the fifty largest markets. In 1970, the networks held 98 percent of all syndication concessions. Allowing local stations to program an hour (from 7:00 to 8:00 P.M.) was meant to enhance revenues for local stations and revive independent production. Furthermore, the rules changes meant syndication rights of independently produced series were not ceded to the network that aired their first run but would be controlled by the studio that produced them. The networks ended up faring quite well after initial fears that affiliates had gained too much from the rules changes.

Coping with the rules changes and the increasing orientation to profits resulted in the least objectionable programming approach and identification with the advertising industry's desire for young and affluent segments of the mass audience. Crime series, miniseries, and made-for-TV movies skyrocketed in the 1970s, and sex and violence proved to be ratings grabbers. The number of shows aired on networks dropped from a high of 155 over four networks in 1953 to 70 over three networks in 1970.

The introduction of the thirty-second ad format revitalized network cof-
fers. By taking the one-minute format and splitting it, the networks could
charge more for two thirty-second ads than they could get for a minute
long ad. This helped them overcome the loss of advertising from the one
hour of programming ceded to local stations and the forfeiting of syndication fees.

But other technologies would further challenge the traditional TV networks, namely the VCR and cable television. Introduced in the 1970s, cable TV moved from a largely rural phenomenon to capture TV households in the urban and suburban spaces of the United States. Similarly, the
VCR's introduction into the American home in the 1980s (40 percent of
homes in 1982, 60 percent by 1988) brought another opportunity to use
television outside the network nexus (McDonald 1990; Sterling and
Kitross 1990).

Over the next decade and a half, TV moved beyond the three network
affiliates and one public station arrangement that had existed in most
communities for so many years. Television, via the expansion of channels
available on cable, became the place where the media industries converged. The development of premium cable channels offering uncensored
feature films, the invention of MTV as an advertising vehicle for the music industry, and the proliferation of talk shows hawking the latest, hottest
star in any aspect of the entertainment industry provided a means for all
media interests to have a stake in television.

/The networks lost audiences to these new forms of television diversion,
and the numbers bear this out. The networks' share of the television audience dropped from 90 percent in 1979–1980 to 67 percent in 1988–1989.
Furthermore, the limitations on content for broadcast networks didn't exist for cable channels. Given the explicit portrayals of sexuality and
graphic violence available on premium movie channels like HBO and
Showtime, the broadcast networks had to up the ante and push the envelope in terms of what was previously avoided or forbidden in their own
programs. While sexual titillation and violence on the broadcast networks
pale in comparison to the cable premium channels, the double entendre
reigns supreme on network sitcoms./

All of these factors led to less differentiation between the "old" broadcasting system and the emerging cable-digital-satellite systems. Indeed,
the course of mergers and buyouts that left no sector of the economy un-
scathed started hitting the networks in the mid-1980s. Their luster diminished by falling ratings and bad investments in other ventures, the networks became vulnerable to takeovers, and all three were snapped up by
conglomerates.

ABC had become the subject of much speculation within the business
press by the early 1980s. An article in *Forbes* pointed out some of its vul-

nerabilities: It had overextended into publishing and recordings and had failures in pay-per-view and cable broadcasting. On the other hand, Capital Cities was a favorite of the business press. Warren Buffett, a major stockholder in Capital Cities who served on the board of directors, started buying ABC stock and made the takeover possible. He got 18 percent of Capital Cities stock from the merger.

The takeover of ABC caused some shock waves at the network. Cutbacks were announced as part of the lean and mean philosophy Smith brought to ABC from Capital Cities. By April 1987, 1,850 employees had been laid off. Labor and management clashes were feared given Capital Cities' approach to labor relations (Mazzocco 1994).

CBS was subjected to a series of takeover attempts inspired initially by political concerns. Senator Jesse Helms tried to engineer a takeover of what he considered a network too liberal for American politics. Ted Turner, founder of CNN, also tried to obtain the network and damaged CBS financially even though it successfully resisted him. CBS finally did change hands in 1985 when Loews Corporation, in the person of Laurence Tisch, ultimately prevailed using the camel nose under the tent flap approach: buying up stock to the point where he became a force that couldn't be stopped.

Meanwhile, NBC was purchased by General Electric in 1985. Why would larger interests take on the networks, which might reasonably be seen as dinosaurs on the verge of extinction? Despite their slide in the ratings, networks were still immensely profitable. In 1988, ABC made $760 million profit on revenues of $3.8 billion, while NBC made $537 million on $3.6 billion in revenues. All three networks moved into cable in some form with varying degrees of success, either directly as in the case of NBC or indirectly as in the case of CBS and ABC. For the latter two, this integration occurred in a second wave of mergers in the mid- to late 1990s.

This second wave was marked by Disney's purchase of ABC/Capital Cities in 1994. Its incorporation into the Disney media empire found in its family such cable stalwarts as ESPN; the Internet venture GO.com; and a whole array of music, magazine, and book publishing interests, cruise lines, theme parks, and other entertainment entities. CBS went through another round of mergers—going first to Westinghouse (an old media corporation that had diversified into other ventures) and then in 1999 to Viacom, a broad-based media company with holdings in many media companies. Considerable synergistic potential lies in cable television channels such as MTV, Comedy Central, and Nickelodeon and their connection to the other media outlets in music, books, and magazines. CBS/Viacom was primed to capitalize on that.

As this was written in fall 2003, the FCC under the leadership of Michael Powell was philosophically geared toward allowing greater concentration of ownership. Powell has gone so far as to say that he is no longer sure there is such a thing as the public interest when it comes to media ownership. He argues that proliferation of cable channels available (at a substantial cost) on most systems provides adequate diversity (Bercovici 2002). A congressional bill passed late in 2003 raised ownership limits of radio and television stations to just under 40 percent of the national audience. This follows a substantial loosening of ownership rules in place since the 1996 Telecommunications Act, which made possible the Viacom/CBS merger and other media-related mergers and buyouts (Nicols and McChesney 2003).

CONCLUSION

"Bigger is better" became the rule of the day in the 1990s as media consolidation was just one part of a massive wave of mergers. Despite assurances to the contrary, the breadth of media holdings in all of these conglomerates (and numerous others, such as FOX and WB) brought about incipient conflicts of interest, particularly with respect to news. (Chapter 4 details the role and evolution of news at ABC and CBS.)

The 2002 buzz about ABC's attempt to lure David Letterman from CBS serves as the best example of how these shakeups and consolidations have virtually divorced media companies from any sense of public service. The attempt to snag Letterman for ABC meant the possible demise of ABC's highly regarded *Nightline* news program. Though *Nightline* actually had higher ratings than Letterman's *The Late Show*, ABC lusted after the show because it had a younger audience that would generate higher advertising rates/At that point, it was eminently clear that television was no longer about reaching large numbers of people with quality programming—the only line that really mattered was the bottom line./

At the beginning of a new millennium, it was clear that television had long since abandoned the kind of high-minded public service ideals reflected in the earliest claims about the role of radio/Network television is no longer about programming that enlightens, inspires, and educates (if it ever was); it is now about generating high advertising revenues. By attracting desirable (young, affluent) audience segments, serial storytelling and soap opera melodrama have become key forms of bait used by television interests to attract those audiences, encourage the consumption ethic, and keep shareholders happy./

The use of soap opera storytelling to achieve high profit margins is the focus of the remainder of this book. To understand how soap storytelling has come to be preeminent in a variety of contexts, chapter 2 looks at the history of soap storytelling and examines why soap operas are truly the commodity form of today's television.

NOTE

1. Mazzocco (1994, ch. 3) gives a full accounting.

Chapter 2

The Soap Opera as Commodity Form

Serial storytelling is as old as mass communication. The evolution of soap opera storytelling began with serial installments of novels in newspapers. By the mid-eighteenth century, serialization of novels in newspapers had become a popular and profitable mode of publishing in both Europe and the United States. Early serials in European newspapers were devised to entice people who normally would not purchase a newspaper. The rise of literary serial narratives was a key factor in the development of literature and publishing and parallels the development of art into a commodifiable and profitable product. Furthermore, the rise of literacy and advances in printing that made books and newspapers cheaper to produce saw published material move from a luxury to a commodity and audiences move from a select few to a mass of consumers (Stedman 1971; Allen 1985; Hagedorn 1995; Hayward 1997).

As movies became a mass consumption medium, they likewise adapted storytelling to installments as a way of keeping customers coming to movie theaters. By 1914 twenty film serials were in distribution; in the next year the number exploded to 150. Film serials were also some of the first attempts at market segmentation, with the introduction of series done specifically for children. Thus, serials were designed to promote the medium in which they appeared, continued consumption of future episodes, and, when transferred to advertising-based media, product or brand loyalty. As serials often helped to introduce a new medium and ensure regular consumption of it, each new mass medium over the last century (film, radio, television) relied on serial forms to develop and maintain mass audiences (Hagedorn 1995). As Robert Allen puts it, "the soap opera is and always has been a narrative text in the service of an economic imperative" (1985, 100).

The term "soap opera" appeared early in the radio era when broadcasters were searching for programming that would reach daytime audiences. Radio had largely been seen as an evening phenomenon, and in the early years programs were broadcast only at night. The desire to expand the number of hours of broadcasting was a consequence of the increasing commercialization of the medium. As demonstrated in chapter 1, a nearly decade-long debate over what purposes this powerful new medium should serve began with the notion that the airwaves were a public resource and that radio programming should serve noble goals such as enlightenment and education. Indeed, many of the early radio stations were owned by publicly minded organizations such as farmers' groups, unions, educational institutions, and churches. The early forerunner of the FCC, the Federal Radio Commission, was initially hostile to the overt commercialization of radio. In 1928 about one-quarter of the programs relied on commercial sponsorship, and the industry's National Association of Broadcasters guidelines prohibited commercials between 7:00 and 11:00 P.M.

The first radio network, the National Broadcasting Company (NBC), took a rather highbrow approach to radio—symphonies and other cultural programming were used to find favor with the FRC as the network expanded its reach. The arrival of the Columbia Broadcasting Company (CBS) and a corresponding campaign by commercial radio interests as they pressured Congress in the late 1920s and early 1930s to make radio more commercially viable began the slow but certain abandonment of public service principles. CBS exploited NBC's reluctance to engage in too much commercialism and created programming specifically designed to attract advertisers. When NBC was launched in 1926, only a few programs were produced by ad agencies; by 1931 only a few were not (Allen 1985). By 1933 the number of "sustaining" hours (programs that had only brief announcements about the sponsoring corporation) had dropped from 76 to 24 percent on NBC, and CBS's aggressive courting of advertisers and mass audiences resulted in it surpassing NBC in the number of affiliated stations by 1935 (Hilmes 1990; McChesney 1993).

Serial programming on radio began with the *Amos 'n Andy* program, which was broadcast in the evening. The show's "narrative indeterminacy" was found to have a positive effect in attracting a loyal audience. As the networks searched for programming that would reach a daytime audience, a 1932 marketing study found that housewives were the most influential persons in the family with respect to buying goods for the household. The medium's importance became clear when a 1934 survey found that the radio was seen by women as second only to the iron as the most essential household appliance.

Armed with these facts, consumer products companies—typified by Procter and Gamble—sought programming that would reach women in the home. As a consumer society developed even in the Depression, Procter and Gamble realized that sales volume could balance the small profit per unit sold and generated demand for its products through advertising, especially on radio. The development of soap operas was an ingenious way to combine the purchasing decision making done by housewives with serial storytelling that had characters using the very products being advertised. A woman by the name of Irna Phillips and the husband–wife team of Frank and Anne Hummert are generally regarded as the pioneers of daytime radio serials, which would become popularly known as soap operas.

Irna Phillips saw the potential of radio dramas not only to bring products to housewives' attention but to generate the whole idea of the "American dream" or the "American way of life," two phrases that came to be pervasive in the 1930s (Lavin 1995). According to Marilyn Lavin, radio soaps were "well suited to play an important role in encouraging mass consumption" (Lavin 1995, 76) by using serial programming to turn housewives into loyal audiences, by providing role models for overcoming the adversity of the Depression era to attain the American dream, and by providing parasocial interaction between characters in stories and audience members at home. Irna Phillips developed *Painted Dreams* in 1931 as the first of many serials she would explicitly design to meet the needs of advertisers.

A successor program, *Today's Children*, saw the development of early attempts at product placements within the shows themselves. Phillips used the wedding anniversary of two characters in the show to get listeners to write in for a picture of them. The return package included advertisements for two different kinds of laundry products. Embedding ads within the story resulted when a survey of listeners found they didn't like the ads because they interrupted the story. For example, Phillips used the preparation of a cake within an episode to promote Pillsbury flour and associate the cake with family appreciation and togetherness as an embedded ad. When the show reached a crisis in lack of sponsors, Phillips ran an announcement at the beginning of the fifteen-minute program urging listeners to buy Pillsbury flour so that Pillsbury would continue to sponsor the show. Phillips recognized that women appreciated the continuity of stories from day to day and designed her characters to become surrogate friends with listeners. She avoided explicit references to the Depression within her stories but did present problems of individuals with individual ways of solving those problems. Phillips's stories were populated by people who could be characterized as middle class, and she used them to show listeners who were making ends meet a glimpse of the American Dream and to project their access to it (Lavin 1995).

Frank and Anne Hummert were the primary vehicles by which Procter and Gamble used radio to push the ethic of consumption. From 1932 to 1960 they produced forty daytime serials and developed "reason why" advertising to correspond to the problem–solution storytelling they devised for their serials. Furthermore, they perfected the assembly line production of scripts by managing story lines and employing a staff of writers to flesh them out. Radio was the only medium to see an increase in advertising during the 1930s, and this helped further the conversion of radio into a commercial medium. Advertisers liked radio for its "personal" qualities—its use of a human voice and the development of characters that helped listeners relate—in contrast to the impersonal nature of print advertising. Networks began to sell half hour blocks directly to advertisers like Procter and Gamble. The Hummerts developed *Ma Perkins* explicitly to promote P&G's Oxydol laundry soap. As a way of measuring the size of the audience, they came up with a mail-in offer of a packet of flower seeds for a dime and got around one million responses. Frank Hummert's background as an advertiser inspired him to use the same type of logic in storytelling that he used to sell products. He developed storytelling that used the approach of defining a problem and providing a product to solve the problem successfully in his advertising work. In the Hummerts' programs, advertisements were not fully integrated into the story as Irna Phillips had done. Instead, they "sandwiched" the narrative between two commercials that associated themselves with the story or a character in it. Thus the narrative was not interrupted by irritating commercials but placed closely to it so that listeners would easily know who the sponsor was. Follow-up marketing research found that listeners' preference for branded products increased with the number of hours spent listening to soaps (Meyers 1997).

Such storytelling and selling techniques endeared people like Irna Phillips and the Hummerts to advertisers and were a major force in the commercialization of radio. By 1939 there were seventy-five hours of afternoon serials per week (Hilmes 1990). Soap operas became the properties of the consumer products corporations that hawked their wares on the programs. The rise of television in the post–World War II era saw the gradual shifting of soap operas from radio to television. By 1960 they were exclusively relegated to television, where they have remained a staple of daytime programming. In the 1990s Procter and Gamble still owned six different series.

The move to television and changes in the American social climate created some changes in soap storytelling. Plots have become more complex, programs have employed larger casts, and stories have delved more into problems of intimacy and relationships. Though they remain highly profitable, as soaps have evolved on television they have required more production costs by using exterior locations, expanding to an hour in length, and generating a "star" system. The changes soap stories have undergone as they transitioned from radio to television also provide a window into the social mood of the times. Moral advice through storytelling continued throughout the 1950s as the shift to television found an increasing emphasis on character development. By the mid-1960s the psychological states of characters—the motives behind their behaviors—had become the primary guide for stories. Soaps of the late 1960s and early 1970s came to reflect the times as social issues of the day and an emerging emphasis on youth took hold. Soaps reached their television ratings apex in the 1970s and 1980s, when there were still more than thirty soaps on television. By 1994 27 percent fewer women in the eighteen to forty-nine age range were watching soaps. But soaps still had drawing power in 2000, as ten soaps still attracted twenty million viewers daily. Contemporary social issues such as spousal abuse, teenage pregnancy, AIDS, and homosexuality are regularly injected into stories (Parney and Mason 2000).

The movement of women into the workplace caused daytime soap producers to try to find a new audience in young people, especially college students, who developed cultlike followings for soaps, viewed as groups in dormitories and apartments. In summer 2000 ABC launched a specific effort to attract younger viewers (college and high school students on summer vacations) called Plunge in This Summer. The network added younger characters to *Port Charles, All My Children, One Life to Live,* and *General Hospital.* Plot lines were explicitly geared toward females between the ages of sixteen and twenty-four. Similarly, CBS took its *The Young and the Restless* in a youth direction, emphasizing young love and peer pressure, and included a story line involving reality TV and teenagers. NBC jumped on the same youth bandwagon by canceling the thirty-four-year run of *Another World* and creating *Passions,* a racier, youth-oriented soap (Parney and Mason 2000).

Despite these efforts, the average age of a regular soap viewer continues to increase; over the last ten years the average age has gone up seven years. Other attempts to boost the audiences for daytime soaps include CBS's Spanish-language version of *The Bold and the Beautiful* as well as adding a Latino character to the ensemble cast. ABC has tried to borrow a page from Latin *telenovelas,* which differ from soaps in the United States by resolving some stories over the course of two months (Bauder 2001).

On the revenue side, television soaps have recently revived the product placement invented for radio soaps with a story line on ABC's *All My Children* involving soap diva Susan Lucci's Erica Kane character. A subplot about her fictional cosmetic company sending a spy into a Revlon factory generated a multimillion-dollar fee for several months of exposure on the program ("Revlon pays for story line" 2002).

In an odd twist, it is generally conceded that prime time soap operas have pushed their daytime predecessors into incorporating exteriors and action sequences in stories (Traynor-Williams 1992). While these episodes are more expensive to produce initially, prime time soaps can recoup the costs through syndication and exportation to other countries. Daytime soaps are only aired once but are produced cheaply enough to be cost effective (Hobson 2003). While prime time soaps and miniseries are covered in chapter 8, it is worth noting that in the 1970s and 1980s prime time soaps proliferated, starting with CBS's *Dallas*, which was first or second in ratings for five years of its eleven-year run. By 1984–1985 there were four evening serials in the top ten shows. The addition of the FOX and WB networks to the broadcasting environment has seen this trend continue unabated (McDonald 1990; Brooks and Marsh 2003).

Finally, the connection between commercial interests and soaps remains strong. The rise of the Internet has seen product placement move into soap chat rooms. Nabisco's placement of coupons and promotions on soap-related websites is reminiscent of the way Irna Phillips and Frank and Anne Hummert generated listener response as a way of measuring the size of the audience (Hayward 1997). Serial installments of advertisements also emerged in the 1990s, with the infamous Taster's Choice "coffee as seducer" serial ads leading the way. Over seven years and thirteen "episodes," viewers watched two apartment neighbors meet and flirt over Taster's Choice (Cavazos 2001).

MARKET-CRITICAL ELEMENTS IN SOAP OPERAS

Defining a soap opera "genre" has been the subject of much work in television studies. A genre can be defined as the set of characteristics shared by a group of television programs that distinguishes them from other types of shows. Genre offers assurance about a show's pacing, storytelling consistency, and expectations about the behavior of characters to both advertisers and the audience. Two overarching requirements of soap opera storytelling seem to be a serial approach to the unfolding of the narrative and the use of strong emotionalism and moral polarization by focusing on the relationships that characterize melodrama.

The work of Jane Feuer goes a long way toward explaining the popularity of the soap opera as a genre and accounting for how the genre has influenced prime time programming. She cites 1970s television as the beginning of the serialization of prime time, which continued through the 1980s. Sitcoms are also one of the genres influenced by soap opera storytelling. Sitcoms, while not specifically offering seriality, do seem to increasingly embody cumulative narration—a series that has historical memory and permits character and relationship development in ways sitcoms of the 1950s and 1960s studiously avoided (Feuer 1987, 1991, 1995).

The five elements presented below, the basis for much of the rest of this book, are derived from a comprehensive review of research on soap operas. The focus of this review was to come up with a set of core concepts or elements that capture the essence of the soap opera's designation as the "commodity" form of television. The emphasis for the characteristics presented here is their relevance to other television programming for attracting an audience and reflecting market values. These elements are not meant to be mutually exclusive. Rather, they interlock with each other and are mutually influential. These factors influence what producers intend for their programs, how they structure the stories they tell, and what the audience derives from soap operas as a form of diversion or fantasy. Dorothy Hobson describes soaps as the "perfect" television form. They are effective at achieving and retaining an audience, are effective in generating press coverage of the program by frequently creating controversy, and most important, bring in advertising revenue. As the ultimate twentieth-century mass media form, soap opera storytelling has become front and center during just about every time block of the day. Hobson also argues that while audiences enjoy soaps, the television industry needs them (Hobson 2003). Similarly, Roger Hagedorn argues that soaps accomplish three primary commercial tasks: promoting continued consumption of future episodes, brand loyalty, and television itself. The five elements are an attempt to link soaps to this value orientation (Hagedorn 1995).

Seriality

The serial nature of the soap opera is its most central market-driven technique. Serial storytelling has been consistently employed when program producers seek to target a program at a new, desirable demographic that group advertisers are seeking (Hagedorn 1995).

Characterized by the use of "teasers" before commercial breaks and "cliffhangers" at the end of each episode, the open-ended nature of serials is what creates the possibility of creative readings and is an important part of how the play element soap audiences bring to their viewing is sustained (Feuer 1991; Livingstone 1994). Such approaches are fundamental to attracting and maintaining an audience and are television's version of developing brand loyalty. What Robert Allen calls the "interepisodic redundancy" of soaps—the way in which new plot developments are revealed to the network of characters in a show over a series of days—is important for soap fans. It allows them to miss an occasional episode and helps them maintain a coherent sense of soap history by seeing how characters react to the new plot twist (Allen 1985).

Extended story lines that may last from two to ten episodes are called "arcs," and the resolution of one arc implies the beginning of another story line. These arcs are generally additional story material to what is happening to the main characters (Mumford 1994; Feuer 1995). This "infinity of the text" (Eco 1985) takes on the rhythms of life and the world in which it is produced and allows variations on a story that never really ends. The speculative fun for loyal audience members is about the "what next?" The game becomes to tune in to see whether guesses and speculations are borne out. It is the brand loyalty or addictive nature of soaps that producers know advertisers desire.

Real-Time Orientation

While story lines can become highly implausible, the rhythm and pacing of soaps are designed to create a real-time orientation in soap operas. This contributes to a sense of realism; the viewers and characters each experience the same passage of time, including cultural holidays and family events like births, deaths, and weddings (Riegel 1996). Soaps create the illusion that the characters and location of the soap exist whether viewers are there or not. This constructed illusion of reality is very important, as it helps approximate for audiences the intensity of a live event and contributes to the sense of being there. Furthermore, the camera motion in a soap opera is designed to resemble the perception of an actual event (Barbatsis and Guy 1991; Hobson 2003). The daily visit viewers make to their soap world is designed to become part of the rhythm of viewers' daily lives and help make watching habitual.

Technological innovations via the Internet and satellite TV make it possible for fans to watch episodes (and study story trends) at their convenience. Fans of *The Young and the Restless* and *As the World Turns* (both owned by Sony) can now access missed episodes for $2 per episode or a $10 per month subscription fee. They are offered through SoapCity.com, a soap website also sponsored by Sony. In 2003, SoapCity.com was getting 3.4 million unique visitors each month, a nearly tenfold increase from 1998 (Healey 2003).

Seeming Intimacy/Play Orientation

The value of intimacy in helping a program capture an audience is reflected in the seeming intimacy viewers can feel with characters they visit on a daily basis. Soaps deal with the concrete problems of modern life and relationships—situations familiar to audiences and thus easy for viewers to identify with. Irna Phillips strove to create soap characters who could be surrogate friends (Lavin 1995; Abercrombie 1996; Rogers 1995). The relation between individual and universal experience allows viewers to feel that they can get into the heads of soap characters (Hobson 2003).

A sense on the viewers' part that they "know" this soap community and its inhabitants goads audiences into "imaginative constructions," projecting their own future plot developments or relating one of the story lines to a situation in their own past or present lives. This familiar, contemporary world becomes a play world for viewers. They are the proverbial fly on the wall, enjoying the spectatorship into the intimate lives of others without involvement in the consequences of the secret world of others to which they are privy. Dorothy Hobson argues that soap fans don't necessarily desire to inhabit the soap world but are familiar enough with the characters and location to find their way around. They know what to expect, and those expectations create anticipation for story developments (Hobson 2003).

Soaps' "ever-expanding middle" due to lack of narrative closure is what facilitates gossip among soap fans, and the popularity of soaps on college campuses is due partly to a preference by college students to watch in groups and engage in commentary and debate (Brown 1990; Allen 1985). At an individual level, Perse and Rubin (1989) argue that soaps offer viewers an opportunity for parasocial interaction as the program becomes an alternative to their own lives.

Viewer feedback to soaps and the significant presence of activity on soap websites and chat rooms reflect the involvement viewers come to feel and the investment they make beyond merely viewing episodes (Perse and Rubin 1989; Hayward 1997). The Internet has extended the ability of soap fans to indulge in their favorite soaps by allowing them to use chat rooms and bulletin boards to gossip with other fans. Some websites offer the opportunity for soap opera mavens to contribute or create their own soap stories or take their favorite soaps in a direction they would like to see them go.

While in years past magazines like *Soap Opera Digest* and *Soap Opera Weekly* offered a combined 1.6 million readers "behind-the-scenes" gossip and allowed them to catch up on missed episodes, the Internet's capability for interactive experiences with other fans brings a play or social element to viewing. The Internet makes it possible for viewers to collectively share their love and hate of favorite and notorious cast members.

Story Exposition

The manner in which a soap story unfolds on screen empowers the audience by giving it an omniscient point of view. Because soaps present different characters' points of view, viewers can get into the heads of soap characters. It can even be said that viewers can come to know the true thoughts and feelings of soap characters in ways they cannot with the people in their own lives. Because soap stories unfold slowly and redundantly, viewers can anticipate and see how characters will react to a new plot twist (Hobson 2003).

The frequent returns from death, bouts of amnesia, and other "carnivalesque" elements of soaps contribute to the sense of play for viewers. These absurdities are acknowledged by viewers, and the ability to infuse a sense of comedy and irony as part of the storytelling adds to the viewer's enjoyment. That viewers can enjoy the program at several levels broadens the audience to those who may be reticent to take them seriously but find them fun for their absurdities and eccentricities (Traynor-Williams 1992).

Soaps get more feedback over a longer time than any other mass fiction narrative, and producers monitor the number of feedback channels that exist today. There has been considerable speculation by participants in online audience chat rooms and fan clubs that program producers and writers visit chat rooms and use viewer mail to help determine how stories should develop.

Themes of Soap Stories

Soaps draw on three basic themes that guide plot and character developments. Conflict and chaos provide tension in soap stories. Clearly defined good and evil allow viewers to take sides and develop "love to hate" sensibilities about characters. And the fact that soaps are set in the upper-middle-class strata is a reflection of projecting the "good life" similar to that found in Depression-era radio soaps.

The world of soaps is not a pastoral world. Soaps' staple story lines are rife with conflict and chaos. But this conflict is rarely geopolitical. Instead it swirls and changes in the interpersonal networks that comprise the ensemble cast of a soap opera. Out of this springs a long list of morality plays and myths that soaps derive and retell in countless ways. The long history the characters have with each other is the breeding ground for these kinds of plot development (Hayward 1997). Although they are far from presenting the ideal family or the ideal community, Tania Modleski (1982) nonetheless argues that the inner and interpersonal conflict in soaps ultimately affirms the importance of family by illustrating the costs of a family at odds with itself. Ien Ang's analysis of the audience for *Dallas* finds that this is the large appeal of soaps: The emphasis on the unavoidable and conflictual elements of interpersonal relations provides the audience with a world that is familiar but does not have to be directly experienced (Ang 1985).

A second common theme in soap operas simplifies a complex world, a world where good and evil are largely clearly defined. But characters can often undergo rather rapid transformations. The monitoring of viewer mail plays an important role in how long a character remains on the show or whether his or her evil streak is due for a transformation. The clear black and white world of soaps is part of their mythological orientation, and as such it emphasizes morality over matters of action (Traynor Williams 1992; Brown 1990; Lozano 1992). Finally, while the audience for soaps tends to live more modestly than the characters in the stories they follow, soaps project a middle- to upper-middle-class lifestyle and world-view. Mary Cassata argues that soaps rarely deal with "the absence of money, the absence of unemployment and the need to budget, save and plan" and maintains soaps are extensions of commercials by presenting the latest in home styles, fashions, hairstyles and luxury items (1985, 52). Reflecting the American dream that hard work brings financial success and status, this is one area where American soap operas differ from their British counterparts. Dorothy Hobson says that American soaps are aspirational in a way that many British working-class soaps are not (Hobson 2003). Soaps reflect the contemporary material value system and trends in fashion and consumption and generally help promote the projection of self through material consumption.

Research on soap audiences provides evidence that soaps cultivate an upper-middle-class worldview among college students who are "ritualistic" viewers. The class correspondence between the soap world and the world of advertising further defines for viewers what is considered "the good life." Such images of affluence serve to socialize the audience to pick up on markers of affluence and result in a tendency toward inflated assessments of affluence in the real world among heavy watchers of soaps, especially among those with less income and education (Carveth and Alexander 1985; O'Guinn and Shrum 1997).

Thus, all three of these story characteristics help make soaps attractive to audiences. Conflict and chaos in stories provide ongoing tension as some plot lines are resolved while leading to yet more developments. Audiences get to cheer and jeer for their favorite good and bad characters. Projections of the "good life" serve the ongoing association of material desire with the American dream, thus creating a perfect environment for advertisers to sell access to the dream of prosperity.

SOAP OPERAS AND THE ECONOMICS
OF MARKET-BASED TELEVISION

The overriding goal of this book is to show how the rules of soap opera storytelling and their relationship to market interests and values influence content trends in news, entertainment, and sports. The elements of soap opera programming presented above are meant to provide a way to systematically link the kinds of stories told and the way stories are told to the market interests and values that guide television and the larger media industries in which it operates.

The way programs are produced, what advertisers expect for their purchases of airtime, and how television programs are judged to be successful are all important factors in what television has become over the last few decades. Soap operas have three characteristics relevant to these concerns:

- Soaps are cheap to produce.
- Soaps are effective in building audience loyalty.
- Soaps are profitable for networks.

It is important to note that we are indeed privileging television's economic priorities over the aesthetic and social values by which television programs can also be judged. Nicholas Garnham asserts that the creative people involved in producing television programs "are subject to increasingly rationalized processes of production within which any room for resistance to the crudest commercial pressures, whether in the name of truth or imagination, has been drastically reduced" (1997, 64).

To shift our thinking from judging programs only on aesthetic criteria, we must begin from the assumption that the product that television produces is not programming but rather the audience, a set of eyes and ears available for exposure to advertising, for the benefit of the advertisers who buy time during program breaks. The most important criterion for a show to be aired and sustained is its marketability, its ability to reach and capture a desired demographic slice of the audience for exposure to advertising. From this position, it is clear that developing loyalty to a program that helps build brand loyalty to the products hawked during advertising breaks is the most manifest goal for the television industry. Follow-up marketing research in the early days of soaps found listeners' brand preferences increased with the number of hours per week they spent with soaps. Research like this that prompted the explosive growth of soaps during the 1930s. Robert Allen concludes that, "The soap opera is, and always has been, a narrative text in service of an economic imperative" (1985, 100).

The cost-effectiveness of soaps begins from the way they are produced. An assembly line approach to script construction solves part of the problem of authorship; the collective nature of story making means the story's progress does not rest with a single person's vision. Nicholas Abercrombie asserts that soaps are produced by methods that "are effectively industrialized, of manifesting a high degree of division of labor and specialization and a demand for rapid and cheap production" (1996, 123).

The assembly line approach to completing scripts is directed by a head writer, who serves as the creative manager of the story. The key is that any individual writer's style cannot predominate—scripts must be indistinguishable. This authorial anonymity contributes to the commodification of soaps. As illustrated by the cases of Irna Phillips and the husband and wife team of Frank and Anne Hummert, soap producers were able to oversee numerous soap operas in the 1930s by guiding the story but leaving the scriptwriters to create the dialogue (Allen 1985; Lavin 1995; Meyers 1997). As television has become a center for profit rather than a source of quality culture, "the increasing rationalization of television production in the name of efficiency has shrunk artistic and journalistic license" (Garnham 1997).

Soaps produced in the United States stand in direct contrast in this respect to soap operas produced in Britain. British soaps are produced in the tradition of public service, and thus story lines in British soaps are geared toward social realism and are set in working-class environments. Set in friendly and supportive communities, British soaps embrace a nostalgic past in which characters offer care and concern for each other. Similarly, the *telenovelas* of Latin America often serve to educate or enlighten audiences on issues of the day like AIDS or economic hardship. On the other hand, soaps in the United States rarely deal with the absence of money or the need to budget or plan household economies. The focus on melodrama and romance in upper-middle-class settings that are the subject of U.S. soap operas reflects a commercial imperative of attracting a daytime audience for exposure to consumer culture from the 1930s onward (Liebes and Livingstone 1994; Cassata 1985).

The loyal audiences built by this approach are the prize that advertisers covet. A 1994 survey by the Times-Mirror Center for People and the Press found that 17 percent of Americans sampled said they were regular viewers of soaps (Greenberg and Busselle 1996). While soaps continue to attract the traditional demographic target of housewives, changes in the workforce beginning in the 1970s caused producers and advertisers to seek a wider audience. The ideal addition to the audience would prove to be young people, and specifically, college students. Not only are college students consumers of household products themselves, they are also the future members of the upper middle class who will possess a great deal of purchasing power. Socializing these young people to desire the comfortable and sometimes luxurious lifestyle that one witnesses in both daytime and evening soap operas is an ideal goal for a program genre whose existence is owed to the successful cultivation of a consumer society.

A ratings decline in the 1970s also brought to soaps more controversial subject matter, especially in the form of more explicit portrayals of sexuality. As part of the drive to attract and maintain young audiences, more exterior locations, more action, and more bizarre developments found their way into soap stories. Jennifer Hayward describes the process succinctly: "To produce a profitable show, networks must increase advertising revenues; increasing revenues requires keeping ratings up; high ratings imply satisfied viewers; and viewer satisfaction demands a compelling show, which means networks must keep tabs on what viewers consider compelling" (1997, 146).

Nonetheless, while television producers are eager to please their advertising sponsors by socializing young people into a consumption ethic and providing an audience for exposure to consumption opportunities, television organizations do not act as charitable enterprises for this function; they are required to generate profit for their own corporate interests. While definitive figures on the profitability of soap operas are elusive, it is quite clear that soaps are profit generators for the networks on which they are aired. Early radio soaps, according to Robert Allen, were very effective at generating profits. They more than held their own against non-serial shows. Even after the initial crush and saturation of soap operas in the 1930s, soaps remained considerably more popular than other types of radio programs. In 1948 the ten highest-rated daytime shows were all soap operas; of the top thirty shows, only five were not soaps (Allen 1985). By 1954 television soap audiences were larger than those for radio soaps. Over one-third of revenues generated by CBS television came from daytime advertising, and CBS was soap king, with the top four soaps from 1952 to 1967 (McDonald 1990).

High ratings means networks can charge more for their advertising time, and thus soaps were and continue to be very cost effective. Expenses are lower than for other types of shows, and the higher ratings mean they generate substantial dollars for networks. For example, *The Young and the Restless* generated $38 million in advertising receipts in the last three months of 2002 despite having a significantly smaller audience than ten or twenty years before (Healey 2003).

Dennis Mazzocco, a longtime employee of ABC who worked in several capacities at the network, including for the ABC soap operas *Loving* and *One Life to Live*, says soaps were "a large source of profits for the networks" (1994, 16). The Broadcast Cable Financial Management Association states that soap operas account for about 12 percent of major networks' profits and continue to draw higher ratings than other daytime programming such as talk shows (Borg 1999). Given that soaps are a relatively small slice of the television schedule, this is a rather surprising figure considering that news, prime time shows, sports programs, children's shows, and other daytime and evening fare are part of the network ensemble of shows and are also profit generators for the network and its parent company.

The proprietary nature of network financial information prevents a comparison of the profitability of prime time soap operas versus other forms of evening programming, but as discussed in chapter 9, the craze of the last few years, prime time "reality" programs, is employing many of the storytelling techniques and structural features found in soap operas. The long tradition of soap operas in the service of corporate profits affects the invention of new program formats by networks that are always in search of the new "trick" to attract viewers.

CONCLUSION

The "grand narrative" of television, the story told in the vast majority of programming, consists of celebrating material consumption and presenting the "American dream" primarily as one preaching that material prosperity will generate substantial happiness and contentment. In looking at soap operas as an economic phenomenon that drives the construction of other television programming, the remainder of this book strives to show how the drive for profits in the era of media conglomeration has put soap opera storytelling techniques at the center of what concerns television producers. Douglas Kellner argues that the economics of television structures both the encoding (the production of media messages) and decoding (the interpretation of those messages by the audience) of media products: "Capitalist societies are organized according to a dominant mode of production that structures institutions and practices according to the logic of commodification and capital accumulation so that cultural production is profit and market oriented . . . determining what sort of cultural artifacts are produced and how they are consumed" (1997, 105).

If the drive for profit is the primary determining factor in what networks produce for audiences, then the "commodity form of television," the soap opera (Potter 1977), should be influential in shaping contemporary programming, whether it is prime time entertainment, sports programming, or news and public affairs programming. As it examines the different kinds of programming influenced by the soap opera paradigm, this book demonstrates that the transformation of television as an arm of the larger cultural industries in the United States has put soap opera storytelling techniques at the forefront of what producers think about as they invent new programs to reach economically desirable segments of the population.

3

The WWE: Machismo, Melodrama, and Money

/Professional wrestling, as it has been shaped by the now dominant World Wrestling Entertainment Incorporated (WWE), presents an archetypal example of how the soap opera paradigm functions in the world of popular culture and television./Like much popular entertainment, the history of wrestling reflects changes in American society, in the role athletes play in celebrity culture, and in the television industry, especially in the last twenty years. Moving well beyond the "don't they know it's fake?" amazement at the success of the professional wrestling industry, this chapter explores how this cross between sports and entertainment has become a major media force in American society.

From its simple origins in carnivals and county fairs to the multishow presentations of WWE events across several television networks, the story of professional wrestling captures the story of much of corporate America, moving from a regional phenomenon to a global enterprise, developing a fan base that moves well beyond working-class males, and facing the continual challenge of keeping the product fresh and at least somewhat unpredictable/The core of this phenomenon lies at its appropriation of soap opera storytelling in attracting and maintaining audiences at several levels. Fans who attend live shows and those who watch some of the regular wrestling shows aired on cable television channels contribute to a set of revenue streams, including ticket sales, advertising income, magazine sales, and spin-off merchandising that make the WWE a very successful media enterprise/In short, the WWE is a superb example of how the "genius" of the soap opera paradigm has been perfected in a way that goes beyond a single television series to develop into a pop culture phenomenon/

A BRIEF HISTORY OF PROFESSIONAL WRESTLING

While pinpointing a particular time and place where "it all started" is difficult when it comes to what we know as professional wrestling, it is generally thought that nineteenth-century England gave birth to the combative sports of boxing and wrestling. Several wrestling styles developed; for example, Greco-Roman wrestling went on to establish itself as a serious amateur sport in the Olympics and in collegiate athletics. As it developed in the United States, the catch-as-catch-can style caught on even though it was barred in England for its brutality in the late 1800s. Wrestling matches in the United States came to resemble barroom brawls, consisting of challenges at fairs and similar events. The problem of early wrestling was that its "last man standing" ethic meant matches could drag on for hours, and audience interest would wane for lack of action (Ball 1990).

The notion that wrestling could be financially lucrative gave birth to promoters, many of whom were saloon owners who added stage halls to their establishments and promoted matches ahead of time to generate interest. The first major wrestling event was held in 1880 at Madison Square Garden in New York before a crowd of three thousand. This match was in the Greco-Roman style, and when the winner was challenged by a catch-as-catch-can wrestler, promoters had to determine a standard style for future matches and championships (Kreit 1998).

A series of problems involving injuries, pacing, and fraud led to the transformation of wrestling from a contest to a show. By the 1920s attempts to ensure people got their money's worth from an event meant that the competition was frequently fixed, and when fans discovered this, they were outraged. Fans were bored by the length of legitimate matches and outraged by the promoters' manipulation of staged matches. Wrestling became somewhat of a laughing stock and disappeared from the "big time" to continue as a working-class sport broken into regional enterprises throughout the country. In 1933 there were six "world champions"; by 1943 there were fifteen. Each promoter controlled a territory and developed his "world" championship free of competition from other regional promoters (Kreit 1998).

Once professional wrestling was determined to be less than a sport, media of the day gave it very little attention. Newspapers didn't cover it at all in their sport sections, and it was not an event that translated well over radio. The arrival of television, however, opened up the potential for wrestling, as its restricted space matched well with what a television picture could provide. As Fred McDonald puts it:

No sport better exploited the visual capabilities of TV than professional wrestling, which generated an enormous following in the first years of the medium . . . wrestling offered movement, spectacle, combat and frequently captivating melodrama of moral conflict as good "clean" wrestlers . . . were pitted against evil "dirty" wrestlers. (1990, 46)

While sports and television were constant companions from television's beginnings as a mass medium, wrestling in particular made frequent, even nightly, appearances on television screens in the late 1940s. At this point television programming was very local—the networks had yet to establish themselves as programming forces, so the vast majority of programming was done at the local or regional level. Of the top ten programs airing in Chicago in 1949, three were wrestling shows. Chicago became a center for professional wrestling and eventually originated two national television shows—*Saturday Night Wrestling*, aired on the Dumont network, and *Wednesday Night Wrestling*, on ABC. There was a revival in the popularity of wrestling in New York City as a result of local telecasting of wrestling shows. The prime time airing of these shows decreased as network control over prime time asserted itself in the 1950s (McDonald 1990; Kreit 1998, Ball 1990).

Early television was often viewed in bars, as not everyone owned a set, and this setting in effect brought wrestling back to its roots and made for conversation in drinking establishments. Crucial to the survival of nonnetwork stations, wrestling shows were an important source of advertising revenue. Wrestlers such as "Gorgeous George" served as celebrity endorsers of local stores and products. Even back then announcers were part of the act, conducting postmatch "interviews" that would set up future matches (Ball 1990).

The televising of matches had a profound effect on the theatrics of wrestling events, affecting character development of wrestlers and the story lines that provided the grist for the conflict between two enemies. Televised wrestling prompted the development of characters and story lines based on stereotypes, especially when it came to foreign wrestlers, and in particular, Russians during the Cold War. It is generally thought that this further move into "entertainment" as opposed to "sport" began to break down the class lines that had developed after the earlier controversies about fixing the matches/Now that it was entertainment, the theatrics and melodrama of wrestling could be seen as tongue-in-cheek and enjoyed by the previously disdainful middle class, which, of course, meant that there was money to be made/

The beginnings of a national circuit came about in the 1940s when promoters recognized the potential for profits and formed the first National Wrestling Association or NWA. Although it was a loose association, the NWA is credited with establishing the first genuine championship in wrestling (Keith 2001). It is estimated that by 1952 there were fifteen million paying spectators at live wrestling events; by 1959, twenty-four million fans were going to arenas to see wrestling in person. But beyond bringing together wrestling promoters from across the country and establishing traveling circuits of wrestling all-stars, the NWA did not work to promote wrestling on a national basis either through national tours or via national television exposure.

Wrestling experienced some decline in the 1960s and 1970s. There is a cyclical nature to wrestling's popularity that presents challenges to those who run what has become a cultural force in American society. What revived the sport was an entrepreneurial interlocutor by the name of Vince McMahon Jr.

McMahon Turns Pro Wrestling into a Cultural Industry

Vincent McMahon Sr. was one of several regional wrestling promoters, who enjoyed his role as northeast promoter of wrestling cards. He was content with the system as it functioned and got along well with his peers throughout the country. When Vince Jr. joined Vince Sr. in 1972, he focused on the television side of the business and worked for the next decade as on-air commentator, expanding the syndication of his show from nine to thirty stations. In 1982 he and his wife Linda bought out his father and began to transform wrestling from an amusing farce into a tongue-in-cheek spectacle, with loud sounds, pyrotechnics, and enhanced scripting of live events. When Vince Jr. snagged a cable deal with USA cable TV network in 1983 (Keith 2001), he had put together the last piece of the puzzle that would wipe out his father's fellow regional promoters (Ball 1990; Dorschner 2000). By that time the priorities of television had overtaken consideration of the paying spectators, as cameras often blocked the view of the people in the arena.

McMahon accomplished all this by luring the best showmen/wrestlers from the other regional promoters and getting early national television exposure when he took over the local NWA wrestling circuit in Atlanta, took its show to "superstation" WTBS in 1984, and established "World Championship Wrestling." In 1985 he went even further toward becoming a national force when "The War to Settle the Score" was aired on MTV—then the still relatively new music cable channel aimed at young people. McMahon also found his way over to NBC, which created the *Saturday Night Main Event* in May 1985 as a once-a-month substitute for the long-running late-night show *Saturday Night Live*. Going even further, McMahon developed the youth market for wrestling in a Saturday morning cartoon show, *Rock 'n Wrestling*, in 1985 (Keith 2001).

The audience base for professional wrestling was beginning to shift toward an increasing number of middle-class viewers. Middle-class teenagers were regarded as having more and more disposable income throughout the 1980s; McMahon's targeting of this key demographic dovetailed nicely with the desires of advertisers, and, therefore, television networks. McMahon's showmanship spawned wrestling's entry into the pay-per-view television world in October 1985 with the inaugural *Wrestlemania* (Kreit 1998).

THE WWE REVENUE NEXUS

In the years since McMahon and his wife bought out his father, Linda and Vince McMahon have created an entertainment juggernaut that is known worldwide. In 1999 Linda McMahon earned $1.6 million in salary and bonuses, while Vince earned $2.2 million and owned 56 million shares of stock. In 2001 the WWE bought out the rival WCW (World Championship Wrestling), an enterprise Ted Turner had started in 1988 by purchasing the NWA and repackaging it when he saw just what a cash cow the WWE was becoming (Kreit 1998). At this point the only competition the WWE faces is from the weekly pay-per-view NWA-TNA (National Wrestling Alliance–Total Nonstop Action), available through satellite and cable systems.

But eliminating the competition hasn't ended the challenges to the McMahons. There have been bumps in the road, most recently in autumn 2002 when a ratings slide resulted in a 30 percent drop in share price for WWE stock. Failed ventures such as the 2001 Extreme Football League (XFL), which was supposed to bring WWE gimmicks to the football field, were a further drain on the McMahon corporate ledger. Similarly, it has been losing money on its six hundred-seat theme restaurant in New York's Times Square. Legal actions against the WWE in the form of a sexual harassment suit; a wrongful death suit filed by the survivors of Owen Hart, whose fall from seventy feet killed him in a 1999 pay-per-view show; and the name change (World Wrestling Federation to World Wrestling Entertainment), prompted by a lawsuit from the World Wildlife Fund, have all affected the profit machine that was the WWE in the late 1990s (Dorschner 2000; Silverman 2002; Piscia 2002).

Nonetheless, the WWE's multiple sources of revenue are designed to ride out rough spots and maintain a loyal following. Understanding how the different revenue streams are developed through the multiple WWE programs aired weekly across several networks provides an understanding of how Vince and Linda McMahon have created the ultimate example of how the soap opera paradigm works.[1]

Live and televised events and branded merchandise are the two primary arms of WWE revenues. Live and televised event revenues totaled

$323.5 million or 76 percent of total revenues in 2002. Over two million people attended WWE events in 2002. And it's not cheap to do so. Floor seats at live events sell for $300—but at least fans get to keep the WWE stenciled logo seat! Arena seats cost $75, and a T-shirt costs another $30 (Rose 2001). Live events have gone global in the last few years; Australia, South Korea, Japan, Malaysia, England, Northern Ireland, and Finland were visited by the WWE in 2002.

These shows serve as the fodder for the numerous cable television shows and twelve pay-per-view shows per year in North America. Nine hours of programming are produced each week. The two primary shows are Monday night's *WWE RAW*, which scores rather consistently as the top-rated cable show, and Thursday night's *Smackdown* program, which also runs two hours. One estimate holds that one episode of *Smackdown* generates $1 million in revenue ("UPN, WWE pin down new 'Smackdown' wrestling pact" 2003). Each of these two primary shows has two accompanying hour-long programs that present highlights and developments that occurred during the primary shows. *Sunday Night Heat* (until recently aired on MTV, now aired on Spike TV) presents itself as an arena show with a different set of commentators than heard on *RAW*. *WWE: The Bottom Line* is a syndicated studio show that presents highlights from *RAW* and *Sunday Night Heat*. The shows associated with *Smackdown* are *WWE:Velocity*, a one-hour "live" show, and *WWE After Burn*, a studio show aired in syndication.

Two other shows round out the WWE lineup. *WWE Confidential* is a magazine show featuring highlights from both *RAW* and *Smackdown*; it often features "superstars" from the past and present. The final program, which has had three separate runs, is the *Tough Enough* reality show, which aired on MTV. This program involved a competition between young men and women to attain a wrestling contract with WWE. The last series aired from October 2002 to January 2003 and was the top-rated cable program on Thursday nights. The two winners selected were given wrestling contracts as the prize. As shown in the analysis of WWE programming in winter 2003, the winners became part of a storyline in *RAW*.

Branded merchandise accounted for 24 percent ($101.5 million) of revenues in 2002. In the last few years, branded merchandise offerings have exploded and now include the toys, apparel, video games, music CDs, book and magazine publishing, home video/DVD, and films. Music CDs were first released in 2000, and WWE Books was launched in fall 2002, with twelve books planned for 2003. *WWE Magazine* and *WWE Raw* have monthly circulations of 267,000 and 173,000 respectively. WWE Films was established in summer 2002 with plans for an animation series, live-action television series, and its first ever pay-per-view movie. Rather constant plugs for these products are made on all the WWE television shows.

The fall 2002 stock slide prompted a series of changes in the story lines, designed to restore the WWE's fading luster. The key to the analysis presented below is that the creative writing team that daughter Stephanie McMahon heads has taken the financial situation of WWE and turned it into a story line by putting several WWE celebrity employees' jobs on the line as they try to revive the sagging ratings. Making the drop in stock price a motivating factor in what goes on at WWE events is just an extension of what Linda McMahon calls "a soap opera action adventure" (Dorschner 2000).

JANUARY 2003—THE ROAD TO *NO WAY OUT*

The "crisis" defined by the drop in stock price and revenues throughout 2002 prompted an attempt to revive sagging ratings by presenting story lines designed to bring back the WWE stars. "Stone Cold" Steve Austin and Hulk Hogan were the primary subjects of discussion on *RAW* and *Smackdown*, respectively. On a quarterly basis, story lines are written so that they reach their climax at the quarterly pay-per-view show, in this case *Wrestlemania*. There are two monthly pay-per-view shows, which provide mini-arcs during this time and serve to further story development as they approach the quarterly spectacular. Given the $35 price tag for television pay-per-view events, this means fans who want to see how story lines develop quarterly will shell out over $100 to do so.

Analysis of a week's worth of three *RAW*-related shows finds fans anticipating the next monthly pay-per-view *No Way Out* as it leads to the late winter *Wrestlemania*. The purpose of this analysis is to show how one week of the *RAW*-related shows develops fan interest in the next pay-per-view and promotes all the other WWE products mentioned above.

As *RAW* is the centerpiece show for the other two shows, this section describes the story line, action, and promotional elements aired for a single week. The two spin-off shows, *Sunday Night Heat* and *After Burn*, are reviewed for how they appropriate the same story lines and promote upcoming live events, pay-per-views, magazine content, videos, and books. Four hours of programming of *RAW*-related material are aired each week, giving hard-core fans a lot to talk about in chat rooms and bulletin boards on the Internet. From a production perspective, the WWE gleans a lot of material from the live *RAW* events to serve as the subject matter for *The Bottom Line* and *Sunday Night Heat.* The same highlights of ongoing story lines are presented three times (once for each program); thus these shows are cheap to produce and serve the same function as airing reruns of network programs: getting more buck for the wrestling bang. Program logs for each of the three shows for the week of January 27, 2003, are provided in tables 3.1, 3.2, and 3.3.

RAW

Advertising laden and promotion driven, *RAW*, as one of the two show-case programs in the WWE stable, comprises wrestling action, backstage plotting, and pre- and post-match story line development. Until a viewer becomes savvy, all of this initially appears as a bewildering array of plots and subplots.

The January 27, 2003, episode of *RAW* opens with a "last week" recap of match results and injuries. Viewers are also reminded that Vince McMahon has given his *RAW* general manager Eric Bishoff one month to bring back the luster to a show that was experiencing a ratings slide. McMahon has put the jobs of Bishoff and his assistant, "Chief of Staff" Morely, on the line, saying that if they can't turn *RAW* around, they will be fired. This was the primary story line for this episode and all those monitored in the lead-up to *No Way Out*, a pay-per-view event that took place on the last Sunday in February 2003. Bishoff had previously announced his intention to lure "Stone Cold" Steve Austin back into the ring after Austin had left the WWE in a dispute with Vince McMahon, which according to *The Encyclopedia of Professional Wrestling* is "one of the biggest money-grossing feuds of all time" (Pope 2001, 169).

The controversy surrounding the return of Austin was the primary story line leading up to *No Way Out* and the subject of backstage story development, an ongoing part of the ring commentators' banter as they described the action, and the focus of in-ring speeches and exchanges between the feuding parties. But the development of the Bishoff/Stone Cold story line went beyond the television shows to embedding additional information in *RAW Magazine*, which contained an interview with Austin. The magazine's interview with Austin was plugged repeatedly in all three shows. Other subplots involving controversies among other WWE wrestlers filled the two-hour show, but the Stone Cold story line was clearly front and center. For each of the other subplots, ring commentators' perspectives, video from earlier matches, and post-match controversies are played for viewers.

The first match between Booker T and Jeff Hardy ends with Booker T prevailing—sort of. Post-match antics find Hardy jumping a victorious Booker T, throwing him out of the ring, and mocking his signature victory "spin." Commentators spice things up during match lulls by talking about the Bishoff/Stone Cold controversy. Before an advertising break, Scott Steiner (a.k.a. Big Poppa Pump and Freakzilla) is seen vowing his revenge of a loss to wrestler Triple H.

Table 3.1. Program Log for RAW

Running Time	Segment Category	Segment Summary
0:00:00	Intro/review	Recap Triple H not cleared to fight, Batista to sub vs. Steiner
0:02:15	Musical intro	Review last week
0:03:40	Match set-up	Jeff Hardy vs. Booker T
0:05:58	Match begins	
0:10:36	Ending/aftermath	Hardy pinned/Booker T does move/Hardy comes back and beats up Booker T
0:11:55	Backstage	Steiner gang
0:12:11	Ads	:30 for WWE (Nathan Jones)/:30 for TNN/2:20 other products
0:15:41	In-ring story line	Steiner enters ring/challenges Triple H/recap last week's match/Triple H, Steiner returns with pipe to beat them—they leave
0:22:15	Ads	:23 for WWE/2:30 for other products
0:25:08	Backstage	D-lo Brown/Hurricane match set-up
0:26:20	Match set-up	Wrestlers enter ring/plug Green Bay show tomorrow night
0:27:35	Match begins	
0:31:33	Ending/aftermath	
0:31:55	Coming up	Update on Stacy Keebler
0:32:05	Ads	3:00 other products
0:35:05	Backstage	McMahon/Hogan recap/Bishoff and Morely discuss 30-day deadline to save jobs (now down to 2 weeks)/Review Jerico/Steebler injury
0:39:10	In-ring story line	Jerico goes to ring to apologize/explain
0:39:40	Ads	3:00 other products
0:42:10	Plug upcoming	Trish vs. Victoria promo/Dudley Boys table match
0:42:41	In-ring story line	Jerico apologizes about chair incident but blames boyfriend Test for injury/Shawn Michaels enters ring/tosses Jerico and Christian from ring
0:52:10	Backstage	Trish seen hitting trashcan
0:52:41	Ads	1:06 for WWE/3:30 other products
0:56:38	Match set-up	Women enter ring
0:57:09	Match begins	Victoria vs. Trish
1:02:48	Match ends	Victoria wins but continues to beat Trish/Jazz enters ring and also beats up on Trish

(*continued*)

Table 3.1.   Program Log for *RAW* (continued)

Running Time	Segment Category	Segment Summary
1:06:36	Coming up	Plug table match
1:06:50	Ads	:28 for WWE/:37 TNN promos/2:30 for other products
1:10:25	Match set-up	Dudley Boys, Lance Strong, William Regal enter ring
1:12:58	Match begins	
1:18:28	Match ends	Three Minute Warning (another tag team) enters, ring brawl ensues
1:19:33	Aftermath ends	
1:20:33	Ads	1:00 for WWE/2:00 for other products
1:23:33	Backstage	Triple H/Batista/others confront Bishoff about Steiner's cheating
1:24:45	Backstage	Tough Enough winners backstage/discuss other controversies
1:27:01	Ads	3:30 other products
1:30:34	Review/match set-up	Tough Enough competition/winners reviewed
1:32:33	Match begins	Nowinski enters ring, accuses Tough Enough winners of making him look bad/Tommy Dreamer enters ring, chases Nowinski from ring/knocks 2 wrestlers out with stick
1:36:15	Backstage	Bishoff's job at stake
1:36:28	Ads	:40 for WWE antidrug/3:00 other products
1:40:08	In-ring story line	Bishoff enters ring/says Stone Cold not here, blames McMahon/will tell his side of story in *RAW* magazine/challenges Austin to *No Way Out*
1:45:18	Austin video	Replays/highlights of Austin's ring action
1:48:11	Ads	:51 for WWE/2:50 for other products
1:52:54	Match set-up	Replays of earlier match—Batista/Triple H vs RVD/Kane while commentator talks about Stone Cold/*No Way Out*
2:03:29	Match aftermath	Steiner comes into ring with pipe after match, Batista/Triple H beat up Steiner
2:04:55	Show ends	

The ad break includes a WWE promo for a new wrestler, Australian Nathan Jones, who among other things has spent time in prison. This promo aired on all the WWE shows yet gave no clue as to when he would begin to appear on WWE shows. Another WWE promotional segment that appeared at some point on all shows was the lineup of the coming live WWE events taking place throughout North America in the following week.

A second match features "D-Lo" Brown and "The Hurricane," and as the wrestlers enter the ring, an upcoming WWE live show in Green Bay, Wisconsin, is plugged. A tease before the advertising break after the match promises an update on the Stacey Keebler injury. After the ad, viewers see highlights of the incident that supposedly injured Keebler, girlfriend of "Test," who was wrestling Chris Jerico. Keebler suffered a concussion when, with all three of them outside the ring, Jerico attempted to hit Test with a folding chair, Test ducked, and Jerico accidentally hit Keebler instead. The highlights conclude with Keebler being wheeled out of the arena on a stretcher with her neck and head in traction.

The next segment returns to the Bishoff/Stone Cold story line as the cameras go backstage to a conversation between Bishoff and Morely, worrying about how they will keep their jobs. Then it's back to the Keebler controversy as Jerico is interviewed backstage about how he feels about Keebler's injury. Apparently contrite, he declares he's going out to the ring to present his side of the story.

Another ad break intervenes, and when the show returns, two more upcoming matches are plugged before the cameras switch to the ring to hear what Jerico has to say about the Keebler injury. In a segment that lasts almost ten minutes, Jerico starts talking about a match with Scott Steiner, while the ring commentators ask, "What about Stacey?" Another wrestler, Christian, climbs into the ring (commentators—"What's he doing here?"). He tells Jerico he doesn't need to apologize for hitting Test's girlfriend because she had no business being near the ring, and he has come out to pull Jerico out of his "depression." Jerico perks up and says Test is at fault, and if he had not been a coward and ducked, Keebler would not have gotten hurt.

The cameras return backstage, where female wrestler Trish is preparing for her match with Victoria by hitting a trash can. The ad break following concludes with a tobacco company–sponsored "whack of the night" from the earlier pay-per-view. The two females enter the ring and begin their match, with the commentators remarking that this is "one of the longest running feuds" in the WWE and that it is all "based on jealousy from what I can tell," with no elaboration beyond that statement. It seems the purpose of the commentators' dialogue is to put a feminine rivalry spin on the match.

Victoria wins the match, but as always seems to be the case, that does not end matters by any means. Even as Victoria continues to beat on Trish after her victory, another woman enters the ring and pummels Trish as well. Jazz, who has been injured, wants revenge because she lost her title.

Before yet another ad break, the tag team table match is teased. The tag team match begins after the ad break when the Dudley Boys take on Lance Strong and William Regal, current tag team champs. Table matches end when the victors drop the losers from high onto a table, breaking it and apparently the wrestler's back as well. When a third tag team enters the ring, a brawl ensues, with Regal and Strong winning and the commentators declaring, "The Dudleys are being punished by the administration of this program."

The segment after the ad break features more backstage intrigue. The wrestling "gang" of Triple H, Batista, and Randy Orton, managed by Ric Flair, is seen complaining to Bishoff about Scott Steiner's cheating. They decide they aren't going to worry about it and then walk away. Meanwhile the director/trainer for the recently completed *Tough Enough 3* (*TE 3*) competition/reality show is seen with the two winners, Matt and John, as he prepares them for their *RAW* debut. The commentators also plug the Triple H/Batista versus Rob Van Dam (RVD)/Kane match coming up.

After another ad break, a recap of the *TE 3* competition serves to set up an exhibition between "these two twenty-three-year-olds." As the match proceeds, it is interrupted by Chris Nowinski, a *Tough Enough* competitor from an earlier series who didn't win. He accuses the *TE 3* winners of "rubbing it in" as the commentators and the neophytes in the ring wonder what he could possibly mean by that. Enter Tommy Dreamer, who chases Nowinski from the ring and tells the *TE 3* duo how lucky they are to be in the ring after only their "fourth day in the WWE business." He welcomes them and promptly knocks each of them out with a bamboo pole he carries with him. A tease before the ad break mentions Bishoff's "two weeks to go" dilemma.

When the show resumes, Bishoff enters the ring to address the crowd. Carrying an envelope (a contract perhaps?) he pleads with the hostile crowd to not be angry with him because "Stone Cold's not here." Bishoff plays a video segment of Vince McMahon saying, "Steve was a friend of mine until he walked off the job. I'm angry. He's got issues." Bishoff says he will tell all—"uncensored, unedited in *RAW Magazine*" and invites Stone Cold to return at *No Way Out* and come back home to *RAW*. Before going to another ad break, a video montage of Stone Cold's ring exploits is shown.

The last segment of the show comes back to the Scott Steiner controversy as his enemies Triple H and Batista get in the ring to battle RVD and Kane. The match is only a prelude to the aftermath, in which Steiner appears in the ring with a lead pipe to get his revenge for a bad beating taken in the previous pay-per-view. Chris Jerico comes in the ring and jumps on Steiner. Then the Batista gang, who had backed off from the pipe-wielding Steiner, beat him bloody.

RAW ran a little over two hours. A breakdown of the show finds that about forty minutes of the program provides wrestling action. Match set-ups, which often develop the story line, run for a little over ten minutes. Backstage story developments and in-ring (nonwrestling action) story line development take up another thirty minutes combined. Introductory segments and preadvertisement teasers take up about four minutes. Over one-quarter of the two-hour show is wrapped up in advertising, five minutes of which is for WWE-related products.

Sunday Night Heat

Sunday Night Heat is an hour-long show that presents highlights from *RAW* and some of the other matches not aired during the two-hour show. The format is similar to *RAW*: Ring commentators describe the action and set viewers up with segments that review current controversies or tease upcoming segments. Outside of the ring action not presented during *RAW*, much of the material from *RAW* is presented on *Heat*, albeit in edited form.

The show begins with the primary story line for the WWE, Eric Bishoff's attempt to bring Steve Austin back to *RAW* and to "save" his job. One new match features Goldust versus Steven Richards, but much of the commentary during the match is about the Bishoff/Austin story line. Viewers get a five-minute match followed by a tease for the Christian–Maven match coming up. Fifty seconds of WWE promotional material during the ad break consists of the Nathan Jones tease and promotion of Jerry Lawler's book.

The return from the four-minute-plus ad break features a tag team match. The end of this match brings a tease for the Jerico/Keebler "chair" story line. After another four-minute ad break, five minutes are dedicated to summarizing Jerico's "apology" and the chasing of Jerico by Shawn Michaels; then there is another four-minute ad break, this time including a pitch for the WWE video *Best of Confidential*, and a JVC "Tower of Power" segment (thirty-seven seconds) features the *Tough Enough 3* exhibition from RAW in which both wrestlers get knocked out by Tommy Dreamer.

The Rico–Spike Dudley match takes up the next segment. Much of the commentator banter however, is about the return of Stone Cold. The resolution of the match is followed by a tease for the RVD/Kane versus Triple H/Batista tag team match, which comes after another four-minute

Table 3.2. Program Log for *Sunday Night Heat*

Running Time	Segment Category	Segment Summary
0:00:00	Introduction	Eight days for Bishoff to save his job
0:00:30	Match set-up	Goldust vs. Steven Richards, continue to talk about Stone Cold Austin
0:01:45	Match begins	
0:06:22	Match ends	Goldust wins
0:06:57	Coming up	Tease upcoming tag team match
0:07:17	Ads	:49 for WWE (Lawler book, Nathan Jones/:50 for MTV/3:00 for other products)
0:11:56	Match begins	
0:16:27	Match aftermath	Brawl continues after bell has sounded ending match
0:16:45	Coming up	Tease Jerico situation
0:17:00	Ads	1:10 for WWE/:55 MTV promos/2:30 for other products
0:21:35	Commentators	Talk about Asian tour
0:27:07	Review/replay	Review of Keebler chair incident/ Jerico apology/Shawn Michaels interrupts Jerico, chased from ring
0:27:12	Coming up	Plug next week's *RAW*
0:27:22	Ads	:37 for WWE/:45 MTV promos/3:00 for other products
0:31:44	Replay	JVC stereo replay of Tough Enough wrestling exhibition
0:32:45	Match set-up	Spike Dudley match
0:33:50	Match begins	Dudley wins (talk about Bishoff's 8 days to save job)
0:38:03	Coming up	Plug RVD/Kane vs. Batista/Triple H
0:38:28	Ads	1:10 for WWE/:35 MTV promos/3:00 other products
0:43:14	Match set-up	Hype main event
0:45:35	Promo for *RAW*	Promote next week's RAW
0:46:00	Coming up	
0:46:25	Ads	:50 for WWE/:25 MTV promos/3:00 other products
0:50:40	Match set-up	WWE anthology CD/*No Way Out* plugs/set-up match
0:52:05	Match begins	Talk during match about Stone Cold not liking Bishoff/*RAW* magazine interview
0:58:00	Match ends	Talk about tomorrow night's *RAW*
0:58:32	Show credits	

ad break. A brief segment follows the street brawl, which comes at the end of the tag team match and plugs the next night's *RAW* and the final segment of *Heat*.

The final four-minute ad break brings the total amount of time spent on ads and promotional material for either the WWE or MTV (the network airing the show at that time) to twenty-two minutes, thirty seconds, or over one-third of the show time. Four and one-half minutes are spent on WWE promos. The ad break concludes with a "WWE Starburst Rewind" (a highlight from last week) and a plug for the *Anthology by Christian* music CD. The commentators end the ad segment with another "teaser," asking, "Will Stone Cold be in the house three weeks from now as we head toward *Wrestlemania*?"

The Christian–Maven match takes about six minutes, during which the commentators continue to talk about Stone Cold not liking Bishoff and learning about that from *RAW Magazine*. The show concludes with a plug for the next night's *RAW*. Similar to *RAW*, a little over one-third of the hour-long show is wrestling action. Program teasers and match set-ups take up about ten minutes of the show

The Bottom Line

The second spin-off from *RAW* takes a different tack from *Heat*. It is a studio show featuring action from *RAW* and *Sunday Night Heat*. This show is hosted by twenty-something Mark Lloyd and begins with a recap of the main story lines: McMahon's charge to Bishoff to "shake the foundations of *RAW*" and Bishoff's invitation to Austin.

In each segment of *The Bottom Line*, Lloyd sets up highlights of particular matches or story lines. In this episode, the Booker T–Jeff Hardy match, the *Tough Enough* winners' "exhibition match" that results in their beating by Tommy Dreamer, the tag team championship between the Dudleys and Strong/Regal, and the brawl between Kane/RVD and Batista/Triple H are covered. Story line material concerns the Keebler injury/Jerico apology and, of course, the Bishoff/Austin comeback.

Commentary from Mark Lloyd and the ring commentators during match and story line segments focuses on the primary story lines. At one point, Lloyd does a thirty-second plug for the *RAW Magazine* interview with Stone Cold, which "will be available on newsstands shortly."

In all, seven segments are sandwiched between six ad breaks totaling twenty-one minutes of the hour-long show, including over five minutes of WWE promotional material, such as ads for the *Best of Confidential* video, the *Anthology* CD, promos for upcoming WWE live events across North

Table 3.3. Program Log for *The Bottom Line*

Running Time	Segment Category	Segment Summary
0:00:00	Introductory piece	Last Week on *RAW*: McMahon's threats to Bishoff; Bishoff announces intention to lure "Stone Cold" Steve Austin; Show intro montage
0:01:25	Studio: Mark Lloyd	Talks about Bishoff/Austin; Steiner beaten by Triple H/Batista/Orton/Flair
0:02:26	Match highlights	Jeff Hardy vs. Booker T—Booker wins. Hardy attacks Booker, after match mocks Booker's 'move'
0:04:08	Still to come	Bishoff's plan teased
0:04:19	Ads	:30 seconds for WWE video/1:30 other products/:30 Promos for WB shows
0:06:49	Studio: Mark Lloyd	Review conclusion of "Tough Enough 3"/Cut to replay of exhibition match/Tommy Dreamer's chasing of Nowinski from ring, hits both wrestlers with pole knocking them out.
0:09:58	Coming up	
0:10:19	Ads	1:20 for WWE—upcoming live shows/highlights of Asian tour/2:00 other products/:30 WB promos
0:14:09	Studio: Mark Lloyd	Review Far East tour/Bishoff two weeks to get RAW straightened out/set up Victoria/Trish match
0:15:14	Match highlights	Victoria wins/Jazz enters ring after match, also pummels defeated Trish
0:18:57	Studio	Comments on match/notes Jazz's injury last Spring
0:19:24	Coming up	Plug Stacy Keebler injury controversy
0:19:36	Ads	:30 for WWE/3:15 other products
0:23:21	Highlights	Replay Keebler accident/interview with Jerico
0:24:48	Studio: Mark Lloyd	Talks about implications of accident and Jerico's apology; scenes of in-ring antics; plug upcoming RAW
0:31:26	Coming up	Plug Bishoff dilemma
0:31:46	Ads	1:16 for WWE/3:00 other products
0:36:02	Studio: Mark Lloyd	Set up highlights of tag team championship rematch
0:36:38	Match Highlights	Table match, no table under ring/trick of Chief Morley

(continued)

Table 3.3.   Program Log for *The Bottom Line* (continued)

Running Time	Segment Category	Segment Summary
0:40:00	Coming up	Plug future tag team match
0:40:19	Ads	:47 for WWE/2:00 for other products/:30 WB promos
0:43:36	Studio: Mark Lloyd	Road to Wrestlemania/*No Way Out* plug/set up Bishoff/Stone Cold update
0:44:09	Highlights	Replay Bishoff at RAW, commentators plug Austin's interview in *RAW* magazine
0:47:21	Studio: Mark Lloyd	Plug *RAW* magazine—available on newsstands shortly
0:48:02	Coming up	Plug matches after break
0:48:10	Ads	:18 for WWE/2:30 for other products
0:50:58	Studio: Mark Lloyd	Set up Steiner revenge motives
0:51:26	Match highlights	Main event from *RAW*, Kane/VanDam vs. Batista/Triple H
0:57:12	Studio	Plug upcoming *RAW*; will we hear from Stone Cold?
0:58:31	End—to credits	

America, and plugs for the next *RAW* and *No Way Out*. As did *RAW* and *Sunday Night Heat*, *The Bottom Line* breaks down into about one-third wrestling action, one-third ads, and one-third story line development and show plugs for WWE products and events.

ANALYSIS

It is useful to remind the reader at this point that the one week's worth of *RAW*-related shows detailed here is only half of the weekly TV presence the WWE achieves. Another four-hour block of programs focuses on Thursday night's *Smackdown*, with equally ubiquitous plugs for pay-per-view events and other WWE moneymaking schemes. It is clear from the detailed look at these three WWE programs that this is a carefully scripted soap opera story. In many ways, the jealousies and rivalries evident in these shows are analogous to the jealousies and rivalries in the familial and interpersonal networks of daytime and evening soaps. Friends become enemies, and enemies get revenge on each other. The WWE is the most dysfunctional family on television, and the web of story lines that result rivals that of any domestic soap opera.

But what makes the WWE approach unique is the conscious linking of what's going on in the story lines to consumption "opportunities" for fans of the show; buying access to the *No Way Out* pay-per-view and getting to the newsstands to buy the magazine with Stone Cold's interview are prompted and encouraged by the commentators throughout the show and WWE promos during ad breaks. The particular ads featuring lines of merchandise are presented at points in the show corresponding to action in the ring (e.g., Christian's music CD is plugged right before his match). Product development and promotion are clearly coordinated with story developments.

The use and reuse of so many video segments makes these shows reasonably cheap to produce, and their airing until recently on several channels (TNN, MTV, WB) allowed fans who missed *RAW* to catch up on developments and had the potential to capture viewers who might not normally venture to TNN (now Spike TV), which is increasingly the "television home" of WWE.

All of these factors make the WWE web of programming a superb example of how the soap opera paradigm functions in today's television. While ratings ups and downs may strike panic in the hearts of the McMahons, at least some of that panic is channeled into revenue by integrating the company's financial woes as part of the story line presented during these shows. Besides, the McMahons aren't stupid. The multiple revenue streams and the constant priming of consumption of WWE-related paraphernalia and attendance at live events tend to mitigate the effects of a ratings drop. No show can ever predict consistently what will be or remain successful. But the McMahons try to at least hedge their bets. Reducing risk in programming is what the soap opera paradigm is all about, and thus it has become an effective form of programming for television producers with their eyes on the bottom line.

NOTE

1. This information has been compiled from the "corporate" section of the WWE website, corporate.wwe.com/media/r_facts.html.

II

SOAP OPERA STORYTELLING IN NEWS

At first glance, one might think that news and soap opera storytelling would mix about as well as oil and water. But in today's media-saturated world, news has come to take on many of the characteristics of soaps. Chapter 4 discusses the history of television news and illustrates that while television news producers initially aspired to bring the prestige and seriousness of newspapers to television, nightly television news programs have slowly devolved into a "show" striving to be as entertaining as any prime time fictional programs.

While once seen as a public service, over the last twenty years news divisions at networks have seen their relatively privileged status within the network negated as the broadcast networks have become mere appendages of larger corporate conglomerates. While once free of the concern for the bottom line, network news operations have become increasingly focused on garnering affluent audiences by providing "infotainment" in the guise of news.

A longitudinal analysis of network news content presents evidence that since the mid-1980s, when the networks experienced a first round of takeovers by corporate behemoths, news operations have moved farther and farther away from "straight" reporting to extensive use of soap opera storytelling techniques. Chapter 5 presents a quantitative analysis of just how much news has appropriated soap storytelling over the last two decades. Chapter 6 gives an extensive textual analysis of how news coverage of domestic natural disasters has changed by looking at two flood stories from 1982 and 1997.

Chapter 7 focuses on one of the most important functions of the news—coverage of democracy. Coverage of political campaigns has been heavily criticized for its increasing focus on the "horse race" of the campaign and candidates' personal characteristics rather than the issues that concern voters. Chapter 7 illustrates that these shifts in coverage are reflective of the evolution toward soap opera storytelling in news.

4

The Evolution of the ABC and CBS News Divisions

Before investigating how television news has come to adopt many of the characteristics of soap opera storytelling, it is necessary to take a look at how the economics of television news organizations has evolved. Examining how television news divisions have decidedly drifted from a public service orientation in decision making and editorial values toward an almost exclusive focus on profit making demonstrates how news storytelling has come to reflect a soap opera orientation. It provides a better understanding of the parallels between the larger corporate concerns with profit and the way news shows are assembled and the editorial value judgments that shape how news stories are told. This chapter looks at the evolution of the news divisions at ABC and CBS, whose content is analyzed for the period 1970 to 2000 in chapters 5 through 7. These two networks were selected for in-depth analysis for distinctly different reasons, each choice a reflection of the particular values and reputation each network came to embody.

CBS, whose reputation as the "Tiffany" network rested largely on its news division, was chosen because for many years it strove to be the *New York Times* of the airwaves. Chapter 1 suggests that economic decisions drove CBS to abandon that notion when it was obtained by larger corporate interests. The movement of CBS away from its reputation as a "serious" news organization can be attributed at least in part to the influence of local television news, especially when CBS hired Van Gordon Sauter, who developed his reputation in local television news, to head the news division in 1982. The replacement of the "old guard"—the generation of newspeople headed by Walter Cronkite—saw the turning out of print and radio reporters who had developed their skills during World War II. They were replaced by a generation that developed within the television industry and was not necessarily "burdened" by traditional orientations to journalism. From a "broadcast of record" to the "theory of moments," this chapter explores how industry changes and the conglomeratization of CBS changed the nature and definition of television news.

ABC's news division had a very different beginning and has followed a very different course. As the oft-regarded inferior "third" network, ABC made choices early on to orient its news in ways different from CBS that, ironically, ended with much the same result in the 1980s and 1990s. ABC's choice to emphasize the visual elements and the manner in which television could portray the drama of news events is best manifested in the power garnered by Roone Arledge, whose success at ABC Sports led him to bring about the transformation of ABC's news division. His emphasis on "story lines" in sports coverage was successful in adding to the drama of live sports broadcasts. He brought this orientation to the way news stories were told on ABC. Along with his contribution to the development of the star system in network news, Arledge's leadership at ABC News ultimately affected all three networks' news operations.

TELEVISION NEWS AT THE DAWN OF TELEVISION

Unlike radio, where news gathering didn't really occur until World War II, television existed for just a few years before there were regular evening newscasts on each of the three networks. Nightly news programs began as fifteen-minute newscasts. In 1948 the *CBS Evening News* with Douglas Edwards premiered in the 7:30 P.M. time slot, while the *Camel News Caravan* with John Cameron Swayze as anchor premiered in February 1949 in a 7:45 P.M. time slot on NBC. In 1954, ABC scheduled entertainment programs during this half hour, which resulted in a ratings drop for the news shows at NBC and CBS. By 1957, both CBS and NBC had switched their shows to 7:15 P.M. Eventually, a shift to an earlier time slot—6:30 P.M.—placated affiliates as they began to schedule local television news shows to precede the national network news. In 1963 CBS and NBC started thirty-minute newscasts, while ABC stayed with fifteen minutes; ABC did not go to a half hour until 1967. CBS Chairman William Paley expanded the evening news to a half hour as a way to make CBS the number one network. The additional time meant opportunities to do more depth stories, background features or "explainers," as Paley termed them. These longer segments and stories in newscasts resulted in increased ratings. Thus the half hour news program became entrenched in the early evening (Westin 1982; Kellner 1990).

Network news at this point was seen as a fulfillment of the public service mandate that came with each broadcast station license. It was not until the late 1970s and early 1980s that news divisions at the networks were expected to be profit centers. Indeed, over the years this situation generated a fair amount of resentment at CBS among the other divisions, which regarded the news division as a "spoiled brat" (Boyle 1988). Following on the successes of Edward R. Morrow's *See It Now* programs, CBS strove to excel in both regular news shows and the longer form documentary, which had produced a number of dramatic television moments such as the exposé of the bankruptcy of Senator Joseph McCarthy's communist witch hunts and the conditions under which migrant workers worked across the country in "Harvest of Shame." Longer stories during newscasts and "quality" documentary work during prime time became the highlights of network television news programming during the tumultuous, news-filled sixties. The shifting values and objectives of network news in the 1970s and 1980s resulted in a move away from this kind of journalism toward a journalism that was expected to garner profits. This value shift continued and accelerated as the network news divisions became mere cogs within networks that were bought by larger media interests, which themselves became holdings of corporate conglomerates. The rest of this chapter examines the internal politics and economics of network news operations at CBS and ABC. This analysis enhances understanding of the nature and direction of change of network news content from 1970 to the present, discussed in chapters 5 through 7.

CBS AFTER CRONKITE

CBS's historical roots in developing news for radio made it possible to quickly develop a reputation for quality news programming on television as well. Walter Cronkite was one of a stable of reporters who made the transition from radio to television. After he replaced Douglas Edwards in the anchor chair, he went on to become the first real icon of television news. The country became used to his authoritative voice as he anchored the news through the civil rights era and through the Vietnam War. His trip to Vietnam and return to declare on air that it was a waste of time and human lives is generally thought to be a turning point in how television and the news media generally would report on the war. Together with CBS News President Richard Salant, Cronkite saw the rise of CBS News as the "Tiffany" of network news. It passed *NBC Nightly News* in the ratings in 1967 and grew throughout the 1970s. In 1961 CBS News had an annual budget of $20 million and 469 staffers. By 1979 the budget was at $90 million with a staff of over a thousand (Boyle 1988). At that point the news division was allowed to run losses—in 1975 "restraint" on news operations kept losses in the news division at $30 million. Also indicative of a lack of subservience to the bottom line before the last quarter of the twentieth century was the development of a policy book that governed how news was to be collected and aired at CBS. The overriding philosophy at CBS was to create a news operation that would be respected for its professionalism and news sense. Generally, the goal was to give news viewers what they needed, not necessarily what they wanted. By giving viewers what they needed to fulfill their roles as citizens in a democracy, CBS news indicated that it would not pander to the audience or commercialize the news.

The policy book was constructed from a series of memos and policy statements that became known as the CBS Standards Handbook. These rules and guidelines prohibited using music, visual re-creations of news, stories sympathetic to advertisers, and other elements of a "show biz" orientation during news broadcasts. As Salant maintained, "This may make us a little less interesting to some, but that is the price we pay for dealing with fact and truth . . . we in broadcast journalism cannot, should not and will not base our judgments on what we think the viewers and listeners are 'most interested' in" (Boyle 1988, 15). This orientation changed in the 1980s when the ownership went through a series of changes; it had ended up in the hands of Viacom by the end of the century.

By the time Salant's replacement, William Small, had himself been replaced by Bill Leonard in 1978, Leonard recalled a conversation with CBS head Kidder Meade during which Meade handed him a piece of paper with CBS's stock price written on it. "That's the bottom line, you're not in the news business anymore," Meade told Leonard (Boyle 1988, 22). Leonard's tenure was a short one. He presided over the squeezing out of Cronkite in March 1981, which resulted in a ratings slide for *CBS Evening News*. When Dan Rather took over the anchor chair, the ratings dropped a full point, causing a drop in advertising rates for the show from $40,000 to $30,000 for a thirty-second slice of time and allowing ABC's *World News Tonight* to take over the number one slot among evening news programs. Each ratings point meant a $12.5 million swing in ad revenues for an entire year. The stakes were so high that CBS conducted research on the impact of Cronkite's departure, which predicted a ratings slide, and the precipitous drop over the summer of 1981 produced a panic situation.

Further cleaning house of the Cronkite/Salant crowd, Gene Jankowski, Leonard's late 1981 replacement, pledged to create a news management team that would be responsive to the company. Changes were rapidly coming in network news. The ascension of Roone Arledge to head ABC News brought challenges as he began to raid competing news organizations for their talent. He tried to lure Dan Rather from CBS; when Rather stayed with CBS, Roger Mudd jumped to *NBC Nightly News*. Furthermore, affiliates upset at the ratings slide for evening news began to assert their power and resisted efforts to expand the news to one hour. The ascendancy of Ronald Reagan to U.S. president brought a deregulatory philosophy to the Federal Communications Commission in the person of Mark Fowler, who regarded television as a "toaster with pictures." Deregulation resulted in the ability of networks to own more stations, and it was the local stations that provided the bulk of the profits for the network as a whole (McChesney 1999).

While network news had been regarded up to that point as a way of fulfilling the FCC-mandated public service provisions, the profitability of local television stations, and in particular their local news operations, was seen by network officials as the source of (financial, not journalistic) redemption for the network. Local television news operations had long since veered from the straight and narrow occupied by traditionalists such as Cronkite. Local news had begun to emphasize emotional content in telling news stories. Human interest stories and self-help stories (which would ultimately morph into "news you can use"), along with blood and guts stories (crime and accident reporting) became staples of local news operations. The role of reporters at these stations was different as well. Reporters became integrally involved in the news and in the communities in which they worked. Local news anchors and reporters more and more became celebrities themselves. Local news archetypes like Geraldo Rivera found their way to network news operations and put themselves into the stories they told.

These developments were often driven by local stations' use of news consultants. These consultants came from a marketing research background and began to shift news judgment to the notion that what viewers wanted mattered most. This led to emphasizing presentation over content, reporter involvement in stories and communities, and linking local news programs to issues raised in prime time dramatic programming (Westin 1982). This was a big shift away from how reporters were seen and heard at the national level. The man brought in to get *CBS Evening News* back to the number one position was someone who had been part of a highly profitable local news operation in California, Van Gordon Sauter.

Interestingly enough, Sauter's role as head of *CBS Evening News* was not necessarily geared toward creating financial discipline at the news division. Instead, he presided over increasing budgets at CBS News, which he invested in *CBS Evening News*. He "borrowed" from ABC several stylistic changes that took CBS news away from striving to be the "newspaper" or even the *New York Times* of the airwaves, thus putting a stake in the heart of the Cronkite/Salant era. These changes brought the use of "bumpers" before commercials to tease stories coming after ad breaks. Sauter brought "market savvy" to *CBS Evening News*—the Minicam, which had revolutionized live reporting at the local level, was introduced in network evening news.

Moving away from a Washington, DC–focused "headline" service, the length of stories was increased so that viewers could be touched by becoming more emotionally involved in the news. Sauter termed this way of storytelling "moment theory." The idea was that using powerful visual scenes in stories would let the viewer realize what it was like to be in the situation being reported. The "moment" occurred, according to Sauter, when "somebody watches something and feels it, smells it and knows it" (Boyle 1988, 139). A "good" broadcast would ideally have two or three of these moments. "Victims" in stories were given prominence; stories were constructed around their point of view. For Sauter, the best TV news was able to convey a person's distress and turn it into a poignant moment. He put it this way: "We moved the broadcast out of Washington. We emphasized stories from across the country. Here we could tell national stories through human experiences and human perceptions more than the statements of bureaucrats and politicians. . . . We emphasized story telling both verbally and visually" (McCabe 1987, 26).

At the same time, Sauter decreased the number of documentaries aired during prime time slots because they were money losers. But his tenure was not about cutting corners. In 1978, the annual news division budget stood at $89 million. By 1982, it had more than doubled to $212 million. Sauter successfully (much the same as did Roone Arledge at ABC) convinced network heads that it was necessary to spend money to make money. Heavy promotion of news programs and catchy news slogans changed the definition of news at the national level. Sauter's vision replaced the traditional CBS notion of itself as the *New York Times* of television or the "broadcast of record" with the idea that *CBS Evening News* should be the *USA Today* of television.

Convinced of the efficacy of Sauter's approach because it lifted *CBS Evening News* ratings out of the bottom, Dan Rather and *Evening News* producer Howard Stringer came to embrace the idea. Rather came up with what he called his "back fence" approach to determining which stories should air and/or be emphasized in the broadcast. The back fence theory consisted of trying to imagine what two "neighbor ladies" (in Rather's parlance) would most likely talk about across the back fence after they watched the news. In one noteworthy case, the Rather team chose to lead with the birth of a royal son in Britain rather than some geopolitical affair that would have led the news under Cronkite's leadership. News from the capital of the world's foremost superpower was now regarded as the "fertile crescent of boring" (Boyle 1988, 139–42).

Decisions regarding CBS weekday morning programming also reflected a distancing from its more traditional orientation to news. The decision to hire former Miss America Phyllis George in December 1984 as coanchor of the *CBS Morning Show* was made by CBS Broadcast Group executives led by Gene Jankowski, whose own background was in advertising sales rather than within the news division. The amount of money spent on the hairdressers, assistants, and limousines at George's disposal—$1 million—was disconcerting to the journalists associated with the show and network. Sauter also brought George Merlis from ABC to produce the morning show. He had been producing ABC's *Good Morning America* for the network's entertainment division. Merlis was brought in to bring "a distinctly commercial sensibility" to his corner of CBS News (Boyle 1988, 212; McCabe 1987). By January 1985, George was proving a disaster, which facilitated the departure of Bill Curtis as her coanchor/host.

This early to mid-1980s series of transitions did not, however, close the book on changes at CBS. A change in ownership beginning in 1985 propelled the news division into further changes, inserting even more entertainment-oriented values into news broadcasts and even greater concerns with having the news operations garner significant profits for the network. This came at a time when CBS ownership increasingly focused on the value of its stock as it became vulnerable to takeovers, at first politically motivated takeovers by Senator Jesse Helms, who thought the network stood as a bastion of liberalism and a symbol of the moral decay of America, then more serious financial challenges from Ted Turner's cable television empire, and ultimately the takeover by Laurence Tisch's Loews Corporation.

September 1983 saw a corporate realignment in face of the takeover threats by Helms, General Electric (which eventually bought NBC), Gannett, and Ted Turner (who dropped his attempt and instead bought MGM). The takeover attempts resulted in the news division having its special status ended and being put on a par with other divisions of CBS. By now Sauter had advanced up the ladder at CBS. Whatever rapport he established with the "newsies" evaporated when he went even more corporate. Sauter was seen as the source of the shift toward commercialism and the bottom line orientation that journalists saw as contributing to the demise of serious news. He would eventually return for another stint to head the news division as well as serve as executive vice president of the CBS Broadcast Group.

The indebtedness CBS took on in fending off the takeover threats resulted in budget cuts at the network. In September 1985 10 percent of the staff were laid off. In May 1986 the news division lost 90 of 1,350 jobs, and a consultant "retreat" organized by Sauter generated resentment from

Rather and the rest of the news division. Even the venerable news show *60 Minutes*, which had been a profitable venture due to its ratings and during one year had made the difference between profit and loss for the whole news division, was slighted by the network as it put together a newer, hipper approach to news magazines in *West 57th*. The news division again saw handwriting on the wall when the network brought staffers from entertainment backgrounds such as MTV and the syndicated show *Entertainment Tonight* to work on *West 57th* and gave it more promotion than *60 Minutes*. This prompted *60 Minutes* producer Don Hewitt to try to own part of *60 Minutes* in a way similar to Norman Lear's ownership of the hit CBS prime time program *All in the Family*. Hewitt attempted to get the news old-timers at CBS to put up a bid for ownership of the news division during the time the network was facing takeover threats (McCabe 1987).

The most earnest, and successful, takeover threat during this period of upheaval came from Laurence Tisch's Loews Corporation. Tisch started scooping up stock in July 1985 while CBS was warding off the threat from Ted Turner. This was initially welcomed by the network, as Tisch indicated at the time that his purpose was to keep "an important American company independent" (Boyle 1988, 298). By October Tisch had secured a 12 percent interest in CBS and refused to sign an agreement that he would acquire no more than 25 percent. Tisch was appointed to the CBS Board in November 1985 and began to throw his weight around. He took over as acting CEO and asked Van Gordon Sauter to resign. The news division initially greeted this move positively, but the appointment of Howard Stringer as president of CBS News was resented by the old guard at the division. Indeed, Bill Moyers resigned from CBS in November 1986 and exiled himself to public television.

Tisch then brought in the Coopers and Lybrand accounting firm to review CBS's business practices. That review resulted in personnel cutbacks, eliminating the medical department and decreasing the company's United Way contribution. A promise to downsize only through attrition at the news division was kept only temporarily. Tisch was reported as wanting to cut $100 million from the $300 million news budget. As these reports surfaced in the press, Rather was furious enough to go to headquarters to complain. In February 1987 a $33 million cut at news was mandated, resulting in 215 layoffs, including 14 on-air reporters, a 15 percent staff reduction. The third cutback in sixteen months demoralized the news division, and many said it began to affect news judgment. They were beginning to discuss which stories could be overlooked, and foreign news was frequently regarded as something too expensive to be covered. These developments prompted a producer at CBS News, Richard Cohen, to write an op-ed piece in the *New York Times*, headlined "From Murrow to Mediocrity." Cohen wrote, "Let's get one thing straight, CBS Inc. is not a chronically weak company fighting to survive. . . . But 215 people lost their jobs so that stockholders would have even more money in their pockets. More profits. That's what business is about" (quoted in Boyle 1988, 331).

In the midst of these cuts, the soaring salaries for network stars also absorbed more and more of the budget. The star system that dominates today's news media outlets was coming into its own. Tisch himself gave Diane Sawyer a big pay hike, and news shows began to be filled with anchor–reporter banter. As an example of how news judgment was affected, the *Evening News* led with the Jessica McClure story—a little girl who had fallen down an abandoned well— and provided Rather with an in-studio prop, an example of the pipe in which she was stuck (Boyle 1988).

As CBS News limped into the 1990s, it had veered far from Richard Salant's goal to be the *New York Times* of the airwaves and it took a sharp turn toward an almost exclusive focus on producing profit for the parent company. Further changes in the 1990s continued to drive the news division in this direction, and a second wave of media buyouts found the entire network sold at first to Westinghouse and then to media giant Viacom.

In 1995 Westinghouse, one of the originators of radio broadcasting, purchased CBS. As this sale was being negotiated, CBS honchos squelched a *60 Minutes* story in which tobacco whistleblower Richard Wigand brought documentary evidence of tobacco company Brown and Williamson's suppression of research linking tobacco to cancer. CBS lawyers, fearing a lawsuit from the tobacco giant at a time when Tisch was negotiating the sale, backed off the story, fearing it would lower the price Tisch could get for the network. It aired three months later (Barringer 1999).

That incident was recalled when Westinghouse sold CBS to media giant Viacom, setting off fears that Viacom would use its new news property to promote its other media holdings and products, which included music, publishing, and movie interests.

While CBS News president Andrew Haywood pledged that his news division didn't "expect to be anybody's handmaiden," a little over a year later CBS was teaming up with MTV to cross-promote shows about the drug ecstasy as a "package that would appeal to parents on CBS and another that would appeal to their children on MTV." Television news operations generally were concerned about news programs' aging demographics (the median viewer age for network news was fifty-seven to fifty-eight). The coproduction was the result of a meeting between Haywood and MTV officials. Haywood was reported as saying he had asked all his top producers to identify opportunities to work with Viacom cable TV properties (Rutenberg 2000).

This joint effort was the harbinger of even more such efforts. Corporate synergy, once viewed as an albatross for television news, was now being celebrated and encouraged. After buying BET (Black Entertainment Television) from African American entrepreneur Robert Johnson, Viacom dropped BET's news operation and introduced a CBS News–supervised newscast (Stanley 2002; Jensen 2002).

Viacom chairman Sumner Redstone also raised eyebrows among CBS newsies in 1999 when he gave a speech in China arguing that news organizations should be cautious about being "unnecessarily offensive" to foreign governments (Pitts 1999).

What else the Viacom/CBS merger portends is speculative, but a news outlet that once asserted itself as an independent, public service–oriented *New York Times* of the airwaves has become a cog in the corporate media profit machine. Chapter 5 explores how all these business deals have affected the way news is presented on *CBS Evening News*.

ABC: FROM "WIDE WORLD OF NEWS" TO DISNEY

Almost from its inception there was a sense that ABC would be a poor stepsister in comparison to the other two dominant networks, NBC and CBS. Indeed, as shown in chapter 1, ABC was born from a regulatory mandate that NBC sell the weaker of its two radio networks as a means of creating more breadth of ownership. For many years ABC would act like a cast-off property, giving news and public affairs short shrift while developing relationships with Paramount Movies and the Disney Corporation. ABC only expanded its evening news program to a half hour in 1967; NBC and CBS had done so in 1963. Lacking the star power generated by the rise of Walter Cronkite to an icon of broadcast journalism at CBS and the popularity of the NBC team of Chet Huntley and David Brinkley, ABC News for many years had an inferiority complex.

But that all changed in the 1970s, as a series of management changes and a decision to invest in the news operation led to the emergence of ABC as a serious news player that would eventually rise to number one in the 1990s. And the man who oversaw that transformation did not come from the world of journalism. Instead, the ascendancy of ABC News was guided by someone much more geared to showmanship, someone who cut his television production teeth on transforming how television covered the sporting world. Roone Arledge became president of ABC News by virtue of the desire of the ABC brass to bring his successful broadcast sports innovations to the news division at the network.

ABC NEWS IN THE EARLY DAYS: ON THE CHEAP

The early years at ABC News were dominated by concerns to keep news program costs to a minimum. In the 1950s the network relied on Fox, Movietone, and Hearst Telefilm newsreel services (whose products were typically shown before feature films in movie theaters) to provide film footage for ABC news broadcasts (Mazzocco 1994). The conservative political orientation of the newsreels fit in well with the political leanings of ABC and, later, Capital Cities ownership. Furthermore, John Daly, a conservative vice president for news, was also the network's only on-air news anchor from 1953 to 1961. He brought in conservative-oriented commentators Walter Winchell and George Solosky, among others.

In 1965 ABC, which was perennially cash poor and subject to numerous takeover offers and attempts, went into merger talks with International Telephone and Telegraph. Federal Communications Commission and Justice Department concerns about how ITT business interests might influence or censor news at ABC caused ITT to back off from its talks with the network. It should be no surprise that a network that had always done things on the cheap found itself regularly challenged with takeover or merger talk. Elton Rule, president of ABC in 1968, instituted a cash management system to try to control costs at the network and increased profits by 10 percent in the first year (Mazzocco 1994). The tenure of Av Westin from 1969 onward brought some technological wizardry to the nightly news program through the introduction of graphics and other visual enhancements to the half hour show. But the biggest source of change at the network was the meteoric rise of Roone Arledge within the company.

Arledge had grown tired of sports by the mid-1970s, after a long stint during which he created *Wide World of Sports*, brought innovation in how the Olympics were presented to American audiences, and took NFL football from an exclusively Sunday phenomenon to *Monday Night Football*. His work at Sports garnered attention among the top brass, and his success and ambition were in mind when he was appointed ABC News president in 1977. The network looked to Arledge to do with news what he had accomplished with sports: using new communication technologies to jazz up the news, creating prime time programs featuring the stars he developed or stole from other networks, and propelling ABC News to the top of the charts by the 1990s. Key to the Arledge strategy in transforming the news division at ABC was borrowing from his sports work the idea of the "story line" (Gunther 1994).

Arledge had transformed the sports division by adding show business values to the way sports were presented. He told his sports producers to introduce the protagonists for each game, identify the obstacles they would face, and identify story lines as the game unfolded. As Lionel Trilling wrote, "Arledge learned about the nature of narrative, the idea that artists must sift through the events and incidents that are, by themselves, shapeless, in order to transform them into meaningful drama. From there, it was a short leap to Arledge's idea that televised sports be organized around what he called a 'story line'" (Gunther 1994, 14). In Arledge's own words, "What we set out to do was to get the audience involved emotionally. If they didn't give a damn about the game, they still might enjoy the program" (Gunther 1994, 17).

It was this fusion of entertainment values with the news that made the news division employees at ABC nervous about Arledge's ascension to president of the division. Indeed, he brought some of his own people from the sports division to work with him in news. The notion that the news is just the news, that a journalist's task is to hold up a mirror to society, was gutted by Arledge's influence. ABC's bold experiment in hiring Barbara Walters away from NBC in 1976 and giving her an anchor's chair next to Harry Reasoner was diminished by what Arledge brought to the news division. The changes began in 1977 and continued through the 1990s.

The way several stories were handled in 1977 presaged how Arledge affected not only news programming at his network but also all of television's approach to news events in the decades to come. A story in the Netherlands about a South Moluccan hostage taking, and coverage of the arrest of the Son of Sam, a serial killer in New York City, prompted once and future anchor for *ABC Evening News* and *World News Tonight* Frank Reynolds to write Arledge about his alarm at Roone's "tabloid" approach to news. Later that same year ABC was criticized by the folks at the "serious" television news operation, CBS, for leading its news program with the death of Elvis Presley. Walter Cronkite also took a few swipes at ABC for its personalization of the Mideast crisis when Barbara Walters interviewed Egypt's Anwar Sadat about a rapprochement with Israel; she got him to declare publicly that he would travel to Israel to negotiate peace with the Israelis. When Cronkite accused ABC of self-promotion, Arledge took it as a compliment and a sign that he was beginning to make waves in the news world (Gunther 1994).

Other changes were a bit more subtle. Arledge got camera work to stop using so much panning, encouraged tight close-ups of newsmakers, and brought in the marketing research that had taken local television news operations by storm. But a big splash was made when the evening news show was renamed and given a lot of bells and whistles with which to work. *World News Tonight* premiered on July 10, 1978, and set into motion a series of other programs that would become staples of the news division. Most significant of these was the late-night television show that became *Nightline*. The 11:30 P.M. slot after local news had been occupied by rerun movies and the dominant variety/talk show, *The Tonight Show*, starring Johnny Carson, on NBC. When the Iranian hostage crisis broke in November 1979, Arledge made a controversial decision to go to regular nightly coverage until the situation was resolved and the hostages were brought back to the United States. The show became named *America Held Hostage*. Many among the news staff were mystified by the decision, arguing that there perhaps wouldn't be enough hostage-related news each night to justify a half hour program. But Arledge's experience with using satellites at ABC Sports created compelling programming in the first few weeks and months of the hostage crisis, resulting in a show that both news makers and viewers sought out. Arledge used satellites to create what he called a global village conversation, pitting officials from the Iranian government against U.S. pundits and officials. Traditionally, networks would interview antagonists in a story or issue separately. This new format meant that each night viewers could see a face-off between the two countries, creating conflict that could be brought into U.S. living rooms with regularity. As the news about the hostage crisis diminished over time, the show was morphed into a show addressing all kinds of public affairs concerns and was renamed *Nightline*.

Other technological innovations surfaced in *World News Tonight*. Arledge created splashy, elaborate openings to newscasts and provided a rundown of highlights of the news. Teasers and bumpers were inserted before advertising breaks to keep viewers tuned during advertisements, as Arledge was fully aware of how the news division's bread was buttered. He convinced the network brass to open their pocketbooks to create all this change. The budget for the news division rose from $65 million in 1977 to $150 million three years later. Thus, Arledge was able to do earlier what took CBS a bit longer to accomplish: spend money to make money. The public service orientation to news, which had disdained profit, was now history. Arledge saw the transformation and expansion of television news at the local level and brought it to network television operations.

Part of the "spend to make" philosophy was dedicated to establishing network news stars to anchor and report for a growing number of evening news shows. Arledge created personality-driven shows in which the presentation of the news was as important, or perhaps more so, as what was being discussed. The hiring of stars was at first a hit-and-miss operation—Arledge had lured *Washington Post* reporter and Watergate "star" Carl Bernstein to ABC but was unable to turn him into marquee value. He lost a bidding war for Dan Rather, who chose to remain with CBS once he was assured he would get the anchor job after Walter Cronkite's retirement. Barbara Walters's disastrous stint as anchor for the evening news show found her and coanchor Reasoner visibly unable to get along, and her attempts to "feminize" the presentation of the news fell flat. But shifting her to a prime time slot in a new show to be called *20/20* created a star vehicle. This show allowed Walters to develop her reputation as an interviewer, and her specialty quickly became the kind of "news" the traditionalists scorn—the celebrity interview. A producer for *20/20* argued "she invented intimacy on television" (Gunther 1994, 152).

The investments began to pay off for the network: *World News Tonight* won the weekly Neilsen ratings in July 1981, and a Sunday morning news show was invented to compete with NBC's venerable *Meet the Press*; *This Week with David Brinkley* premiered in the fall of 1981. About the only bad move Arledge made was a quickly aborted three-anchor format for *World News Tonight* featuring Frank Reynolds in Washington, Frank Robinson in Chicago, and Peter Jennings in London. The lack of a center for the show and introductions to introductions from anchor to anchor to reporter were unwieldy for a half hour news show. Nonetheless, Arledge's changes and successes at ABC had raised eyebrows throughout the television news community—with network brass in awe and more traditional broadcast and print journalists appalled: "Following Arledge's lead, all the networks now packaged and sold the news with graphics and music and promotion. They all looked for stories with drama and impact not just in prime time but also for their newscasts. His approach to the news, once deemed heretical, had become mainstream" (Gunther 1994, 175).

That "top of the world" feeling Arledge had become accustomed to—celebrity status, limousines, fine foods, and the other perks that came with his success—was seen in a few short years as excessive when ABC and Capital Cities Broadcasting merged in 1985. The resulting change in management brought the philosophy of Capital Cities, which had been so successful at generating profits at the local television stations it owned, to the entire ABC enterprise. Sales and marketing increased in importance; keeping operating and labor expenses low alienated news staffers and tempered some of Arledge's spending on stars and global technological reach. Capital Cities' longtime tap into the U.S. political system and relationship with the FCC facilitated its expansion of television holdings. People in the news division looked at how Capital Cities ran news operations at its local stations and wondered whether the sensationalistic focus on crime, violence, and government corruption would become a staple for the network news division. Profit margins at the local stations reached 55 percent in 1984 and averaged over 50 percent into the 1990s (Mazzocco 1994, 68).

The immediate fallout of the Capital Cities merger was the elimination of seventy-five people from the eleven hundred–strong staff in the news division. Arledge resisted cuts by arguing for the make money to spend money philosophy that had worked with his former bosses. Arledge wanted to continue to increase revenues rather than cut costs, and argued that news shows in prime time were far cheaper to produce (by about half) than an equivalent amount of entertainment. NBC and CBS were also losing money networkwide, and the old broadcast networks suddenly appeared as dinosaurs threatened by the competition from cable television's specialty channels (including CNN, the then relatively new twenty-four-hour news kid on the block).

Arledge for a time rose to the challenge of his new ownership team but faced difficulties with the star system he had created. Ted Koppel, whose career was made by the *America Held Hostage/Nightline* late-night news venture, began to demand a greater say in his shows, to the point where he negotiated his own production company with the network and allowed *Nightline* to drift into a more conventional interview program while he put his efforts into prime time specials.

ABC's fusion of news and entertainment continued in these years with a heavily criticized attempt to hype news stories through dramatizations and recreations. A July 1989 re-creation of the passing of a briefcase between an alleged American spy and his Soviet counterpart was considered a serious breach of journalistic ethics. Despite (or perhaps because of) the encroaching infotainment orientation to news, ABC became the highest-rated news service in 1989. It had become more advertiser friendly and was garnering profits similar to the sports and entertainment divisions. The prime time show *20/20* had been retooled into a "news you can use" show emphasizing consumer-friendly stories and middle-class concerns advertisers were eager to reach. By reaching younger, upscale viewers, ABC was charging 20 to 30 percent more for advertising time than CBS.

When the news budget hit $395 million in 1991, Capital Cities began another round of cost cutting, attempting to take $50 million from the budget. By 1992 there was a 10 percent reduction of the news staff, and $25 million was cut from the news division (Gunther 1994, 334–41). ABC left the exit polling consortium of networks and newspapers that provided early projections of election outcomes. It began to form alliances with other global news operations to share footage, thus facilitating the closing of bureaus around the world. But perhaps the biggest breach into news integrity was ABC's announcement that it would begin to use more video news releases (video footage and sound bites supplied by parties interested in shaping the tone of news stories) to "enhance" its news coverage (Mazzocco 1994, 131).

Capital Cities grew weary of its fights with Arledge, and by October 1991 things reached a head. Robert Weissmasser was brought in to bring fiscal responsibility to the news division as executive vice president of ABC News. In April 1992 Arledge was diagnosed with prostate cancer, further eroding his power as head of the news division. But audiences kept tuning in—*World News Tonight* continued into a fifth year of leading the nightly news ratings wars in 1993 and provided an annual profit of $50 million. *Nightline* chipped in with $20 million in profits, and *20/20* made $40 million for its parent company. The prime time news programs that Arledge had fathered—*Prime Time, 20/20,* and newcomer *Day One*—increasingly took on tabloid characteristics with high-emotion stories. Monetary success for the news division was accompanied by a shift in journalism that may have attracted crowds but was otherwise seen by critics as a sellout: "The defects of ABC News were evident—the journalism was sometimes shallow, pictures overshadowed words, the range of ideas expressed was narrow, and drama, more than enlightenment shaped some stories but these flaws were common to all television news" (Gunther 1994, 363). Indeed, the same round of merger mania seen in CBS's takeover by Viacom hit ABC/Capital Cities when it became part of the global media giant Disney.

The $19 billion deal, announced in late 1995, was approved by the FCC in January 1996, with Disney chairman Michael Eisner pledging, "ABC News will continue to operate in the public interest, without corporate interference" (Lieberman 1996).

That assertion proved problematic rather quickly. The Disney purchase of ABC also created changes at the top. Roone Arledge moved up to senior vice president, and David Westin became president of ABC News in 1997–1998. Several instances of conflicts between the news division and Disney took place in the late 1990s. ABC backed off a story about tobacco companies Philip Morris and RJ Reynolds adding nicotine to the tobacco in their cigarettes beyond what was naturally present. Threatened with a lawsuit, ABC apologized. A *Prime Time* story about an exposé of the Food Lion grocery chain's repackaging of expired meat was vigorously defended, and a jury's judgment against ABC was ultimately lowered by the judge to a symbolic fine.

But ABC's *Good Morning America,* freshly transferred back to the news division from the entertainment division, rather quickly took on the role of shill for other ABC/Disney programs and products, starting off with puff pieces about Disney World (Rosenberg 1997).

Two other instances of corporate conflict with news values occurred between 1998 and 2000. The first concerned ABC News investigative reporter Brian Ross's story about Disney World employees who engaged in pedophilic acts with children in the theme park. Encouraged initially to pursue the story, Ross soon got requests to extend the story to other theme parks. He did, and found that in comparison Disney was negligent in checking employees for criminal records. Over four months, the back and forth between Ross's investigative team and David Westin ended with Westin killing the story (Stevens 1998).

Just days before Westin killed the story in September 1998, Eisner gave an interview on public radio and indicated his preference for ABC reporters to not cover Disney at all: "The way you avoid conflict of interest is to, as best you can, not cover yourself" (Smillie 1998). So, in just less than three years, Eisner had gone full circle, from saying the "right thing" to allay journalistic and public concerns at the time Disney bought ABC to abandoning any pretense of news division independence.

Another controversy stoked the notion that television journalism had become harlotry. Disney/ABC's part ownership of an online pet store—pets.com—became a news item when *Good Morning America* interviewed a sock puppet referred to as the "pets.com sock puppet" on at least two occasions in February 2000. The staff involved in the *Nightline* and *Good Morning America* segments pleaded ignorance, but most critics were unforgiving (Kaufman 2000).

May 2001 saw a further diminution of ABC News when Disney ordered layoffs of 125 among the news division staff of 1,200 (Rutenberg 2001). The replacement of *20/20* by a Disney-produced drama/evening soap, *Once and Again*, added insult to injury. In the same month ABC News was heavily criticized for a blatant tie-in of Disney's movie *Pearl Harbor*. Local news outlets, *Good Morning America* and *World News Tonight,* and the ABC News website all did duty in promoting the film, which critics derided as a soap opera treatment of what was up until then the most deadly attack on American interests (Rosenberg 2001).

ABC's devolution into "infotainment" became complete when it won out over other TV news competitors to interview Gary Condit, a congressman whose affair with an intern who then disappeared had become the latest reality soap opera that television news obsessed about. And Disney's preference for entertainment over news was made more evident when it tried to lure David Letterman's late-night show from CBS in March 2002, threatening the future of the highly regarded *Nightline*. This was an example of advertising demographics trumping audience size. *Nightline* actually drew higher ratings than Letterman's show, but the audience for *Nightline* skewed older, while Letterman's skewed younger. Advertising aimed at a younger audience brings higher revenues than ads aimed at more mature audiences (Lowry and Jensen 2002).

Late 2002 found ABC, like CBS, testing the waters about a merger with cable news heavyweight CNN. Trying to catch up to NBC, which had ventured into cable news with MSNBC and CNBC, both networks had decided that their news divisions were too bulky to justify a half hour nightly news show and a couple of prime time slots per week (Hall 1996). Although such deals had not come off as of mid-2003, it seems only a matter of time before a broadcast news operation merges with a twenty-four-hour cable news channel. Another merger or two will further reduce the diversity of news sources while enhancing corporate profits and create even more synergistic promotional gimmicks within the corporate family that houses the news organization.

As Lawrence Grossman put it, journalism as a public trust is a "rapidly disappearing perspective. News is just a dot on the balance sheets of Disney, Time Warner, Viacom and Fox." Danny Schechter, former ABC News producer, cites the effects of merger mania on news content: "There's been a merger between the news business and show business. It's the Monicaization of news. The entertainment culture is overwhelming the information culture" (both quoted in Smillie 1998, 13).

WHAT CONGLOMERATIZATION HATH WROUGHT

Looking at the transformation of CBS and ABC news divisions in the context of the increasing conglomeratization of the U.S. media system reveals just how much news values have changed over the last quarter century. The emphasis on the bottom line has come to pervade all news operations—print, broadcast, and cable. Once deemed a profession, journalism, in the eyes of many contemporary analysts, has become just another source of eye candy. This has been especially true for many years at the local television news level but also at the national level over the last two decades (McManus 1994; Underwood 1993; Krajicek 1998). Before moving on to the analysis of network news over the last thirty years, it is useful to draw on analyses of local broadcast and print operations that have experienced similar transformations as a means of defining the current state of the news media in the United States.

John McManus's analysis of local television news organizations concludes that there are four ways in which market logic shapes local television news reporting: seeking images over ideas, seeking emotion over analysis, exaggerating to add appeal and drama, and avoiding extensive news gathering (McManus 1994, 162). The primacy of image in television was best understood by the team that guided the packaging of President Reagan (Hertsgaard 1988). The idea that images can overpower words came to be gospel among television producers as they sought out compelling visual angles and scenes for evening newscasts. Inevitably seeking emotion over analysis flows from a concern with images. Avoiding complexity by keeping stories short may be an artifact of the growth of the remote control, but as is evident from the influence of people like Van Gordon Sauter and Roone Arledge, it also leads to reducing news to morality plays with an emphasis on story lines that tell of struggles between good and evil. Exaggerating to add appeal and focusing on deviations from the "normal" as a means of keeping the novel or unusual at the forefront re-

sults in an emphasis on oddball and crackpot stories that reflect the carnivalesque elements of a soap opera. But McManus's last point, about
avoiding extensive news gathering, is perhaps the most important factor
for this discussion; it fully reveals the form over substance philosophy
that pervades all television news operations. A quote from a television reporter sums up this issue: "Reporters are film-makers. We're making little films. It has to have a flow—a beginning, middle and end . . . a well
rounded, complete production. Newspaper reporters are information oriented. They are trained to get a whole lot of information. They ignore the
production side. That's because they don't understand it's the production
that's important" (McManus 1994, 155).

These factors make coverage of crime a staple of television news, especially at the local level. The rash of crime stories throughout the mid-
1990s, at a time when law enforcement statistics showed that crime had
actually decreased, is an example of an entertainment orientation to television news that is far removed from the mirror theory of journalism,
which holds that all journalism is supposed to do is hold a mirror up to
society. In 1993 crime stories doubled on the networks, and murder stories tripled at a time when crime was declining. Resulting polls showed
that fear of victimization increased among the population. One poll found
one-third of the country citing crime as the number one concern. Reporters are not the only ones to blame—the drive for profits reflects the
concerns of industry moguls and stockholding owners as well as editors,
publishers, and photographers (Krajicek 1998, 5). Choosing the interesting over the important means that: "As best suits the situation, the media
will either employ a Pollyana naivete or the carnality of a road worn biker.
Stories are presented as morality plays, which allow the media to occupy
the choir loft of moral sanctimony from which it can cheer the good guy
and hiss the bad guy" (Krajicek 1998, 14).

According to McManus, the trend toward what he calls "market journalism" began in the late 1960s, when local news became "whatever is interesting." News consultants at local television stations provided much of
the impetus to please, rather than merely inform, audiences. Local news
operations and their stations became highly profitable and propelled the
deregulation frenzy that began in the 1980s under Mark Fowler, Reagan's
head of the FCC. Fowler brought the laissez-faire economic philosophy of
Reagan to the media world. He eliminated the practical requirement to
limit advertising to sixteen minutes per hour. He discarded the working
requirement that 5 percent of a station's broadcast week be devoted to
news and public affairs. He dropped the requirement that stations ascer-
tain the most important issues and problems by surveying the communities they served. Shortly before Reagan left office, Fowler suspended the
longstanding Fairness Doctrine (in place since 1949), which required that

television news present all sides to a controversy. Fowler's characterization of television as a "toaster with pictures" no doubt accelerated the
trend toward reducing news viewers to customers, defining news as just
another product and potential profit source.

News consultants, marketing research, corporate takeovers, and deregulation are all major contributors to the transformation of news from a
public service to a cavalcade of hairdos, visual razzamatazz, and archetypal morality plays. Looking back at the history of journalism, one can
find other eras in which such emphases were labeled as "yellow,"
"tabloid," or "sensational journalism." The brief period of muckraking
from the mid-1960s to early 1970s can now be seen as a moment in which
journalism served its function to "comfort the afflicted and afflict the comfortable" (Bennett 1988) and spoke truth to power. The slow corporate
takeover of all the media since then has transformed the function and purpose of news programming in the world of television. Doug Underwood's analysis of the years following that period argues that news executives put a brake on the journalism of the 1960s and early 1970s by
beginning to emphasize marketing the news. The declining readership in
newspapers and television news' losses to cable and other video diver-
sions in the 1980s put journalism on a track toward defining successful
news operations as those with large audiences and creating "consumer-
friendly" newscasts rather than having an emphasis on citizen enlightenment (Underwood 1993).

Underwood's surveys of working journalists are quite revealing in this
light. He found that journalists at large chain papers were the most alienated by the changes they had seen occur in their workplaces. Aggressive
newsroom management by people with nonjournalistic backgrounds has
resulted in market-oriented values guiding "news products." Cutbacks in
coverage of government and the reduction of news staffs have resulted in
a loss of depth and a softening of news coverage. Treating the reader as a
customer is the product of increased profit and marketing emphasis at
newspapers and television newsrooms. Journalists working under this
new reality maintain that the greater profit emphasis is not compatible
with the pursuit of journalistic values and treating the reader as a citizen.

CONCLUSION

The history of network television news presented here is meant to provide background and context to the analysis of the evolution of network
news since 1970 that will be presented in the next three chapters. By looking at some of the economic forces and changes imposed on television
news over the last thirty years, one can gain a better understanding of

why the content of television news programs has come to reflect the values associated with the soap opera paradigm. The increasing concerns with profitability at the corporate level reached down into the heretofore sacrosanct news divisions beginning in the late 1970s, accelerated in the 1980s, and reached an apex in the 1990s. This trend wrought significant changes in how the news was selected and presented over this same period. Aspects of presenting the news identified in this chapter, from Van Gordon Sauter's "theory of moments" to Roone Arledge's "story lines," reflect the employment of techniques first successfully pursued in soap opera storytelling. Bringing serial elements to news broadcasts, emphasizing "live" or "you are there" sensibilities for viewers, telling news stories in a personalized, intimate manner, and framing the perspectives of an ensemble of "players" are examined as the following chapters look at how network television news has changed. The next chapter, using quantitative techniques, details how news has increasingly employed the five characteristics of soap opera storytelling since 1970. To put flesh on the quantitative analysis of CBS's and ABC's changes over this period, chapter 6 presents some qualitative analyses of a specific kind of story: coverage of natural disasters. Chapter 7 looks at coverage of political campaigns over the same time period with a qualitative analysis of the 2000 presidential primary season and the controversy surrounding the close election contest in the fall of 2000. The news media, as a key linchpin in the vitality of democratic decision making, are examined to determine how they have substituted a soap opera approach to covering campaigns for a serious, deliberative look at the issues and candidates voters are facing. The soap opera paradigm's effect on our electoral system demonstrates just how pervasive the use of soap opera storytelling techniques has become.

5

TV News:
The Show's the Thing

As described in chapter 4, television journalism has gone through many changes in the five decades of its existence. Once populated by reporters coming from print outlets, television news has increasingly become more entertainment oriented, and the staffing of on-air positions is often made without any regard for the journalistic background of those who appear on the twenty-four-hour cable services or network news. This chapter uses the elements of the soap opera paradigm identified in chapter 2 to examine how network television news has adapted them to presenting the news of the day.

The analysis of the evolution of network news from 1970 onward shows how the change in the status of network news from a public service obligation to a source of profit for the conglomerates that own the networks has resulted in changes in how the news is presented and the kind of storytelling that takes place in these programs. The focus of this chapter is a quantitative data analysis, which will illustrate how television news has come to adopt many of the characteristics of soaps since 1970, and in particular from the mid-1980s onward, when the media mergers began to pick up steam. This analysis takes on two forms. First, there are aspects of how the show is structured and presented that employ soap opera-like qualities. This discussion of *program* elements focuses on serial elements within the news program such as introductory segments, teasers before advertising breaks, promotion of other network news shows and the degree to which news shows put an emphasis on projecting a "live" or "you are there" orientation.

The second analysis looks at *story* elements that reflect soap opera values. Each story within a broadcast was examined to determine whether and how the soap opera elements—seriality, real-time orientation, intimacy, story exposition techniques, and soap story characteristics—are present in the story.

NETWORK NEWS: A THIRTY-YEAR LOOK

The data reported here comprise a longitudinal study of network television news. Newscasts were sampled from 1970 at six-year intervals: 1970, 1976, 1982, 1988, 1994, and 2000. Two-week samples of the weekday nightly newscasts from two networks for each year listed were obtained from the Vanderbilt Television News Archive in Nashville, Tennessee. Two networks, ABC and CBS, were analyzed. In the years 1970, 1982, and 1994, two weeks in mid-March were sampled. To get a flavor of the coverage of presidential political campaigns (presented in chapter 7), the years 1976, 1988, and 2000 were sampled in mid-October. Only one broadcast (on ABC) during the selected sampling periods was unavailable from the Vanderbilt Archive, and that was due to the newscast being preempted by a baseball playoff game. Another edition of ABC's *World News Tonight* was abbreviated in the same week due to a baseball playoff game.

Depending on the variable, the unit of analysis is the broadcast (for program elements such as introductory segments, teasers before ad breaks, length of ad breaks, promotion of other news shows, and "live" segments) or the news story (for storytelling elements such as intimacy, story exposition, and story characteristics). These data were coded by the primary researcher. An intercoder reliability study was conducted on a 10 percent sample (twelve in number) of newscasts by a second judge to affirm the consistency and reliability of the primary researcher. Variables that were measured more directly, such as timing the length of each story, ad break, and "live" segment within stories, were done twice by the primary researcher and were not subjected to a reliability study. Cohen's kappa was used to correct for chance agreement and yielded substantial agreement. Reliability figures were computed for the seven elements identified previously: for elements of seriality, .97 was obtained; for real-time orientation, .88; for seeming intimacy, .85; for story exposition, .83; for conflict, .85; for good/evil, .80; for upper-middle-class orientation, .80. Some of the data reported here are measures of time dedicated to various sections of newscasts. Working definitions for these segments are as follows:

- *Introductory segments:* Material that introduces the program by providing a tease for upcoming stories. Segments may involve the anchor, graphics, and/or video. This segment ends with the anchor's introduction of the first story.

- *Teasers:* Segments before advertising breaks using the anchor, graphics, and/or video that promote stories following the advertising break.
- *News promos:* Promotion of other network news shows either during advertising segments or during the news show itself. Promotions of other non-news network programs are not included.
- *News time:* All news stories added together. This does not include introductory segments, before–ad break teasers, and advertising time.
- *Advertising time:* All advertising break material, including all network (news or otherwise) promotions during advertising breaks.

For the second part of the analysis, a "story" in a newscast is defined thus: A *story* is a distinct segment of a news program that addresses a specific event or item in the world. It can be a reporter-narrated story, an anchor voice-over of video, or an anchor-read item (usually labeled a "brief.") There can be several stories on a single event. These are distinguished by the use of different reporters on the story.

From this analysis it is expected that the following hypotheses will be supported:

1. Time during network newscasts dedicated to advertising, teasers, network promotions, and introductory segments will increase from 1970 to 2000.
2. Total news time will decrease from 1970 to 2000.
3. News stories will increasingly employ each of the soap opera storytelling techniques of seriality, real-time orientation, seeming intimacy, story exposition techniques, and soap story characteristics. Furthermore, these techniques will increasingly be used in combinations within news stories.

Based on the analysis presented in the last chapter, it is expected that both networks will reflect these trends, though differences in the way the two networks present the news may exhibit differences in the degree of change. Of particular interest in this area are the key leadership changes in the ABC and CBS news divisions in the late 1970s and early 1980s in the persons of Roone Arledge at ABC and Van Gordon Sauter at CBS. As noted in chapter 4, these two individuals, through Arledge's "story line" orientation and Sauter's "theory of moments," represent the shift to soap opera storytelling based on their work in television sports and local news, respectively.

PROGRAM ELEMENTS IN NEWS AND
THE SOAP OPERA PARADIGM

The data presented here look at introductory segments in newscasts, teasers before advertising breaks, promotion of the network's "brand" of news products within the newscast and during ad breaks, segments during news shows that project "live," and total time dedicated to news and non-news content during a broadcast. For each variable, a table representing the variable's behavior over time is presented. Table 5.1 defines use of introductory segments in nightly newscasts over the thirty-year period examined. The data contradict the predicted relationship. In 1970, both networks offered fairly lengthy introductory segments. A closer look at the 1970 segments, however, provides a stark contrast to what was happening in 2000. In 1970, each network provided a rundown of the entire newscast's stories in an "index" format; a brief word or phrase identifying the story is presented along with the reporter who will be featured in the report. By 2000, introductory segments were forty-five to sixty seconds long and included anchor comments, graphical flourishes, and video teasers. While Table 5.1 shows that these differences over time are significant, the relationship is not linear and instead is somewhat U-shaped. The 1970-era introductory sequences were quite long—about sixty seconds for ABC and about twenty seconds for CBS. A much more stripped-down approach to newscast introductions, especially by CBS, was employed in the 1980s, with a sharp rise in the 1994 and 2000 broadcast samples.

Table 5.2 illustrates the use of teasers in news shows before advertising breaks to encourage viewers to not leave the channel during the break. The relationship over time is more in line with what was predicted. Except for 1976, there was an increase in the amount of time given to teasers before advertising breaks. There is a pretty sharp jump in the number of seconds used to tease stories from 1988 onward. The network data show that ABC has always been more aggressive in plugging coming stories than CBS, which has also used thirty-plus seconds per broadcast to tease coming stories. A strong R-squared of .593 (table 5.2) emerges in this relationship, and the test for linearity was significant at the .000 level. In 2000, CBS was using an average thirty-seven seconds per broadcast for teasers, while ABC averaged forty-nine seconds per broadcast.

Table 5.1.   Length of Introductory Segment in Newscast (Mean Values, in Seconds)

Network	1970	1976	1982	1988	1994	2000
ABC	60.2	47.8	27.6	4.8	31.2	55.6
CBS	18.1	3.0	3.0	9.7	9.4	48.4

Between group F = 18.94, R-squared = .009, P = .000

Table 5.2.   News Story Teasers (Mean Values, in Seconds)

Network	1970	1976	1982	1988	1994	2000
ABC	23.3	9.2	26.6	38.6	32.3	48.7
CBS	1.6	0	19.7	37.9	36.5	36.8

Between group F = 61.28, R-squared = .593, P = .000

Table 5.3 presents the effort television networks make in promoting the news "brand" of their networks. It describes the use of within-program promotions of other news shows on the network. Typically, the anchor will follow a report with a comment (for example, "Later on *48 Hours,* you can see the entire interview") or note coverage of a public affairs event (such as a presidential debate or state of the union address) that the network will be providing later that evening or week. The table shows that news promotions during newscasts before 1982 were nonexistent. Since that time, there has been a steady rise in the amount of time in a newscast dedicated to promoting other network news products. The relationship is linear at the .000 level with an R-squared of .352. The last two years sampled, 1994 and 2000, saw a marked increase in the use of such promotions, to a two-network average of seventeen seconds in 2000.

This relationship is more dramatic when one looks at promotions of other news shows during advertising breaks (see table 5.4). The relationship is linear, and a slightly higher R-squared resulted: .375. There were no news show promotions during ad breaks at all in 1970 and 1976.

Table 5.5 reports the increasing use of "live" segments in newscasts over time. The relationship expected is not very strong due to a sixty-four-second average for ABC in 1976. This average is due primarily to one lengthy live interview with a baseball manager during a story about the World Series. The length of live segments stayed flat until 2000,

Table 5.3.   Promotions of News "Brand" During Newscasts (Mean Values, in Seconds)

Network	1970	1976	1982	1988	1994	2000
ABC	0	0	5.0	10.1	1.3	27.3
CBS	0	0	0	0	13.0	6.0

Between group F = 16.42, R-squared = .352, P = .000

Table 5.4.   Number of News Promotions During Ad Breaks (Mean Values)

Network	1970	1976	1982	1988	1994	2000
ABC	0	0	0.4	1.0	0.2	1.6
CBS	0	0	0	0	1.3	0.6

Between group F = 15.00, R-squared = .375, P = .000

Table 5.5.   Live Segments During Newscasts (Mean Values, in Seconds)

Network	1970	1976	1982	1988	1994	2000
ABC	0	63.6	21.5	9.7	15.1	83.5
CBS	0	0	0	21.0	9.4	24.9

Between group F = 3.49, R-squared = .052, P = .000

when there was a huge spike in the length of live segments. This jump is reflected largely in ABC's eighty-four-second average per newscast for that year. In this sample, ABC consistently employed more effort to use seemingly "live" material. A weak linear relationship results from this. Thus, while a steady increase in going "live" was expected, the data show a substantial jump in the final year sampled compared to the five previous years sampled. Part of this result can be attributed to the fact that technological advances in television now make live segments easier to include in a newscast. And indeed, surveys of journalists and producers at local stations show that technical ability to "go live" can result in overkill. Reporters say producers seek to use expensive technology to present live stories just so use of the technology can be justified (Tuggle and Huffman 1999, 2001). This research also shows that producers feel going live is an important competitive enhancement designed to attract and maintain viewer attention.

The next two tables illustrate how the use of non-news items described above affects the amount of news time in a broadcast. Table 5.6 shows that the amount of time dedicated to news stories in broadcasts has been decreasing since 1982. In 1970, both ABC and CBS had over twenty minutes of news stories in a half hour broadcast, with CBS averaging over twenty-two minutes. After a small bump up in 1982, both networks began to reduce the amount of newscast time for stories, so that by 2000, ABC was averaging just over eighteen minutes and CBS was averaging eighteen minutes, thirty seconds of actual news stories within a broadcast. This relationship is statistically linear with an R-square of .427.

Table 5.7 shows how time has been allotted to all the non-news elements described above over time. It groups advertising time, introductory segments, teasers within a newscast, and news promotions within

Table 5.6.   Total News Time During Newscast (Mean Values, in Seconds)

Network	1970	1976	1982	1988	1994	2000
ABC	1,228	1,209	1,246	1,229	1,217	1,089
CBS	1,339	1,344	1,377	1,243	1,187	1,114

Between group F = 29.91, R-squared = .427, P = .000

Table 5.7. Total Non-news Time During Newscast (Mean Values, in Seconds)

Network	1970	1976	1982	1988	1994	2000
ABC	446	347	434	407	460	557
CBS	246	237	263	410	423	571

Between group F = 39.95, R-squared = .506, P = .000

news blocks together into "non-news." There is a steady increase in non-news time from 1976 onward, with a big jump in 2000. As noted in chapters 1 and 4, both ABC and CBS were sold to larger conglomerates after 1994. (CBS actually changed hands twice in the mid- to late 1990s.) Part of the drop in news time is reflected in an increase in advertising time, perhaps an indication of the "bottom line" orientation to news that Disney and Westinghouse/Viacom brought to the network news divisions they acquired as part of a larger deal. From 1988 to 2000, ABC's advertising breaks increased from nearly seven minutes per half hour to over nine minutes, while CBS increased advertising time from close to seven minutes to nine minutes, thirty seconds.

The increases in teasers before advertising breaks, promotion of other network news shows, and the sharp rise in the lengths of introductory segments account for the other portions of "non-news" content in nightly news programs. It should be noted that news and non-news elements do not add up to thirty minutes total because advertising aired after the credits at the end of the show was not counted even though it fell within the half hour time block. Thus, the amount of advertising per half hour of news is actually greater than the data reported here indicate.

DISCUSSION

Many of the changes in the way news is presented that have been discussed here reflect the soap opera paradigm in terms of identifying a number of ways in which news uses serial elements within news broadcasts. Introductory segments, teasing upcoming stories before advertising breaks, and promotion of the network news brand during both the news and advertising breaks—though not exclusive to the soap opera form—reflect attempts to grab and hold viewers to a program or a particular network for news. The increase in advertising time is a reflection of the subsuming of network news under increasingly large corporate umbrellas and how the conglomeratization of network television has brought substantial distance from a public service orientation to the news—more show, less news.

All of this suggests that the soap opera paradigm has affected the way news is presented during nightly news programs, especially in the last fifteen years. It is during this decade and a half that we have seen both of the networks used in this study change from being stand-alone networks to becoming parts of media conglomerates. CBS was initially bought by Westinghouse in the late 1980s and then Viacom in the 1990s. ABC was purchased by Capital Cities (an electronic media corporation) and then later in the 1990s by Disney. The controversy in late winter 2002 about whether Disney would abandon ABC's *Nightline* if it acquired CBS late-night talk show host David Letterman is a reflection of how these media conglomerates regard their news operations. If news programs are now regarded by their corporate owners as just another source of profit, stripped of any public service obligation, is it any wonder that they would increasingly take on characteristics of soap opera entertainment?

The increases in self-promotion of the network news "brand," the increases in time devoted to teasing stories later in the newscast, and lengthy, technologically sophisticated introductions to news shows all fit within the framework anticipated by the soap opera paradigm. This part of the examination of how news programs have evolved reveals a drop in time dedicated to news stories of nearly three and a half minutes since 1982, clearly diminishing the time available to describe an increasingly complex world.

Moving on to how these news operations tell the stories of the day, one expects that these non-news elements that reflect a soap opera orientation will be complemented by an increasing use of the other elements identified above—seriality in stories, the use of "real-time" reporting, seeming intimacy, the manner of story exposition, and the characteristics and themes of news stories—as news operations try to create brand loyalty among viewers and attract new viewers by using vivid, emotional tactics in the telling of the news.

SOAP OPERA STORYTELLING IN THE NEWS

This section looks at aspects of news stories that reflect a soap opera orientation to the news. Each of the five elements is analyzed for its contributions to the news. But since the elements often complement each other, this section also tries to get a feel for how they have been used in concert over time to create a rather different way of presenting the news. The influence of the Arledge era at ABC and the shorter but nonetheless significant tenure of Van Gordon Sauter at CBS seem to reflect the beginning of an increasing use of the soap opera elements. One should note from the outset that many of these elements, in particular seriality and story exposition, are not necessarily negative aspects when presenting news stories. Some of these elements inevitably become part of news stories because they help tell the story in an accurate way. Thus, an increase in a particular element is not necessarily a "bad" thing. But the ways in which news pumps up emotion, focuses on individual travails or interpersonal disputes, and reduces government or political news to power squabbling tend to take away from presenting a macro or "big picture" analysis, which is so often crucial in presenting the news.

Since the unit of analysis for this portion of the study is the *story*, the analysis must account for the possibility that there may be substantial variation in the number of stories broadcast over the thirty years this study covers.

Two tables help provide a picture of how the number of stories in a broadcast has evolved. Table 5.8 shows that the average number of stories in a newscast dropped rather consistently from 1970 to 2000. ABC's news programs went from a high of fifteen stories in 1976 to nine in 2000. CBS's high of nineteen stories in 1970 fell to eleven by 2000. While some of this drop may be attributed to the increase in "non-news" time shown in table 5.7, one might also reasonably expect there to be longer story lengths as fewer stories are told in newscasts. Table 5.9 shows this to be the case.

CBS's shortest stories occurred in 1970, when it averaged seventy seconds per story. In 2000, an average story was coming in at one hundred seconds (one minute, forty-one seconds) Likewise, in 1976 ABC had story lengths of 78 seconds on average. By 2000, it was running stories averaging 134 seconds (two minutes, fourteen seconds).

For both the number of stories and story lengths, the change over thirty years is largely linear; decreases in stories and increases in story lengths occur incrementally over the six years sampled from 1970 to 2000. The most significant implication coming from these data is that longer story lengths will allow for more opportunity to incorporate soap opera storytelling elements. Longer stories enable portrayals of intimacy, more elaborate story

Table 5.8. Average Number of Stories in a Newscast (Mean Values)

Network	1970	1976	1982	1988	1994	2000
ABC	13.1	15.2	15.2	12.1	11.1	8.5
CBS	19.3	16.9	14.1	13.0	14.8	11.3

Table 5.9. Average Story Length in a Newscast (Mean Values, in Seconds)

Network	1970	1976	1982	1988	1994	2000
ABC	96	78	82	102	113	134
CBS	70	84	100	98	87	101

exposition, and portrayals of story themes such as conflict and triumphing over adversity. The findings below generally posit increases in stories using soap elements over time. The fact that the number of stories per broadcast was falling only serves to enforce the growing influence of soap opera storytelling in presenting the news. That is, with a smaller number of stories in the soap opera era of TV news, the number of stories exhibiting soap opera characteristics is actually a higher percentage of all stories in the later years of this study. With this in mind, one can now identify how the soap elements were identified and coded story by story.

The means used to identify the presence of a soap opera element in a news story was to identify rather specific characteristics of each element in terms of how it is reflected in the news. These criteria provided the basis for the high degree of intercoder reliability results reported earlier.

Seriality: The most obvious example of seriality in news stories is coverage of a story over multiple days. Usually day-to-day coverage opens with some statement of continuation from previous days such as, "There was continuing violence on the West Bank today . . . ." The end of the story may reflect the idea that the story is not over, and viewers should expect further developments.

Real-time orientation: As previously demonstrated, the use of live segments, which most of the time are labeled on-screen as "live," has increased. But that is just one aspect of classifying a story or segment of a story as having a real-time orientation. Often "live" or, more broadly, immediacy is *suggested* in a news story. The presence of a reporter sitting at the anchor desk with the anchor conveys a sense of "live" even though the show may very well have been recorded. Reporter-anchor exchanges with the reporter in a remote location also project immediacy even if they are not done live.

Seeming intimacy: This element has multiple indicators or cues that suggest to the viewers that they are seeing unobtrusive behavior in which people are "letting their guard down" and presenting the inner thoughts and emotions of those involved in the story. The use of emotion, whether described or portrayed on camera, is an obvious indicator of intimacy. In stories involving crimes or disasters, the use of victims or victims' relatives to tell their story also reflects a sense of intimacy. Stories that are primarily about the personal lives of people who are not celebrities or otherwise well known, and stories that use hidden cameras, project the "fly on the wall" orientation that is crucial to this element. Highly charged personal discourse among news "actors"—people viewers are familiar with—also projects intimacy to viewers. This is especially true in political and governance stories in which issue disputes become contests of will between powerful political players. Behind-the-scenes portrayals designed to project a microscopic look at a situation also qualify for designation as intimate storytelling; "insiderism" is a close relative of intimacy. Finally, news stories that try to show how the viewer may be affected reflect an attempt to make viewers feel they should pay close attention because they may face the same situation. This is typified when anchors or reporters relate the story to viewers through the use of "you" or "your family or loved ones."

Story exposition: This rather broad category is meant to capture how the story is told through the participants involved. Several stories surrounding a singular event or issue go beyond a single perspective, just as in a soap opera it may take several days before all the characters' reactions to a plot twist are revealed. In news, getting to the different motives of the individuals or groups involved or portraying the several sides or angles of a story reflects an attempt to give a fuller telling of the story. Reporting on the reaction from other countries and groups in international news and using reporters in multiple locales for different takes on the same story is a way to try to bring a fuller picture to the issue. Summaries of trials that have not been given day-to-day coverage are meant to provide some context to current developments. Multiple perspectives on the news are also achieved by doing a "macro/micro" analysis—looking at the big picture or structural view of an issue while also presenting everyday or micro examples flowing from the big picture perspective. A story about the plight of seniors obtaining the drugs they need will, for example, often look at the political process or debate trying to arrive at a solution to help seniors and then will be accompanied by some examples of senior citizens having a hard time making ends meet because of high drug expenses. Finally, on fairly rare occasions, an anchor may segue between two stories linking them in ways not apparently obvious to viewers, thus making a connection viewers may not have perceived as relevant.

Story characteristics: There are three subcategories for this element: conflict/chaos, clear delineations of good versus evil, and projecting or promoting an affluent society. News is often built around situations of conflict; in fact business as usual is usually not news, whereas deviations from normality are identified as newsworthy. But the mode of presentation of a story can heighten the degree of conflict in a story. Stories that present pro and con perspectives in a she said/he said mode reflect the personalization of an issue dispute. Much of what is cast as political reporting can best be characterized as a "food fight," in which the conflict is emphasized and the issue being disputed is backgrounded in the story.

The issue of good versus evil would seemingly be out of bounds for the news, as such characterizations of actors or actions in a news story would violate norms of objectivity. Nonetheless, a societal shift toward judging issues in almost exclusively moral terms can be seen in how the news often reflects the U.S. government's judgment about another nation or group. In some stories, overcoming adversity can be seen as a triumph over negativity or "evil." Recent coverage of foreign affairs has taken on tones of moral judgment as political leaders cast enemies in the starkest of terms. Stories about military conflict or citizen intervention to prevent or stop a crime are also examples of heroism that fit nicely under this category.

Stories on the economy are generally couched in language that includes the middle economic strata (which are very broadly defined in the United States). Reports on the stock market and evaluations of the economy are often done in ways that give the impression that income and wealth distribution are less skewed toward the affluent than population statistics might reflect. Reports on new, upscale, high technology gadgets aimed at people who have more disposable income beyond the average household are another indicator of celebrating affluence. In other words, news projects products that people cannot necessarily afford to buy. But these stories encourage viewers to at least aspire to possessing markers of "the good life." Finally, an increasing use of news from the world of sport and cultural celebrity brings tabloid elements into news stories. Though the stories about the glamorous may not always portray them as happy, the display of material possessions identifies just what the good life can bring materially.

Having laid out the criteria for identifying these elements in news stories, it is appropriate to look at how each of these elements has evolved over the last thirty years of network news. The tables present the data for each element. The numerical data presented in each table are percentages of stories per broadcast for each year studied.

Day-to-day reporting on a continuing story is common in television news, so it is no surprise that there have been elements of seriality in TV news throughout the thirty-year sample investigated in this study. ABC and CBS evening news programs averaged about 20 percent serial stories in 1970. These averages stayed in the 20 to 30 percent range until the year 2000, when there was a dramatic rise in the percentage of serial stories to about half of all stories broadcast on both CBS and ABC. Table 5.10 illustrates this increase in the percentage of serial elements per broadcast. Because the first five sample years contain roughly the same averages, the R-squared is rather small—.113. Because continuation stories are part of the real world of events, that there is not a steady increase should not be surprising. The rise in the year 2000 can be seen as an increased emphasis on following stories day-to-day as well as perhaps a function of the cutbacks in reporting crews the networks have undertaken since being bought by conglomerates; fewer reporters means fewer stories are selected for coverage, and those that are selected represent an investment for the networks that encourages them to stay and follow the story to a point of resolution.

Table 5.10. Percent of News Stories with Serial Elements

Network	1970	1976	1982	1988	1994	2000
ABC	19	34	36	18	26	46
CBS	22	22	17	22	29	45

Between group F = 16.81, R-squared =.113, P =.000

Table 5.11. Percent of News Stories with Real-Time Elements

Network	1970	1976	1982	1988	1994	2000
ABC	0	4	2	2	1	14
CBS	0	0	1	4	2	1

Between group F = 11.40, R-squared = .086, P = .001

Real-time elements in news stories consist of clearly labeled "live" reports or seemingly live exchanges between the anchor and reporter. The previous discussion of program elements revealed that the time of live segments used in the news has increased significantly in 2000 beyond the modest use of live segments from the earlier years sampled. Table 5.11 reinforces this finding, mostly due to a rise in ABC's use of a real-time segment in 2000 in about 14 percent of stories. Again, the overall relationship, though weak, is in the expected direction.

Projecting a sense of intimacy in news reports is a key indicator of how the soap opera paradigm has been employed by network news, because unlike seriality and real-time orientation, intimacy is not a traditional news value or mode of news storytelling. Thus for this element one expects to see a gradual increase in its use to tell a story. The data, as represented in table 5.12, affirm this anticipation. The first three years sampled—1970, 1976, and 1982—showed little in the way of intimate portrayals of people's personal dilemmas or pain and did not focus on the private lives of prominent politicians or celebrities. From 1988 onward, however, there was a spike in the use of storytelling which employs a sense of intimacy to viewers. This parallels the purchase of the networks by larger companies beginning in the mid-1980s. By 2000, ABC's news stories projected intimacy in nearly 30 percent of stories, and CBS used intimacy in nearly 20 percent of stories broadcast in 2000. This increase over

Table 5.12. Percent of News Stories with Intimacy Elements

Network	1970	1976	1982	1988	1994	2000
ABC	5	8	4	8	21	29
CBS	2	1	5	25	14	18

Between group F = 61.46, R-squared = .336, P = .000

time is significant, and the resulting R-squared is .336 at a .000 level of significance, affirming the expected rise in this element.

Story exposition is an element of soap operas that actually can translate into better reporting of a story. This category is primarily populated by stories that present multiple perspectives on an issue by using sources representing different points of view or by airing several stories from different parts of the world or the country to convey a sense of completeness. Table 5.13 shows that story exposition elements were increasingly used as the networks became part of larger corporate operations. From being present in less than 3 percent of stories per broadcast in 1970, by 2000 40 percent of stories on ABC and 23 percent of stories on CBS brought elements of story exposition to their evening news programs. The increase is particularly noteworthy beginning in 1988. The expected relationship over time is strong—the R-squared is .542, and the test for linearity is significant at the .000 level.

The final set of soap opera elements tested for their presence in ABC and CBS evening news casts comes under the umbrella of characteristics of soap opera storytelling—the degree to which stories include conflict and chaos, capture sides in a conflict as good or evil, and project a sense of an affluent society. Each of these subcategories was coded separately for each story in a newscast. Since this is one of the primary news values—stories that are attractive to newspeople because they provide a basis for a more vivid story—one could reasonably expect news stories throughout the sampling period to use conflict as a hook in presenting the news. The data summarized in table 5.14 show that this is the case. Conflict in news stories was present from 1970 onward. By the late 1980s and throughout the 1990s the use of conflict as a key point in storytelling about doubled to over 20 percent of stories on each network conveying a sense of conflict. Given the slight dips in 1976 and 1982 (probably due to the substantial number of reports on the Vietnam War in 1970), the strength of this relationship is not as strong as that seen with other elements—.209—but the relationship is statistically significant, indicating that the rise in the use of conflict is not a chance development.

Stories that in essence contrast "good" versus "evil" actors or agencies appearing in the news stand in contrast to stories about conflict in the sense that such a valuing of the sides of a story runs counter to traditional

Table 5.13.   Percent of News Stories with Exposition Elements

Network	1970	1976	1982	1988	1994	2000
ABC	3	5	10	20	27	40
CBS	1	0	11	24	18	23

Between group F = 143. 10, R-squared = .542, P = .000

Table 5.14.   Percent of News Stories with Conflict Elements

Network	1970	1976	1982	1988	1994	2000
ABC	16	5	7	12	23	21
CBS	6	5	11	24	21	23

Between group F = 33.25, R-squared = .209, P = .000

"objective" journalism. Nonetheless, network news started exhibiting these elements around the time the pace of media conglomeration reached its peak in the 1990s. Table 5.15 shows that good-versus-evil contrasts in the news were rare in the years before 1990, and then there was a jump in stories using good versus evil. This is especially noteworthy in 2000, when the sampled period included the bombing of the USS Cole in the Arabian Peninsula country of Yemen, a bombing broadly thought to be committed by Osama bin Laden and his terror network. Perhaps a comparable period in news could be found in the Cold War fifties, when television news was in its infancy. At that time, a lot of news footage was captured by the companies that provided newsreels for exhibition in movie theaters before the main feature. Not conventionally identified as news, newsreels were a combination of entertainment and information whose narration often used the pejorative terms of political leaders in describing threats from "the Reds" in the Soviet Union and the "growing yellow horde" of China. Today, terrorism is the new evil "ism" around which diplomatic and defense policies are set.

The percentage of stories on either network using good versus evil storytelling never rises above 5 percent of all stories broadcast. Though the relationship is statistically weak, we can say with some certainty that there has been a rise in the number of stories which single out good and bad individuals or countries as a way of pumping up the emotion of a story.

The final storytelling characteristic explored in news over the last thirty years focuses on the degree to which economic affluence is projected or celebrated in news. A shift to portraying American society as primarily affluent can be seen as a function of the kind of audiences the news is trying to reach. For many years the news has included information about daily stock market activities, seemingly as a barometer for the health of

Table 5.15.   Percent of News Stories with Good/Evil Elements

Network	1970	1976	1982	1988	1994	2000
ABC	1	0	0	0	5	2
CBS	0	0	1	2	1	3

Between group F = 8.70, R-squared = .069, P = .004

the economy. Though many consumers of news now have a stake in the stock market through retirement savings, in prior decades stock owner-ship was more exclusively the province of the determinably affluent. Table 5.16 illustrates that images of an affluent society were very sparse throughout the first three years sampled for this study. From 1988 onward however, there was a dramatic increase from the meager use of affluence in broadcasts. In the more recent three years sampled—1988, 1994, and 2000—between 6 and 8 percent of stories contained elements of affluence. While there is a statistically significant relationship over time, there is not much of a linear rise but rather a sudden jump in the era of conglomera-tization from 1985 onward. Thus, the relationship over time is weak, with an R-squared of .121.

Having looked at the elements of the soap opera paradigm separately, a question inevitably arises about whether groups of these elements are present in news stories. As mentioned in chapter 2, it is reasonable to con-clude that the elements complement each other in many ways. A "live" presentation can enhance the vivid emotion present in a story and make viewers feel closer to those involved in the story. Seriality in news stories helps present a continuing "character development" that may encourage viewers to see "good" and "evil" sides in stories portraying conflict. In-deed, it can almost be expected that the soap story elements are grouped in a set of stories during the newscast rather than spread throughout. Some news situations are more amenable to this kind of storytelling than others. The final table provides some evidence that the stories containing soap elements often include more than one. This idea was tested by ag-gregating the elements present in each story. As there are seven elements coded in this study, three elements or more was the criterion for deter-mining whether any single story in a newscast genuinely drew upon soap opera storytelling techniques in a substantial way. Table 5.17 presents this analysis and shows there is a marked increase in stories utilizing three or more soap storytelling elements in concert from 1988 onward. Again, the timing of this increase is noteworthy. By 1988, both CBS and ABC had al-ready been merged or bought out by larger corporate entities—Capital Cities in the case of ABC and Loews Corporation with respect to CBS. In the years 1988, 1994, and 2000, both broadcasts had at least 10 percent of stories using three soap opera elements. Prior to those years, an average

Table 5.16. Percent of News Stories with Upper-Middle-Class Elements

Network	1970	1976	1982	1988	1994	2000
ABC	1	1	1	8	7	8
CBS	1	2	1	6	6	3

Between group F = 16. 71, R-squared = .121, P = .000

Table 5.17.   Percent of News Stories with Three or More Elements

Network	1970	1976	1982	1988	1994	2000
ABC	8	0	7	10	13	21
CBS	0	0	6	14	10	14

Between group F = 13.04, R-squared = .193, P = .001

of less than 10 percent of stories in a newscast could be identified as having at least three soap elements (and in 1976, no sampled stories contained three or more soap elements). Thus the percentage of stories in the later three years sampled doubled from the earlier years. An R-squared of .193 indicates a moderate relationship over time. Furthermore, nineteen of the twenty broadcasts in 2000 contained at least one story with three or more elements (fifteen of twenty in 1994 and 1988), while in 1982 only six of the twenty editions of the news contained a story with three or more elements.

DISCUSSION

The data from this study offer substantial support for the idea that network news programs have increasingly employed elements of soap opera storytelling designed to heighten the emotional involvement of viewers in the stories they are watching. As attempts to describe what is going on in the "real world," conventional definitions of journalism rest on putting up a mirror to society. The use of soap opera storytelling techniques in TV news suggests that much more is going on as the networks assemble their news programs. Nightly news production teams clearly have incorporated entertainment values in presenting the news, especially in the last fifteen to twenty years, during which the network news divisions have deviated from the traditional public service context in which they were originally conceived. The data presented here illustrate that this shift has prompted news producers to find new ways of telling news stories more geared to their corporate parents' desires for serving bottom line, rather than democratic governance, values. Pumping up the emotion, creating a sense of "being there," and emphasizing conflict are the news tactics consistently employed in greater percentages of stories from 1988 onward.

This situation points to an obvious crisis of journalism—a profession that has seen its independence wither away in the face of corporate conglomeratization. If news is now more about making money than providing a public service that enriches democratic debate and deliberation, it is not difficult to see that this crisis is also a major issue for the fulfillment of democratic governance. The most important requirement for a democratic political system is an informed populace. If news is more about entertainment than creating informed citizens, democratic participation and decision making will no doubt suffer as well.

Although some elements were identified as not hostile to good television journalism, it is clear that news producers place a high value on having viewers "feel" something about the news of the day rather than learning what they need to act as intelligent citizens in democratic discourse. A dispassionate approach to the news has been determined to be fundamentally boring and thus not in sync with serving the interests of the bottom line. In other words, for today's television news, it is more important to please stockholders than it is to educate citizens.

Because the traditional function of news to inform contrasts with the entertainment functions of other television programming, the next two chapters continue to focus on how television presents the news of the day. Chapter 6 presents a detailed look at how television news has changed the way it approaches natural disasters and their impact on the citizens' lives that are disrupted by them. Natural disasters present prime opportunities to pump up the emotional elements of the story. The examination of television news and soap opera storytelling concludes with a look at how coverage of political campaigns has come to resemble a mini-soap opera by looking at coverage from the 1976, 1988, and 2000 campaigns included in the study of the evolution of network news and from a qualitative look at the 2000 primary season. Both of these chapters present case studies that illuminate the meaning behind the quantitative overview just presented.

6

Floods of Tears: Natural Disasters in the News

Coverage of disasters such as floods, hurricanes, and tornadoes has become a staple of television news. Visually compelling, this coverage conveys the desperate situation many people find themselves in when faced with such calamities. As such, these stories are ripe for soap opera-like treatments. How television news has approached the telling of these stories and how the telling of these stories has changed in the last twenty years can provide a window into how the soap opera paradigm has affected the way these stories are presented to audiences.

Two separate flood stories, airing fifteen years apart, allow comparisons of how the incorporation of soap opera storytelling techniques has influenced network television news coverage. While some differences in the characteristics of the floods being covered may have affected the way the networks approached these stories, it is quite apparent that news judgment—in the form of allocation of time during a newscast dedicated to an ongoing story, the resources dedicated to covering the story, and the particular narrative strategies employed in relaying the story—is a significant factor in how network coverage of such tragedies has changed.

In 1982, floods hit Ohio, Indiana, and Michigan and caused substantial property damage and general disruption; this was the greatest flooding in the region since 1913. The hardest-hit area was in and around Ft. Wayne, Indiana, where two flooding rivers converged. Stories of the flood began to hit the airwaves on Monday, March 15. ABC's *World News Tonight* ran stories throughout the week, the final one on Friday, March 19. The *CBS Evening News* coverage of these floods extended into the next week as well, with a final story on April 3. ABC ran a total of five stories, ranging from one minute, forty seconds to four minutes, one second in length. CBS's eight stories ranged from two minutes, twenty seconds to two minutes, thirty-nine seconds.

The 1997 flood was called a hundred-year flood and covered a much larger area than the 1982 flood: Minnesota, North Dakota, and the Canadian province of Manitoba. There was a freakish quality to this flooding that hampered those fighting it: The flood was the result of a quick thaw following a blizzard that had hit the region, and the icy conditions made the situation more harrowing. Stories on this flood aired for a longer period due to the extensive area it affected. The story ultimately centered on Grand Forks, North Dakota, after covering smaller communities.

ABC's coverage ranged from April 5 to April 27 (with a final follow-up story on May 25), while CBS followed a similar pattern of coverage from April 5 to April 23 (with a follow-up story on June 29). ABC ran thirteen stories in all, five of them "briefs" (anchor-read reports of thirty seconds or less without an on-site report). CBS ran a total of twelve stories, five of them briefs. The briefs offered day-to-day continuity of the story even when nothing meriting a fuller piece transpired. Thus, these briefs kept the serial element of the story alive even when there were no significant developments.

It is quite clear that one difference between the two flood stories is that both networks devoted greater resources to covering the 1997 flood, sending multiple reporting crews at the height of the flood. The 1982 flooding was covered by Meredith Viera and, on the weekend, by Frank Currier for CBS and David Garcia for ABC. Eventually, ABC's stories were introduced by Frank Robinson, who was part of the three-anchor team employed by ABC at that time. He did not do any actual reporting and instead did the on-site introduction to Garcia's reporting.

The 1997 flood stories at ABC were initially handled by Erin Hayes, but as the flooding extended and eventually reached and devastated Grand Forks, North Dakota, three more reporters—Ron Claiborne, Bill Blakemore, and John Donvan—were brought in, with Lisa Solters on weekend reports. At CBS, initial reporting was done by Randall Pinkston. Over time, Bob McNamara, Bill Plante, and Frank Currier became part of the team of reporters covering the story.

To be sure, the visit by President Bill Clinton to Grand Forks was a reason for the increase in time dedicated to the story; Donvan and Plante were White House reporters who followed the president (see sidebar on how presidential visits were covered for each flood). Nonetheless, the dedication of considerably more reporting resources is a reflection of the multiperspective approach to news and the evolution toward focusing on a smaller number of stories per broadcast. Like the presentation of a new development or plot twist in a soap opera community, multiple reports give viewers a greater sense of omniscience—seeing several angles of the story from different perspectives conveys a greater sense of completeness, much like when soap viewers learn the reaction by a number of characters to a new wrinkle or development in the soap narrative.

Thus, while the two floods being compared show some variation in the extent and length of the flooding and coverage, there are both similarities and differences in their treatment by the two networks. Both floods garnered the attention of the presidents in office at the time, Ronald Reagan and Bill Clinton. Both floods produced stories about the resilience of people in coping with the flood and the aftermath. Stories about both exhibited substantial emotional response from those affected. What is different between the 1982 and 1997 flood coverage is the degree to which the presidents were made part of the story, the tone of the resilience of the people, and the degree and emphasis of emotion exhibited in the stories.

The comparative analysis of these two sets of coverage focuses on the degree and manner to which they reflect elements of soap opera storytelling; examples of seriality, real-time orientation, seeming intimacy, story exposition, and story themes are present in the telling of these stories, though substantial variations are evident between 1982 and 1997. It is important to keep in mind that the two networks by 1982 were under the guidance of the men who ushered in many of the changes in news at CBS and ABC, Van Gordon Sauter and Roone Arledge, respectively. The changes these men brought to the evening news programs are identified in chapter 4 as embodying an increasing preference for soap opera storytelling. As previously mentioned, the soap opera paradigm is an evolutionary phenomenon, and one should not expect 1982 to be devoid of soap opera storytelling techniques. One can see Sauter's "theory of moments" at work in 1982 as well as Arledge's emphasis on story lines. The value of comparing the 1982 and 1997 floods lies in how changes afoot a decade and a half earlier were played out in ways that make the soap opera approach to news more discernible and definitive in 1997. It is this transitioning and perfecting of the soap opera paradigm to which this chapter now turns.

What the two sets of stories have in common is that they follow a similar narrative path. The stories seem to be presented in three phases. The preparation and bracing for the flood is followed by stories of areas affected by the water and the evacuation of severely affected areas. The final phase ensues when the water retreats and recovery begins. Looking at both floods, such a narrative transition seems inevitable, almost prescribed. It is as if producers are saying, "OK, first we show the resistance to Mother Nature, then we show the limitations of fighting her. Last, we show the victims, and we conclude with a determination to get back to normal." The task of the reporters is to then go out and find stories that will fulfill this narrative

PRESIDENTIAL VISITS TO DISASTERS

Since the advent of television, how the presidency is viewed and how presidents use public events have changed. This is because television news has become an important factor in how government communicates with the public. Staging events designed to maintain the president's image as a leader has become an integral activity to the everyday functioning of the White House, and the primary object of that planning is television news.

The role of television in the modern American presidency is unprecedented. Only Franklin Delano Roosevelt's fireside chats, broadcast over the radio airwaves in the 1930s, provide a comparison with another medium in terms of how presidents attempt to establish a direct relationship with the American public. Pre-television presidents weren't necessarily required to have a pleasant visage or be movingly articulate in the way required of presidents from the 1960s onward. The public image of the president is now not only equated with how successful a president is seen to be but also with how he performs in times of crisis, whether domestic or foreign in nature.

The 1982 and 1997 floods offer a lesson on how both television news and the officeholder have come to view the importance of presidential visits to disasters. Ronald Reagan and Bill Clinton, though coming from different parties and worldviews, were both thought of as masterful communicators who used television effectively enough to be elected twice. However, as the fifteen years separating these two stories demonstrate, there is a growing sophistication with which the president's handlers have used visits to natural disasters to ensure flattering media coverage.

Reagan's appearance in Ft. Wayne, Indiana, was part of a day of visiting disaster areas; tornadoes in Oklahoma were also visited (although interestingly, there was no coverage of the Oklahoma visit on either ABC or CBS news shows). Reagan's appearance in Ft. Wayne occurred on March 16, one day after the first reports on network news. The coverage consists of video footage of Reagan without any corresponding "sound bite" from him commenting on the disaster or the federal government's response.

On *CBS Evening News*, after a brief mention of the visits in Dan Rather's lead-in, Meredith Viera reports:

VIERA: The President got a bird's-eye view of some of the damage caused by tornadoes in Oklahoma. But as Air Force One approached Ft. Wayne, the view changed to that of a city devastated by flooding. (*CBS Evening News*, March 16, 1982)

The video coverage consists of shots of Reagan in the helicopter interspersed with scenes of the flooding shot from the helicopter. At the end of the report, it is noted that no announcement on what kind of aid will be forthcoming has been made. On ABC's *World News Tonight*, the story includes brief footage of Reagan's visit to a Red Cross shelter as well as his survey of the disaster from a helicopter:

GARCIA (reporter): On his way back to Washington this afternoon, President Reagan stopped for a look at the worst flooding since 1913. The water level [is] over 10 feet above flood stage. The president scheduled a visit at one of the Red Cross emergency shelters to see how the victims are doing. With millions of dollars in aid requested and up to 3,500 people still out of evacuated homes, the president wanted a first hand assessment. (*World News Tonight*, March 16, 1982)

Garcia's report defines a clear purpose for the visit—Reagan is there to determine how the federal government should assist local governments in coping with the flood—but little else is presented in terms of Reagan's empathy for victims or whether citizens of Ft. Wayne are comforted by the visit. The only time Reagan's voice is heard during the stories on the Ft. Wayne flooding is four days later when the waters have receded. A *CBS Evening News* story conveys the following segment of a telephone conversation between the president and Ft. Wayne's mayor, Winfield Moses:

FRANK CURRIER (reporter): Ft. Wayne's mayor thanked the President for his disaster declaration this afternoon in a telephone call to Camp David.
MOSES: Look forward to the difficult task now of trying to clean the city up from this terrible flood.
REAGAN: Oh well, this is great. The rain has stopped? (*CBS Evening News*, March 20, 1982)

The accompanying video is taken from the mayor's office, and no shot of Reagan on the phone is presented. Thus, for the Ft. Wayne flood story, the coverage of the president's visit is rather brief and mundane. This stands in sharp contrast to the way Clinton's visit to the Grand Forks area during its flood is covered. While Clinton's visit is also a one-day story, the nature of that coverage is very different and highlights how television news producers as well as White House communication strategists use opportunities like natural disasters to provide an image of the president as comforter and healer. Both CBS and ABC presented the president's visit as part of a package of reports

(continued)

on the flooding on April 22. While these would be the only stories involving the president (CBS had earlier covered the visit of Vice President Al Gore in a brief on April 11), the extent of the coverage far exceeds that given to Reagan's visit to Ft. Wayne.

ROBERTS (anchor): The lead editorial in today's *Grand Forks Herald* is addressed to President Clinton. It says "Welcome to Our Nightmare." This is some of what the president saw today (scenes of flooding from the air shown) as he surveyed this modern day Atlantis in the middle of America. As Bill Plante reports, the president promised residents of the flooded Red River Valley financial aid and offered them moral support.

PLANTE (reporter): The president's staff said he had come to show people here that the administration cared, to give them a boost after what they had been through. John Alexander, who came with his daughter to hear Mr. Clinton, filled sandbags for two days only to see the river wash them away.

ALEXANDER: I could not imagine devastation. We're looking at the whole Grand Forks—50,000 people—having to move out. That's a lot of people to move at one time.

Plante: The president's aerial view from Marine One brought home the scope of the disaster, block after block of homes and businesses awash in the mud brown water. But Grand Forks mayor Pat Owens told Mr. Clinton, the river hadn't drowned people's spirits.

OWENS: I believe within our communities, the people that have lost their homes and possibly lost their business and all their possessions, have had a tear in their eye and wiped it and went on to help the other people within their community, which has just amazed me. I tell you I'm so proud to lead this community. (voice breaks)

PLANTE: It will be weeks before the people in this shelter go home, if they still have homes. Mr. Clinton reached out to them.

CLINTON: What makes a community a place to live in is not the buildings, it's the people. The spirit and faith that are in those people (followed by shot of resident looking upward at president). Water cannot wash that away and fire cannot burn that away and a blizzard cannot freeze that away. And if you don't give it away, it will bring you back better than ever and we will be there with you every step of the way. Thank you and god bless you.

PLANTE: Whatever consolation the people here drew from the president's visit, it's the promise of even more federal aid which gives them the most hope. (*CBS Evening News*, April 22, 1997)

The noteworthy use of emotion by the mayor of Grand Forks and both reporter Bill Plante's and Clinton's use of words make the story somewhat poignant. The anchor's mention in the lead-in that the president is there to provide moral support adds to a theme in the story of providing solace to a stunned population. The lengthy quote from Clinton's speech to flood victims and the video of upward gazes by audience members clearly enhance the president's image as comforter and healer. The presidential visit received similar banner treatment on ABC:

JENNINGS (anchor): President Clinton today toured the vast inland ocean that now engulfs Grand Forks, ND and a lot of places which are smaller. The president said people are in the fight for their lives as he promised hundreds of millions in federal aid to help them recover.

DONVAN (reporter): There was a need in Grand Forks today that this president knows better than most how to satisfy. It was the need for sympathy.

CLINTON: I don't recall ever in my life seeing anything like this and I have been very impressed by the courage and the faith that all of you have shown in the face of what has been a terrible, terrible dilemma.

DONVAN: Not only did Mr. Clinton come to see for himself from the air how a river turned into a sea that has swallowed up whole towns, he also sat down and listened.

MAN: The citizens here have no basic services in sewer and water.

DONVAN: This was a meeting with local officials—mayors and health inspectors and fire wardens. None has slept much this week, many were near tears talking to the president.

MAN: You hold them in your arms and you tell them it will be alright which you probably know it won't be. But you keep fighting.

DONVAN: But there was also humor. Pat Owens, who lost her home, is the mayor of Grand Forks.

OWENS: This morning when I was getting ready to come here to meet the president, Mayor Straus [mayor of East Grand Forks, Minnesota] and I were talking. He didn't have water, he still doesn't have water at this point. I thought what do I wear? (laughter)

CLINTON: It looks good. (more laughter as he reaches over and touches her arm) (*World News Tonight,* April 22, 1997)

Much like the story on CBS, the president is cast as providing sympathy and a comforting ear to hear the stories victims have to tell. Two

(*continued*)

moments of emotion are exhibited as Donvan talks about local officials "near tears" and a man describes comforting a citizen or child in his arms. Quotes from Clinton in each story combine a sympathetic tone and a tone of resilience and recovery. In other words, he tells them how much strength they have shown and expresses confidence that they will triumph over the tragedy.

Coverage of a presidential visit has clearly changed in the fifteen years separating these two stories. One should not conclude that all the differences between the two stories are due to the adaptation by network news of soap opera storytelling techniques, although these two stories provide a compelling example of the president as the "great comforter."

It is not just a matter of news producers picking a theme for a story and building the story around it. The way a president's public appearances are handled also has a lot to do with the way the president's media handlers construct opportunities for the president to look "presidential." Certainly the growing sophistication of White House communications strategists plays a significant role in the way these stories are presented. While Reagan's media handlers were judged masters of the process in their time, the Clinton White House strategists make those efforts seem almost amateur given the way they constructed events to demonstrate Clinton's warmth and compassion. White House strategists set up meetings and media access so that the president's role as comforter could be amply demonstrated.

The media created visual moments such as the interspersing of views of the public looking up at Clinton and selected the most poignant comments and moments from his meeting with emergency and local government officials. The public was clearly in an emotive mood and sought comfort in the president's presence and words. The 1997 flood story shows how the needs of the media and of the White House strategists combine to fully demonstrate the use of soap opera storytelling techniques.

structure. This chapter looks at each of these phases of reporting for both floods to show that the coverage of the 1997 flood reflects more elements of soap opera storytelling than does the coverage of the 1982 flood.

RESISTANCE AND DETERMINATION

Most flooding, unlike tornadoes and earthquakes, involves some warning and preparation time. (Similarly, there is often some advance notice about hurricanes, allowing people to board up and take shelter or evacuate.) As the water rises farther up the river, flood plains and areas near rivers are vulnerable, and attempts to prevent possible flood damage are undertaken by emergency crews and citizen volunteers. This was the case in each of the floods examined here; the early stories appearing on the two networks focused on the determination and resilience of the affected communities. In each case, citizens are seen sandbagging and working to protect the more vulnerable. These stories are accompanied by quotes expressing a determination to fight the flood and lessen its harm to the community.

Stories from the 1982 flood typically begin with summary leads that tell the story in brief. Between anchor Dan Rather's introduction and reporter Meredith Viera's lead sentence, most of the essential facts of the first day of flood stories are captured:

> RATHER: Over wide areas of the upper Midwest, one of the worst winters on record is causing some of the worst flooding in 69 years. Four thousand homeless in Michigan, Ohio and Indiana . . .
> VIERA: Fifteen percent of Ft. Wayne Indiana is under water. Along streets in the northwest section of town motor cars have been replaced by motor boats. (*CBS Evening News,* March 15, 1982)

World News Tonight takes a similar approach, introducing the story and quickly moving to the efforts to resist the flood, drawing on the words of local citizens to paint a picture of a community coming together:

> DAVID GARCIA (reporter): In the worst flooding since 1913, volunteers took advantage of a respite from the rain to reinforce Ft. Wayne's defenses against the rising tide, bolstering each other with camaraderie.
> WOMAN ON SANDBAGGING CREW: Oh I love Fort Wayne. And I like when the community gets all together. Like this. It's great. (*World News Tonight,* March 15, 1982)

Later in the story, Garcia quotes a woman who has to evacuate:

> WOMAN: It's rotten, it's just, there's no words for it really.

In a story on March 17, ABC's three-anchor format comes into play, with anchor Frank Reynolds doing a studio introduction while on-site anchor Max Robinson introduces a story by David Garcia on how students have been recruited to fight the flood:

> REYNOLDS: Across much of the Midwest right now, the big worry is the weather. Floods and tornadoes already have caused numerous deaths and

millions of dollars in damages. The devastation is widespread but the most critical point remains in Ft. Wayne. Max Robinson is there tonight. Max?

ROBINSON: Frank, the next 48 hours are critical here in Ft. Wayne. The three rivers that run through the city are expected to crest at record levels. Ten percent of the city is already under as much as 6 feet of water with property damage already 16 million and climbing. Today the number of evacuations ordered doubled at 8,000 and by the time the flood waters crest as many as 20,000 may be homeless. Right now it's a battle against time. David Garcia reports. (*World News Tonight,* March 17, 1982)

But much of the story reflects a determined population. Garcia notes the use of high school students to aid the sandbagging effort:

STUDENT: It's the thought of if it would happen I'd want everybody to help me so I think I have to help other people.
STUDENT: Well someone has to do it we are just as able as anybody else. (*World News Tonight,* March 17, 1982)

Those affected by the flood express both fear and ironic relief:

WOMAN: The dike up there is crumbling and over there it's just coming through, so I'm pretty scared.
WOMAN: Never been in a flood area and I almost dropped my flood insurance. That's what got me and I've got it. (*World News Tonight,* March 17, 1982)

These stories indicate a journalistic concern with facts and figures while also portraying the experiences of those caught up in the flood. Resilience and determination, frustration and fear are the contradictory emotions felt by both local officials and ordinary citizens. The use of youth as a booster to the community stands in contrast to how youth are presented in the 1997 flood. Youth are also given prominence in the recovery stories surrounding the 1982 flood, when high school volunteers "adopt" a home or family to assist in the recovery effort (*CBS Evening News,* April 3, 1982).

While preparation for the coming flood is also a theme in 1997 flood stories, the words used to describe the activities of the local communities are filled with more emotion, and the images and words of local citizens involved are more emotion-laden. This initial CBS story on the 1997 floods reflects a different way of telling a flood story:

RANDALL PINKSTON (reporter): Fighting fatigue and the rain and (unintelligible) weather, volunteers in eastern North Dakota and western Minnesota are in a race against time, trying to build dikes higher and faster than the rivers are rising. (*CBS Evening News,* April 5, 1997)

Throughout the story, Pinkston interlaces his narrative with sound bites from those affected:

ROSE DUPREE: It's a darn scary thing because there's nothing you can do for water. You can't stop it (Crying) It's scary, really scary. (The camera also comes closer in to a full face view as she speaks)
UNIDENTIFIED WOMAN: I know it's not easy to see this. (Crying on shoulder)
MIKE STULTZ: We never had a chance, the water just came up so fast. (*CBS Evening News*, April 5, 1997)

These quotes typify how those affected by the flood are used to project greater emotion than in those stories from the 1982 floods. While most of the 1982 stories rely on local government officials for information and on-camera quotes, the 1997 flood stories look more at everyday citizens, such as this CBS story that focuses on a couple who were airlifted out of their water-trapped farm:

PINKSTON (reporter): Throughout the Dakotas and Minnesota, spreading floodwaters and ice are trapping more farms and communities. For some victims who want to leave now, the only way out is by air. Today, just north of Morehead, Minnesota, the national guard rescued Malcolm and Harriet Tuchman. (*CBS Evening News*, April 4, 1997)

Quotes from Harriet Tuchman tell her story and convey her emotion:

HARRIET TUCHMAN: My doors were froze about that far up. (motions with hands) There was solid ice on our outside doors. (How did they get you out?) They had to chop us out.
PINKSTON: And the Tuchmans are no strangers to harsh weather . . .
TUCHMAN continues: We've been in floods before. We've been in it seven times already but not with all this ice.
(later in story)
TUCHMAN: I don't even want to think about it. It's terrible. It's a mess. It's a mess. Don't want to talk about it. (*CBS Evening News*, April 4, 1997)

At the same time, early flood stories also include sound bites from regular citizens reflecting determination to hold off the waters and relief that some of their preparatory efforts had paid off:

VOLUNTEER: If we wouldn't have built these dikes, while the snow was blowing, they would have gone over, they would have washed off and pretty much [the] whole town of Monte would be under water.

WOMAN: It was close. It was dangerous for everyone to be down there doing what they did. But it was wonderful. (*CBS Evening News*, April 7, 1997)

CITIZEN: Fighting the blizzards and the rain and everything, we've had everything thrown at us. Keep plugging away. (*World News Tonight*, April 7, 1997)

A story from CBS on April 10 provides an archetypal example of how the 1997 flood stories reflect a different storytelling orientation. This story focuses exclusively on a woman's efforts to help her elderly parents survive the flood:

BOB MCNAMARA (reporter): Every morning now, after the freight trains pass, Michelle Rohrs walks the tracks for more than a mile, bringing her parents food, mail and encouragement . . .

MICHELLE ROHRS: I think they're kinda getting stressed now.

(a bit later)

MCNAMARA: Her father, Ted Rohrs, refuses to surrender. (*CBS Evening News*, April 10, 1997)

The story then describes what they are doing to save the buildings and farm equipment. After this factual interlude, the story returns to the human drama:

MCNAMARA: In this part of the country stubborn streaks and stiff upper lips are as much a part of the human condition as frost bite and snow tires . . .

PAULA ROHRS: It makes you feel pretty lonely again. It does, it feels more isolated out here, so it's um, we're gonna continue to fight, and hold the house. (*CBS Evening News*, April 10, 1997)

McNamara closes the story with this:

MCNAMARA: Ted Rohrs found another generator to run another pump, to stay dry another day. But if the water rises a foot and a half, it will not only be over his mailbox, his fight with the river will be over, too. (*CBS Evening News*, April 10, 1997)

This extended narrative contrasts with stories from the 1982 flood, which accomplished several vignettes of victims in stories of similar length. This story captures how network news uses human interest stories to convey the emotional experiences of people trying to survive a disaster. The 1982 floods took a more "big picture" approach to telling the story of a flood—rattling off statistics, conveying the thoughts of local officials, with only a few brief quotes from some of those directly affected. Whereas in the 1982 stories citizens' comments are used to add some color, in the 1997 stories the news is offering more of a focus on those directly affected. In two cases, single families or individuals are made the focus of the story rather than the window dressing to a story that deals mostly with explaining the extent of the flood and the possible damage. Statistics are fairly rare in the 1997 flood stories, whereas they tend to make up the leads to the 1982 stories.

So, while the 1982 stories reflect a more traditional journalistic concern with conveying the news about the flood, the 1997 stories focus more on individual victims of it. Camera work in 1997 uses tighter framing of these victims and is more likely to show them crying. While resilience and determination are a part of stories from both floods, the stories in the next phase of the coverage show a more subdued response when the reality and extent of the flooding hit the community.

RESIGNATION AND EVACUATION

Whereas the early stories begin to address the need for evacuation, in the second phase the narrative takes a sharp turn to victimhood as the full force of the water hits the community (in each year, news stories focused on the largest city affected by the flood: Ft. Wayne, Indiana, in 1982 and Grand Forks, North Dakota, in 1997). Stories focus on evacuation efforts and estimates of damage to the surrounding area. In the 1997 floods, the days following the initial flood reports include several short (thirty seconds or less) stories giving a brief update of the flood's progression. In the 1982 flood stories there is less of this because the flood itself lasted a shorter amount of time.

> FRANK ROBINSON (anchor): Ft. Wayne's biggest river crested at 25 feet this morning but the crisis is hardly over. Three leaky dikes, built over 60 years ago, are all that stand between the city and disaster. While the repair work continues, the weather forecast calls for 2 to 4 inches of rain by tomorrow night and each inch of rain adds another foot to the flood waters. (*World News Tonight*, March 18, 1982)

In 1982 at this stage, concerns with property damage begin to emerge. The primary sources for these stories are local officials, emergency workers, or businesspeople. The following story on *CBS Evening News* uses both narrative and quotes from individuals to convey the desperation, but in marked contrast to the use of emotional words and images in 1997, these stories have a tone of resignation rather than anger or depression:

> RATHER (anchor): In Ft. Wayne, a citizens' army heaved and tugged sandbags today, still trying to save the dikes that are the last defense

against flood waters. It's like rebuilding the pyramids, Mayor Winfield Moses said.

VIERA (reporter): The battle cry in Ft. Wayne today is "save the Pemble-ton dike." Last night, it began to literally disappear, threatening a 25 square block area. (*CBS Evening News*, March 18, 1982)

The wordplay by both Rather (rebuilding the pyramids, Moses said) and Viera (battle cry in Ft. Wayne) is an attempt to invigorate the story with some out-of-place metaphors. Splashy language and vivid imagery seem more like an attempt to be quippy rather than to sensationalize a story. At once expressing some of the futility no doubt existing in Ft. Wayne at that moment while also conveying that residents still have a lot of fight in them, the story ends up expressing the contradictory moments one can find in virtually any news story. But the quotes from the local officials reflect a realization within Ft. Wayne that not all will be well:

MAYOR: The difficulty is that these dikes are made out of river sludge that was put here in the 1940s and it turns almost into a toothpaste.

INSURANCE AGENT: I think we have a rather depressed area here in Ft. Wayne and as a result people are being conservative with their money and really didn't expect this to happen.

FED EMERGENCY OFFICER: I think the damages are much higher than we had in 1978. Of course the river is three feet higher. (*CBS Evening News*, March 18, 1982)

Similar tales of transition from determination to resignation can be found in the coverage of the 1997 upper Midwest floods. The longer period over which the 1997 floods made their way through the region inevitably meant there would not always be a full news story each day. This "short" from ABC on April 11 gives a continuity to the story without delving into a full report:

JENNINGS (anchor): It may still be news for most of the country but we don't need to tell the people in the Midwest about the winter that just won't go away. Snow has been falling throughout much of the upper Midwest, complicating efforts to deal with the floods. (*World News Tonight*, April 11, 1997)

Consider this brief by CBS's Dan Rather on April 15:

RATHER (anchor): People in the upper Midwest are still waging their battle with the rising Red River. The National Guard today helped evacuate hundreds of people barely one step ahead of surging flood waters. The Red River is already 20 feet above flood stage in some spots and melting snow is expected to add more than six inches by tomorrow. (*CBS Evening News,* April 15, 1997)

As the flood spreads downstream, stories begin to focus on those victimized by the flood while also anticipating the arrival of the flood waters at the largest city that would be affected, Grand Forks. This "victim" story focuses on the difficulties rural communities will face now and in the future, as farmers anticipate what it will mean for their growing season. The story also conveys the solid, stoic manner in which they draw upon faith and experience to get them through the devastation:

CAROLE SIMPSON (anchor): ABC's Ron Claiborne is in Minnesota where farmers are coming to the unpleasant realization that the worst may actually be yet to come.
CLAIBORNE (reporter): At a church service today in hard hit Ada, Minnesota, the strain, the stress of the difficult week could be seen on the faces (camera does tight close-ups on church goers), could be heard in the voices.
MAN IN CHURCH: The flood came, flowed past my door. I did not ask why. I asked for strength, I asked for help. You gave it to me. (voice breaks) (*World News Tonight,* April 13, 1997)

Later in the story, a farmer in the area says:

FARMER: If it was just water, it would be gone now and the soil could start drying. But now you have to melt the ice and the soil is saturated. It's just going to take some time. (*World News Tonight,* April 13, 1997)

Again the contrast to the way stories are approached in the 1997 floods is instructive with respect to soap opera storytelling. This story focuses on individual-level experiences of the flood as opposed to more sweeping statistical pictures generated in the stories about the 1982 floods. Stories about the 1982 flood did not go to churches to get images of people seeking spiritual solace for a natural disaster. It is not unreasonable to assume that people in Ft. Wayne in 1982 looked to their faith communities for comfort from the flood, but the employment of such a strategy in 1997 indicates that reporters were seeking out such perspectives and imagery. Editorial and reportorial decision making were geared toward pumping up emotion and having viewers empathize with flood victims by telling their stories and watching them shed tears. It is not until the recovery and clean-up phase that the 1982 stories begin to reflect the exploitation of emotion that is evident almost from the beginning in how the 1997 flood story was told.

As the flood approached Grand Forks, both networks "cued" the impending disaster for their audiences, pointing out the large numbers of people who would be affected in the city. Two brief stories capture this sense of impending doom for the people of Grand Forks:

> JENNINGS (anchor): In North Dakota, the Red River is again proving the forecasters wrong. At least twice they have declared the flood has reached its peak. Not so. Tonight, the waters are again at a new high and weary residents are building last minute levies to protect their homes if they can. Next stop for this flood, Grand Forks. (*World News Tonight,* April 17, 1997)
>
> PAULA ZAHN (anchor): In the upper great plains, Grand Forks, North Dakota and its 70,000 people are getting ready for disaster. The rampaging Red River is expected to crest tonight at 25 feet above flood stage. Some dikes have already given way and desperate sandbaggers are trying to save other levies from the same fate. There is a plan to evacuate the entire city if more barriers give way to the Red River. (*CBS Evening News,* April 18, 1997)

Adjectives like "weary," "rampaging," and "desperate" in the anchor voice-overs of images from the affected areas add a sense of emotion even to these brief updates. As continuing narratives, they also signal viewers that more, and the worst, is yet to come. These transitional briefs are important elements in keeping the story alive for viewers. In the next few days, the flood story in Grand Forks becomes a major focus for the nightly newscasts as the networks no longer depend on a single reporter to cover the scope and magnitude of the disaster. A visit by the president brings the number of reporters on the scene to three for each network.

FROM MOURNING TO RECOVERY

The final phase of coverage of the floods provides an emotional view of those returning to their homes to determine the extent of the damage. In the 1997 stories, this phase seems to start with the arrival of the president, whose visit is meant to provide assurance of help from the federal government. In the 1982 stories, the presidential visit comes earlier in the flood and thus takes a different tone (see sidebar). Different emotions are portrayed, ranging from shock to sadness to sometimes relief when a featured citizen learns of the fate of his or her home or small business. The greatest display of emotion in the 1982 flood stories comes in this phase as people begin to return to their evacuated homes to survey the damage. Stories on consecutive days on ABC and CBS reflect this transition to grief and recovery:

ROBINSON (anchor): In the Midwest, it's raining again and that's the last thing Ft. Wayne needs after 7 days of flooding. But as David Garcia reports, rain or not, many of the flood victims have started to come back.

GARCIA (reporter): West Main Street at the peak of the flood. West Main Street this morning (visual comparison showing water has receded). The flood waters are dropping a half inch per hour. . . . Bolen Baugh is just getting over a heart attack last fall. He lost his job after the attack. Now, his home.

BAUGH: I'm completely wiped out, yes. It really didn't hit me until a couple of days ago. Then the bottom just kind of falls out of you, you don't know what you're going to do.

Garcia then transitions to a woman who "took out flood insurance a week ago."

MILKIE: Just had that gut feeling mostly.

GARCIA: But most don't have flood insurance and are devastated . . .

HUSBAND: We don't have nothing. (breaks down)

WIFE: I mean that's the only thing that keeps us going. We got two kids we gotta find 'em somewhere to live. (voice breaks) (*World News Tonight*, March 19, 1982)

This story uses tightly framed shots of each victim and the sound bite is lengthy, despite the few words uttered as each individual pauses to wipe a tear away or recover his or her voice after it breaks. A story a day later on CBS reflects a similar theme—receding waters, promises of aid from the president, and an emotional turn to some of the hardest-hit residents:

LESLIE STAHL (anchor): Tonight marks the start of spring and the end of winter in the Northern Hemisphere. And in one small corner of the United States, Ft. Wayne, Indiana, it brought some relief for flooded out residents . . .

CURRIER (reporter): Ft. Wayne's mayor thanked the President for his disaster declaration this afternoon in a telephone call to Camp David.

Moses/Reagan on phone:

MOSES: Look forward to the difficult task now of trying to clean the city up from this terrible flood.

REAGAN: Oh well, this is great. The rain has stopped?

MOSES: The rain has slowed down. It certainly will not cause us a problem. The rivers are going down. The evacuees with a little luck will be able to go back to their homes on Monday.

ERIC JOHNSON: From what it looks like now we look like we made it, and hopefully that's gonna be the end of it.

CURRIER: Others were not as lucky.

MARY HIRE (in car): How about . . . you think it's up to my clothes in the closet?
RESPONSE: I would say it probably was.
HIRE: Oh dear.
CURRIER: For Mary Hire, forced from her home a week ago by flood waters, the first return visit was an emotional experience (shown crying on man's shoulder) but after the tears there were smiles, her living room soaked by six inches of water, was still intact.
HIRE: Well, I still got a lot to be thankful for, you better believe it. You know, it could have been worse. (*CBS Evening News*, March 20, 1982)

A follow-up story on CBS March 22 went further in conveying the reaction of Ft. Wayne residents as they returned to flood-damaged homes:

VIERA (reporter): The water is gone now, the flood is over, but for some folks along Edge Hill Ave. it's not easy going home. Ruth Mosely spent this morning picking through her possessions, putting aside what's ruined. She and her son had three pumps going at one point last week but they couldn't stop the water.
MOSELY: (tightly framed in camera) We have a grandson that lives in Gatlinburg, Tennessee and whenever he comes down here [he] looks for his little toy box that has a turkey on the outside and when I looked down the stairs and there was his little soldiers and his balls floating around (voice breaks). That's what cracked me up. Everything else is, you know, trash and treasures.
VIERA: Robert Dolahite lives a couple of doors down from Ruth Mosely. Today, the city condemned his house, the foundation simply crumbled. Dolahite lost 50 years' worth of trash and treasures. (Question to him) Is this the hard part, coming back?
DOLAHITE: (tightly framed and crying) I don't know if my wife will be able to come back.
VIERA: Dolahite says he doesn't want his wife to come back and see their home like this. It's the house he grew up in, the house where they've retired.
DOLAHITE: It makes you sick. We'll fix her up and come back. We've been here all our lives, it's hard. (lots of pauses as his voice breaks)
VIERA: Dolahite spent time . . . sitting on his neighbor's front stoop just puffing on his pipe. The shock still comes and goes; he says it will take a while before it goes away for good. (*CBS Evening News*, March 22, 1982)

The most heartrending tales come from people who are either retired or near retirement. The reporter's narratives give us a quick background to some of their stories, accompanied by their emotion-laden reactions. Stories such as these probably serve to enhance any nationwide effort to collect material aid for these flood-afflicted areas. The "official" story, which occupies so much of the early reporting on the 1982 flood, gives way to focusing on the hardships individuals are facing and will face in the immediate future. While the stories open with promises of federal aid, they leave viewers with an opportunity to place themselves in the shoes of these victims and thus have a greater "feel" for what they have been through.

The 1997 floods took a longer period of time to play out. While many of the interim days were covered in the newscasts in the form of briefs, once the flood hit Grand Forks, the networks were in full swing and sent a number of reporting crews to cover a visit by President Clinton and the flood's effects on the city of seventy thousand. In an interesting twist to the 1997 flood stories, both networks relied on emergency workers to tell how it personally affected them and their families. Probably because most victims at that point were still staying in emergency shelters, reporters found that those emergency workers who were escorting them around the devastation in boats had their own personal stories to tell about how the flood was affecting average folks.

Erin Hayes's reporting for ABC uses powerful language and imagery to set up her extensive quoting of sheriff's deputy Greg Dravansky to put a human face on the flooding devastation:

> HAYES (reporter): This is an occupied city, surrendered to forces of nature that are still hard to fathom. There are 15 square miles of city, of city, under water. Thousands and thousands of homes and businesses, schools and churches. Everything is awash in deep, filthy, powerful river water. Life as anyone would know it in a city has stopped here.
> DRAVANSKY: It's hard to see a community that once had streets where traffic flowed and kids played and people worked in their yards and you see nothing, there's nobody here it's almost like—will they ever come back?
> HAYES: All weekend they ran from the river stunned. The river rose to its record level and then it kept going.
> DRAVANSKY: I don't think there's any words to describe it. It's total devastation.
> HAYES: Greg Dravansky is a sheriff's deputy. Like so many rescue workers here, he too has a home submerged. A family trying to figure out what their life is going to be. This is his city and he does not recognize it.
> DRAVANSKY: It doesn't seem real. It's not real. You feel like you're going to wake up and find that it's a bad dream.
> HAYES: What strikes you when you travel through here is that there are no voices, no sounds of life in a city. Just an odd and very sad silence. Erin

Hayes, ABC News, Grand Forks, North Dakota. (*World News Tonight*, April 21, 1997)

A story on CBS two days later uses local bank president Randy Newman to capture the devastation to both his business and his family home:

> NEWMAN: My neighbor came running over to me and said your building's on fire. . . . That's a terrible feeling. I feel that my home is in shambles, my family is uprooted. You lose three buildings and your employees. Quite frankly, we lost a community. That's a very large death in your family. It's gonna take me a while to get over it. (*CBS Evening News*, April 23, 1997)

Still, the news provides some moments of relief and hope—seeing good in little things like the rescuing of family pets. The assignment of several reporters to the Grand Forks area enabled this kind of assessment of the damage both at the official level and through the stories of local residents coping with a disaster that caused a major upheaval in their lives. As an interesting contrast between 1982 and 1997 flood coverage, the portrayal of young people offers a different take on the aftermath of the flood. Coverage of the 1982 Ft. Wayne flooding focuses on the hard work and volunteering of students to help the community fight the flood waters during the peak of the flood and later to help affected residents clean up their homes. Students' perspectives on the 1997 flood are cast in a different light. As a follow-up to the Grand Forks flood in 1997, an ABC report on May 25 captures high school graduation day in Grand Forks:

> CAROLE SIMPSON (anchor): It was a bittersweet graduation day for the students of Red River High School in Grand Forks, ND. ABC's Lisa Solters spent the day with a group of students who have already learned some of life's most difficult lessons.
> SOLTERS (reporter): Seventeen-year-old Ben Holbrook thought his graduation would be one of the happiest times of his young life.
> HOLBROOK: I know I've graduated. Right now I'm just gonna go through the motions, just get it done. . . . we got it right about up to here. (pointing out the flood level in his basement) (*World News Tonight*, May 25, 1997)

Quotes from other students indicate a sense that they have been deprived of something, while their principal points out that the students played a role in sandbagging:

> ANDY KVERNAN: This is supposed to be the funnest month of your whole high school career. We didn't get to experience that.

REBECCA LESMEISTER: The longer it went on the sadder it got because [I] realized there's no last band concert and everything's ended.
PRINCIPAL DARYL BRAGG: We had 800 students on the dikes putting sandbags in place on the final couple days before the levies broke. (*World News Tonight*, May 25, 1997)

The tone throughout this piece contrasts markedly with the portrayal of the Ft. Wayne high school students who were extolled for their hard work and generous spirit. These different images of high school students could be cast as generational differences or as an artifact of the way their stories were used by reporters. Nonetheless, the 1997 report also seems to represent a larger trend evident in the differences between the two flood episodes. The flood of 1997 has a more negative cast and tone to it in news reports when compared to the 1982 flood coverage. The Ft. Wayne flood coverage is characterized by more resilience and determination to recover than the 1997 flood coverage. Perhaps this is due to an apparent larger degree of devastation in the 1997 flood, but it might also signal an inherent tendency in news to focus on the tragic elements of these stories rather than on a more upbeat determination to resist and recover from the power of nature. Such a tendency can be seen as consistent with soap opera storytelling, with its focus on the melodramatic and tragic. The differences in the characteristics of each flood—with the 1997 flood being more severe—leave that open to question. Nonetheless, the portrayal of the reaction of students to each flood can be seen as a metaphor for the overall approach both networks took to each of these stories and how the reporting of disasters has changed in the life of network television news.

FLOODS AND THE SOAP OPERA PARADIGM

It is now appropriate to look at the five elements of soap opera storytelling and determine their utility for explaining how network news approaches this kind of story. As mentioned previously, these two flood narratives are compared with the understanding that even in 1982 network officials and news producers were already beginning to change the character of network news. Thus, stark changes are not to be expected, but rather there should be further evolution of soap opera storytelling in the 1997 coverage.

Seriality: The continuity of this story is clearly evident in both situations analyzed. Although the 1982 flood was of shorter duration than the 1997 flood, each network provided five full reports during the time the flood reached its peak in 1982. In the more enduring flood of 1997, day-to-day reports were not sustained over the nearly twenty-day period during which the flood hit different parts of the northern Midwest. Out of a total of twelve stories aired on ABC over the period from April 5 to April 27, five were short updates of twenty-three seconds or less. On CBS, eleven stories were aired from April 5 to April 23; five were twenty-five seconds or less. These short stories served as arcs for the larger narrative about the flood of 1997, keeping the story on viewers' minds even when there was not a lot of substantially new material to report.

Real-time orientation: This element is also a reflection of the day-to-day coverage, but more important, the networks began to use technology to give viewers a sense of being there. The way anchors introduced the stories created a sense of talking to the reporters live even when the interaction took place earlier and was taped for broadcast. The narrative of the story—resilience, victimhood, and recovery—also provided viewers with a reassurance that normality would eventually be restored, thus allowing both the networks and the audience to "let go" of the story.

Seeming intimacy/involvement: In this area are the greatest differences in the way that the 1982 and 1997 stories were told. Though emotion was expressed throughout both flood narratives, certain aspects of the way the story was told helped to pump up the emotion in the 1997 flood stories. Tighter close-ups of victims, more obvious use of emotionally touching moments, and use of officials and emergency personnel to convey some of that emotion were clearly more pervasive and distinctive in the 1997 flood stories than in coverage of the 1982 flood. In 1997 the use of emotion in news stories began with the early stories of the flood. In 1982 it was not until citizens began to return to their homes that substantial emotional reaction became part of the flood narrative.

Story exposition: The length of stories and the multiple perspectives provided in several reports in the 1997 stories mark a different way of telling the story from the coverage of the 1982 floods. In 1982 use of one reporter per day and a rather consistent time frame for each story of about two to two and one-half minutes suggest producers' concern with telling more stories within the news show than the approach taken in 1997, when multiple reports appeared on significant days within the story, creating substantial amounts of time in a daily newscast dedicated to the story.

Another significant difference was the addition of a personal narrative about how the floods were affecting local officials and emergency workers. For the most part, the flood stories from 1982 chose victims who were not part of the official story. In 1997 the use of a fireman who was escorting the reporter in a motor boat provided a means by which to convey how the fireman and his family were personally affected by the flood. These were not stories of heroism or competence (or incompetence) but contemplated the future of the community in the eyes of the official/victim. The multiple reports done during the height of the flood in Grand

Forks conveyed a sense of telling a more complete story than the solo reporter, single-story approach found in 1982.

Story characteristics: Because these stories affected the whole community, a focus on middle-class concerns is less apparent. But the other two subelements of this category—good versus evil and conflict/chaos—are more present. Mother Nature was clearly cast in a villain role; in both cases these stories tended not to cast any human decision making (such as permitting development in flood-plain areas) as problematic. Rather, the forces of nature and the cruel, indiscriminate way in which natural acts affect large numbers of human beings were consistent themes—good people versus bad nature. This seems especially true in the 1997 stories, with the freakish weather element of a half spring/half winter battle that complicated preventing and dealing with the floods.

The conflict/chaos theme leaned more toward chaos as news focused on the disruption of normality and how people coped with that disruption. And the portrayal of chaos was limited as well; the human factors of coming together as a community and strangers helping strangers served as a counterbalance to the disruption of normality. The long-term losses to businesses and the long-term prospects for recovery were also part of the chaos caused by nature. This was where the themes of resilience and recovery provided assurance to the larger audience that governments and communities can successfully cope with these types of disasters. The final stories addressing each flood demonstrated a difference in how the networks closed the narrative. Fort Wayne was seen in recovery: it could still host a statewide basketball tournament. On the other hand, the Grand Forks portion of the 1997 flood provided a mixed-narrative closure by focusing on the graduating high school seniors and how their year was far other than normal. Both regret and resilience were expressed by high school seniors: a life-goes-on ending rather than a recovery or "happy" ending.

CONCLUSION

The differences in the telling of these two flood stories tell a lot about the utility of the soap opera paradigm in explaining how network news has evolved over several decades. The more traditional journalistic approach seen in the 1982 flood coverage, while not devoid of soap opera moments, stands as a contrast to how the 1997 flood was used as a news story to pull viewers' heartstrings and to keep the narrative of the flood at a human level.

The dedication of substantial technological and human resources to tell the story of the 1997 flood also stands as another contrast to the 1982 flood coverage. Having several reporting teams on the ground conveys a fuller, multiperspective picture of the flood and allows for the telling of both the "macro" or big picture statistical elements and the "micro" or human elements.

The more dramatic use of the president's visit to the devastated areas in 1997 exemplifies the symbiosis between the media and the White House communications strategists in projecting the president as both a national symbol of strength and reassurance and a father figure offering comfort to victims.

The differences in the 1982 and 1997 flood narratives make a convincing case for the evolving nature of the soap opera paradigm as it exists in the television news world. What was demonstrated through the statistical analysis in the previous chapter is borne out in this more in-depth look at how network news approaches coverage of natural disasters. News is not just the news; it is much more than a mirror held up to society. It is a constructed narrative that presents words and images designed not so much to inform as to get people to feel compelled to tune in on a consistent basis. Soap opera storytelling fills that function quite well.

7

All My Primaries:
Political Campaigns
and Television News

For some time now, the conduct of campaigns and television news coverage of political campaigns have been criticized for their emphasis on colorful, vivid imagery and coverage of the political and "insider" aspects of a campaign while de-emphasizing the issues facing the country.

Much research has focused on how campaign coverage focuses on the "horse race" aspect of politics—tracking polls that purport to show day-to-day or week-to-week changes in the standings of the candidates, money issues such as who has raised or spent more and who has more to spend, and the degree to which the campaign devolves into a popularity contest. Coverage of issues ends up getting short shrift, and voters' decisions end up being based on criteria that may or may not predict what the president will do once in office.

It is generally assumed that campaigns prepare the winning candidate for assuming the presidency. The notion is that the intense scrutiny, the constant avoidance of saying anything that will upset the campaign apple cart, and the reduction of complex ideas into bumper sticker-like expressions all help the winner step into office prepared for the challenges he or she will face.

The horse race approach to coverage leaves citizens unable to adequately sort out where the candidates stand on the issues. News consumers are more capable of handicapping the outcome of the election than they are able to articulate where the candidates stand on any number of issues. Television news tends to boil down coverage of the campaign to a few basic themes and endlessly regurgitates new pieces of information about those themes. The tendency of television campaigns to simplify the complex and turn the campaign into a test of wills and accusations between candidates is a relatively new development that parallels the ascension of television news (as opposed to national news weeklies and daily newspapers) as the primary source of news for most Americans and the growth of television advertising–driven campaigns.

One of the primary functions the media serve in campaigns today is winnowing out the pack of candidates who start out well in advance of the primary season. Using poll numbers, fund-raising figures, and judgment about how voters will react to candidate perspectives the news media consider marginal, television news differentiates "serious" (those with the potential to win the nomination) from "token" candidates. One reason for dismissing several candidates as long shots is to make the task of covering the race more manageable from a news perspective. Television news just doesn't have the resources to cover all the candidates equally, so news organizations select those with the greatest potential to secure the nomination as the front-runners.

Over the last few decades of presidential primaries, large fields of candidates have been reduced to a few (usually two) deemed worthy of coverage. This also helps serve the needs of presenting the campaign as a soap opera. By reducing the field to two or three at most, news organizations can then give each candidate regular coverage. And this coverage inevitably will focus on the personal characteristics of the candidates and their "pasts" with each other, providing the glaring coverage that leads to "gotcha" incidents in which the candidates' gaffes are analyzed and dissected for their implications on the rest of the race.

These characteristics of campaign coverage on television news programs find kinship with soap opera storytelling characteristics. This chapter draws on data from the evolution of news study presented in chapter 5 to look at how television coverage of politics has changed since the 1976 presidential race. It also examines the three weeks of coverage of the early 2000 presidential primaries to bring textual analysis to understanding how coverage of campaigns has come to take on the characteristics of soap operas.

POLITICAL CAMPAIGNS IN THE NEWS

Before moving to an in-depth look at how reporting on the 2000 primaries used elements of the soap opera paradigm to structure the way the campaign was presented in news shows, data from the evolution of news study can provide highlights of how television news coverage of politics has evolved. As part of the three-decade analysis detailed in chapter 5, one presidential election year in each decade was selected. Two weeks in

October for the years 1976, 1988, and 2000 were sampled specifically to allow some historical perspective on how TV news coverage of campaigns has evolved.

One thing that is immediately apparent when looking at political campaign news for these years is the drop in the number of stories concerning the campaign. The figures for 1976, 1988, and 2000 are eighty-three, forty-nine, and twenty-nine stories, respectively. A look at the average length of each story for each network shows there is no relationship between the number of stories on the campaign and the average length of stories. Both networks aired their longest stories in 1988, with ABC averaging over three and one-half minutes per story (three minutes, thirty-three seconds) and CBS over two and one-half minutes (two minutes, thirty-three seconds). The shortest stories are found in 1976 (one minute, forty seconds for ABC; two minutes, nine seconds for CBS). Average story lengths in 2000 are three minutes, two seconds for ABC and two minutes, eighteen seconds for CBS. Although a smaller number of campaign stories doesn't exactly translate into longer stories, 1988 and 2000 clearly outpace 1976 in story lengths, while there were more stories in 1976. This apparent discrepancy is due to a greater number of "briefs" or anchor-read stories in 1976.

Keep in mind that statistical interpretations of the three campaign years and two networks are limited due to the small number of stories when broken down by network and year. Thus, any conclusions here are based on a cautious interpretation of the data. The most remarkable finding from analyzing campaign stories in 1976, 1988, and 2000 is the virtual absence of any soap opera elements in stories from 1976. Only four of the seven elements—seriality, intimacy, story exposition, and conflict—register any codes in 1976.

Eleven of the eighty-three stories in 1976, eleven of the forty-nine stories in 1988, and fourteen of the twenty-nine stories in 2000 contain serial characteristics. As a percentage of total campaign stories, this is roughly 13, 22, and 38 percent, respectively, for the years 1976, 1988, and 2000. This lends support to the idea that seriality in campaign stories has increased over the last thirty years.

Real-time elements in campaign reporting are used rather sparsely in the years studied. There were no real-time elements in any of the 1976 stories. For 1988 and 2000, only two stories per year project a real-time orientation. Similarly, intimacy in campaign stories occurs at minor rates; one story from 1976, five from 1988, and four from 2000 contain some aspect designed to give viewers an intimate look at the campaign and candidates.

Story exposition, identified in chapter 5 as one of the soap elements that may correspond with quality journalism, is present in the 1988 and

2000 campaign stories in a meaningful way. Only one story in 1976 uses story exposition techniques. However, 24 percent of stories in 1988 and 44 percent in 2000 employ story exposition elements in campaign stories.

As might be expected from campaign coverage, conflict as a story characteristic occurs regularly in political campaign stories. About 4 percent of stories in 1976, 18 percent of stories in 1988, and 16 percent in 2000 exhibit conflict in campaign coverage. The final two elements, good versus evil and projections of affluence, do not register any codes for any of the three years studied.

The final consideration of how coverage of political campaigns has evolved looks at how the elements are used in concert in a single story. Using the criterion of three or more elements in a story, for the later two years sampled (1988 and 2000), each has over 30 percent of the stories about the campaign containing three or more soap elements, with a slight increase in 2000 (34 percent) over 1988 (31 percent). None of the stories from 1976 registered three or more elements.

What is clear from this brief look at a quantitative study of how campaign coverage has evolved is that soap opera storytelling techniques have been a prominent feature of how television news presents political campaigns in the era of conglomeration. A nasty 1988 campaign featuring attack ads, name calling, and other conflict-ridden tactics comes on the heels of the first round of media consolidation in the mid-1980s. The 2000 campaign follows a second round of mergers and buyouts in the mid- to late 1990s. While the 2000 campaign had the fewest stories of the three years studied, those stories generally contained more soap opera storytelling techniques. The news agenda during campaign 2000 was crowded with international conflicts and crises in the form of the bombing in Yemen of a U.S. naval ship and a spike in violence in the occupied territories of Israel/Palestine. While this may somewhat explain the smaller number of stories, most analysts of campaign news coverage have noted a drop in news about politics.

QUALITATIVE ANALYSIS—THE 2000 PRIMARIES

Campaign 2000 provides a good opportunity for presenting a textual analysis of the campaign as covered by television news outlets.[1] The fact that there was no incumbent running in this race means there was a potential for both parties to have a lively race for the presidential nomination. While that was only briefly the case for the Democrats, nonetheless the potential for a heightened sense of conflict and drama was clearly exploited by the television news services.

The analysis of the primary season begins after the Iowa caucuses in the week before the New Hampshire primary. After months of preprimary coverage, polls, and speculation, this moment is the first real expression of popular will. Three weeks of television news programming were monitored for this analysis. Beyond looking at the nightly news networks, cable news programs such as CNN's *Inside Politics* and the Sunday morning news talk shows such as *Meet the Press* on NBC and ABC's *This Week* were recorded. Going beyond the thirty-minute nightly newscasts helps uncover the role pundits and opinion columnists play in television news, get a sense of how news shows whose sole subject is politics cover the campaign, and reveal the role twenty-four-hour cable services play in portraying the campaigns in ways consistent with soap opera storytelling.

Even a relatively short, three-week period of monitoring campaign coverage brought up numerous instances of soap opera techniques in television coverage of presidential politics. Before moving into analysis of specific instances of this, a digest or synopsis of the campaign saga is presented to illustrate how routine, daily coverage of the primary season can be seen as an ongoing melodrama. An analysis of CNN's coverage of the postelection controversy illustrates how twenty-four-hour news services approach and anticipate a breaking story.

"ALL MY PRIMARIES": A SYNOPSIS OF
THE EARLY 2000 PRIMARY CAMPAIGN

Starting the day before the Iowa caucuses, a lingering advertising spat between George Bush and his main rival in Iowa, Steve Forbes, underlies concerns that Bush may not do as well as expected. Shortly after Iowa, media coverage will reduce the race to four men, two in each party, despite the continuing campaigns of Forbes, Alan Keyes, and Gary Bauer. In the meantime, John McCain, who has skipped Iowa to focus on next week's New Hampshire primary, is leading Bush in recent polls there. In the Democratic race, the conventional wisdom has concluded that Gore has become a better candidate since Bill Bradley entered the race last fall. There is general consensus that Bradley may have peaked and that Gore's organizational strength will effectively thwart the Bradley insurgency.

The rest of the week brings another round of speculation about New Hampshire in light of Gore's "solid" win and Bush's "respectable" showing in Iowa. McCain becomes a big player—his performance in the polls and in a Republican debate follow an incident in which he is asked a hypothetical question about his reaction if a pregnant teenaged daughter sought an abortion. The Saturday before the New Hampshire primary, Bush calls in "reinforcements" by having his parents campaign on his behalf. In the Democratic debate, speculation swirls about whether Bradley will go on the attack and the risks inherent in such a strategy. Coverage of New Hampshire anticipates the role of independent voters and their would-be suitors, McCain and Bradley.

The second week of the primary season finds Bradley backing off some of his attack strategy as polls show no positive feedback for it. Tuesday's reports before the New Hampshire polls close find McCain is "having a good day," and even though networks don't report exit polls, they begin to consider what the apparent McCain victory will mean for the rest of the race. Pundits speculate whether the visit by Bush's parents may have diminished the presidential stature of their son. As the Republican race shifts to South Carolina, Bush's visit to the very conservative Bob Jones University sets off controversy and criticism from McCain. Things get personal on the Democratic side when Bradley demands an apology from the Gore campaign for a comment by a Gore aide about Bradley supporter Senator Bob Kerrey being a "cripple."

Later in the week, George Bush tries to undercut McCain's ties to veterans (a sizable group of voters in South Carolina) with an appearance before a veterans' group in which an activist veteran accuses McCain of not supporting veterans' issues. When a poll shows McCain ahead in South Carolina, Bush runs ads undercutting McCain's integrity on his campaign finance proposals. McCain then counters that Bush's kowtowing to religious conservatives in South Carolina has moved Bush too far to the right after starting out as a "compassionate conservative." The attacks and counterattacks continue unabated.

The third week of coverage finds the Bush campaign in makeover mode as he becomes the "reformer with results" and reacts angrily to a McCain ad comparing Bush's lack of honesty to the Clinton administration. Bush had earlier tarred McCain by equating McCain's tax proposals with Clinton's tax cut plans. McCain's "favorable" media coverage is seen by the Bush camp as evidence of a "liberal" media preference for him. The vitriol and emotion are heightened when "push polls" from mysterious sources become a major story as McCain uses the dramatic story of a female supporter whose son gets upset when he answers a push poll critical of McCain. Though the Bush campaign denies it is the source of the push polling, McCain calls on it to stop. At the end of the week, McCain decides to cease airing any more negative ads and calls on Bush to do the same. McCain's decision is seen as risky even though running negative ads undercuts his claim to be a "different" kind of politician.

POLITICS AND THE SOAP OPERA PARADIGM

Monitoring the first three weeks of the presidential primary season reveals a great deal of resonance with soap opera storytelling. It is important from the outset to note that none of the shows monitored devoted much coverage to discussion about issues affecting voters' lives. Exceptions to this are the interview segments with the candidates on Sunday morning talk shows. Even then, such discussion tends to focus on the political effects of various policy positions, such as what they might mean for candidates' poll standings. For the most part, coverage of politics has become a highly personalized battle to try to control a candidate's image in media coverage.

Coverage of politics clearly follows a serial pattern. Use of teasers to open shows reflects a way of bridging one day's reporting to the next. Daily programs such as CNN's *Inside Politics* have a rather standard approach to opening the show:

JUDY WOODRUFF (anchor): The leading Republican hopefuls resort to ad warfare, but have the candidates gone too far?
(begin video clip)
SENATOR JOHN MCCAIN: When he was—had a 30-point lead we were buddies. He used to put his arm around me and embrace me. Then we beat him in New Hampshire. Now I am a hypocrite.
(end video clip)
BERNARD SHAW (anchor): Is the thrill of competition getting a little too personal? (*Inside Politics*, February 8, 2000)

This lead also reflects the personal nature of the coverage and the seeming intimacy that coverage projects. McCain's claim that he and Bush were buddies is one of frequent reminders that competing candidates in the same party can become enemies in a short amount of time. Just as plot turns in regular soaps revolve around betrayals and backstabbing among associated or related characters, the kind of debate that takes place in primary season can quickly devolve into emotional, highly personalized exchanges.

Likewise, when voting is taking place, reports before the polls close lead viewers to a conclusion about the results without actually reporting those results. Peter Jennings's lead-in to the February 1 edition of *World News Tonight* is representative of how networks fulfill their pledge to not report exit poll results before the polls close:

JENNINGS: In New Hampshire tonight, the voters are reshaping the presidential campaign of 2000. . . . Senator John McCain appears to be having a very good day. The polls are not closed. We won't project winners until they are. . . . But based on turnout, especially of voters who say they are independent, John McCain has had a much better day than Texas governor George W. Bush. The Democratic race . . . is simply too difficult to characterize as of now. (*World News Tonight,* February 1, 2000)

Such an approach reflects how coverage of the campaign is focused on an up-to-the-minute, "real-time" orientation. This segment effectively updates the viewers on the day's events while also bringing back a redundant theme of the week—the competition among candidates (McCain and Bradley in particular) for independent voters in New Hampshire. Thus the broadcast brings in an ongoing story line while also projecting a future that is apparently known but yet to be fully revealed. The voluntary agreement by networks to not discuss results before polls close is both an attempt to show themselves as respectful of democracy and a way of stretching out stories over several hours or days. Thus, before the results are made official, the networks can begin speculating about the implications of this vote for the next primary. This redundancy of story lines in the Republican race is accompanied by a suspended story line in the Democratic race—"too close to call," although even here reporters begin to speculate that indeed John McCain, and not Bill Bradley, has captured the independent voters.

Redundancy in story lines occurs *within* shows such as *Inside Politics* or *Meet the Press,* which dedicate large amounts of time to discussion of the campaign. For example, in light of Bush's loss to McCain in New Hampshire, Bush undergoes a makeover of sorts by "re-theming" his political career from "compassionate conservative" to "reformer with results." After an initial report from the Bush campaign, *Inside Politics* revisits the issue through reports on polling, a discussion with representatives from both the Bush and McCain camps, and a journalist chat segment featuring press pundits:

> JUDY WOODRUFF (anchor): Having lost a round to the underdog and falling again in the polls, George W. Bush did come out swinging today at John McCain, now a heavyweight since New Hampshire. . . . It is Bush, says Bush, who knows how to govern and how to get results. He spoke this afternoon to supporters in Wilmington, Delaware.
> (begin video clip)
> BUSH: In this race, there's only one person who can stand up and say, I'm a reformer with results; of the major candidates, only one person who doesn't have a Washington, D.C. zip code, somebody who comes from outside the system but somebody who's got a record of reforming and a record of results. (*Inside Politics,* February 7, 2000)

Later in the show, reporter Candy Crowley revisits the same issue in her report:

CANDY CROWLEY (senior political correspondent): Well, we began to see it at the end of last week, Judy, after the New Hampshire defeat. . . . I think you can see behind me what—which way they're tacking. And that is that Bush is now portraying himself as the reformer, saying, look, I have some results here. I reformed the education system in Texas. I reformed the tax policy in Texas. I reformed a number of things there. (*Inside Politics*, February 7, 2000)

The degree of story exposition and its redundancy over time feeds both the needs of political junkies and more casual followers of the campaign. Redundancy yields more details for the junkies; focusing on the strategic and tactical shifts in campaigns is a means of giving viewers the intimate, omniscient point of view of a campaign, just as the viewers of soaps are in a position to see the forest for the trees by following the implications of a story line. Redundancy also ensures that more casual viewers will eventually hear the story. In this case, Bush's makeover—revealed through reporters, pundits, and the actual characters involved—receives multiple treatments both within shows and over several days.

Another form of involving viewers can be found in how polls serve the function of a Greek chorus in political campaigns. Poll results favorable to McCain are seen as a reason for the Bush makeover—especially a poll showing McCain doing better against Gore in a hypothetical fall campaign matchup. Similarly, poll results after Bradley becomes more aggressive in his campaign show no benefit and perhaps some backfire. Soon after, he mellows his rhetoric.

At other times, the Greek chorus role is played by the pundits appearing in the journalist talk segments of both CNN and the broadcast network Sunday morning talk shows. The segment below reflects a speculative discussion about how the public will react to a shift in McCain's advertising strategy. The truth value of this commentary is clearly suspect, as no data are provided to justify the assertions being made:

GEORGE WILL: I don't think they were working. First of all, if they were working he'd had, as Ralph Reed said, about 18 days of it to work. So he wins both ways, he gets the negative ads, he gets the points for pulling them. But he made the ad, the one that runs the White House in the background and says, "This man Bush is like Clinton." He finally said something that the average voter said, "That's just not true." No one believes that down there. So that—that boomeranged and went right back at McCain's strength. He's supposed to be the straight talker and that's not straight talk.

SAM DONALDSON: But ladies and gentlemen, negative ads work. I mean, that—that's why they run . . .

GEORGE STEPHANOPOULOS: Being against negative ads works as well. I mean that's what—and you've got to in some ways admire McCain for the flair. . . . But what he's hoping is people will say, "Man, this guy is a victim. Let's go out and show that Republican machine." (*This Week*, February 13, 2000)

As mentioned at the beginning of this section, there is very little discussion of issues that concern voters' lives. In the absence of reporting on issues, programs place a high priority on largely personal issues. In the three weeks of politics monitored for this project, several story lines emerged that generated multiple-day coverage: Bradley's health, McCain's answer to a hypothetical question about a pregnant teenaged daughter, Bush's parents' campaigning for him in New Hampshire, McCain's reaction to Bush's use of a veteran to besmirch McCain's credentials as an ex-POW, the mutual accusations between Bush and McCain that the other is "like Clinton," and a mother's emotional retelling of an anti-McCain push poll phone call her son, a McCain admirer, answered. The family angle surrounding Bush's parents and the emotional unfolding of the push poll story deserve a closer examination.

The appearance of George and Barbara Bush in New Hampshire on behalf of their son leads to speculation in the week following the New Hampshire vote, which Bush lost to McCain. Several reporters speculate that the appearance may have backfired—the appearance of the former president saying "this boy, this son of ours is not going to let you down" (*World News Tonight*, February 2, 2000) actually may have diminished his son's stature:

JENNINGS: Do they (McCain campaign) think that Mr. Bush ran a good campaign against them?

LINDA DOUGLASS (reporter): Well, one of his top aides told me tonight they think Bush ran a bad campaign in New Hampshire. They say it was a terrible mistake for him to bring his parents in, that it simply reinforced the image that McCain was trying to develop that Bush may not be all grown up, Peter. (*World News Tonight*, February 2, 2000)

Similarly, on CNN's *Inside Politics*:

JEFF GREENFIELD: Any regrets about bringing his family in on the grounds that it made him look like Junior?

CROWLEY: You know, I know that the McCain campaign thought that. No, there isn't. This is a pretty close family. This is a guy who would welcome his dad. As I am told, the parents called and said, you know, we can come up, or you know, we really want to come up. And they let them come up. And that—there's no regret there that I can see. (*Inside Politics*, February 1, 2000)

And on February 2:

> JEFF GREENFIELD (senior analyst): And I have to say the pointing out by Bill Schneider that bringing the Bush family to New Hampshire may have backfired because it painted Bush as sort of Junior—the president referred to him as my boy. I was a little surprised to see him introduced today by Dan Quayle, because while Dan Quayle may be popular among some conservatives, if you're worried about an image that you don't quite have the gravitas to be president, I would just have to say that's a curious choice for the man to introduce you. (*Inside Politics*, February 2, 2000)

The function of reporters and pundits in bringing the campaign to voters gives viewers an experience of being inside the campaign. The great deal of "insider" commentary is meant to help viewers understand the implications and consequences of the latest poll result or advertising campaign. The insiderism of all this gives viewers the *sense* of being in the know about the "behind the curtain" aspects of political elections. Similarly, the unusually long sound bite given to a mother who told the story of her son and the push poll phone call brings a different sense of intimacy:

> LINDA DOUGLASS (reporter): At a town hall where people stood up and gushed their support for John McCain, Donna Duren told him that his candidacy has turned her teen-age son's life around.
> DONNA DUREN: My son has now found himself a hero.
> DOUGLASS: Then last night, she said, her son answered a phone call from someone who claimed to be taking a poll.
> DUREN: But he was so upset when he came upstairs and he said, "Mom someone told me that Senator McCain is a cheat and a liar and a fraud" and I was almost in tears. I am so mad. I was so livid last night, I couldn't sleep.
> MCCAIN: I will—I will tell you that what you've just told me has had a very profound affect on me. If they want to win, fine, but we don't need to do that to any Americans. (*World News Tonight*, February 10, 2000)

The strong emotions exhibited by both the mother and McCain provide a special sense of intimacy. The use of close-ups during McCain's statement provides an opportunity for viewers to relate to feel McCain's outrage. The dramatic and entertainment value of this approach is obvious. The value of such an approach for democratic decision making is suspect to say the least.

The kinds of stories told about campaigns clearly draw from the same themes seen in soap operas. The emphasis on conflict and the often chaotic locomotion of campaigns make for a never-ending series of mini-plots that bring a microscopic focus to the strategic elements of campaigns. The virtual reduction of a large field in the Republican party to two candidates facilitates even greater seeming intimacy as networks do round-robin coverage each night of the four designated (two in each party) principal candidates. Here, achieving the desired level of intimacy in coverage is also a mitigating factor in focusing on only a few designated "serious" candidates. McCain's openness was a hit with reporters who traveled with him, and the seeming intimacy and knowledge about the "real" John McCain resulted in lots of generally favorable coverage. In other words, the McCain media strategy matched nicely with the soap opera values reflected in coverage.

Finally, while political reporting rarely identifies "good" and "evil" candidates, it certainly covers with relish the accusations and recriminations between candidates about negative attacks, advertising, and misrepresentations of candidates' pasts by their rivals. And political coverage is obsessed with who's up and who's down. As McCain and Bradley each found out, they were pushed into being more aggressive and negative than their "clean politics" advocacy allowed. Bradley was virtually encouraged by the press to be more aggressive and then criticized for it. McCain suffered when Bush charged politics as usual after a McCain ad linked Bush to Clinton.

DISCUSSION AND IMPLICATIONS
OF THE SOAP OPERA PARADIGM

A simple change in how the role of media in politics is perceived has a turnkey effect on the way reporting of politics is conducted. By considering the construction of television news as *scriptwriting* rather than journalistic *reporting*, it is not hard to see why soap opera elements enter into the storytelling and affect how the story unfolds.

The use of raw material by producers to reflect certain scenarios can be seen in how reporters use that raw material to construct a personalized, emotion-charged picture of presidential campaigning. Two examples below provide a window into how journalists and pundits serve as "scriptwriters" for the ongoing campaign:

JOHN KING: Gore leads comfortably five weeks before the primary here, but California is one of Bradley's major targets; the stakes: enormous.

GORE: On March 7, California will have a very decisive voice in picking the Democratic nominee.

KING: Already, the campaign looks and sounds a lot different from the long months in Iowa and New Hampshire. No more barns, less hand-to-hand campaigning, much more of a focus on constituency group politics.

GORE: I am proud to have the heritage of a father who lost his seat for re-election because he had the courage of his convictions to stand for what is right, including for civil rights in this country.

KING: The issues in California are as diverse as its people.

GORE: I will move heaven and Earth to confront the problem of global warming.

KING: Topics discussed at this Los Angeles community college forum ranged from gangs and gun control to gay rights.

GORE: We are called upon to be a brave people in embracing what we know to be right, but difficult. (*Inside Politics,* February 3, 2000)

Consider this "advice" provided by CNN analyst Jeff Greenfield to Bill Bradley on getting tougher with Gore:

GREENFIELD: I think you have to say to him, you know, the whole political world is expecting you to attack the vice president tonight. And the problem is, since you didn't do it when things were going so well, it's going to sound like sour grapes.

One thing you can do is get up and take responsibility for what's happened. You can acknowledge the fact that you haven't drawn the distinctions. You can promise the vice president a fight over the next several months to make sure he knows you're going to stay in the campaign. And then, senator, it's your choice. You can talk about ethics and you can talk about hypocrisy. If you choose not to do it, you simply have to reaffirm your belief that voters want a different kind of campaign. It's a tough call for Bradley to make. (*Inside Politics,* January 26, 2000)

In the first example, writers use the raw campaign fodder to craft a script that can shorthand issues and focus on strategic/tactical concerns. The use of Gore sound bites to lend authenticity and the sense of being there reflects the careful crafting that goes into such pieces. The story is visually rich as it moves back and forth from Gore's appearance in a town hall meeting to images of California, which accompany reporter John King's voice-over.

The second piece is drawn from the frequent journalist commentary and exchange segments. "What Bradley should do" is a construct of what the pundits assert he is lacking. What is noteworthy is the sort of Catch-22 that Jeff Greenfield shows Bradley as facing. The conundrum he faces is largely a construct of media assessments of Bradley's chances. The message is, go negative and then we will point out how it conflicts with your clean politics campaign.

The point is that the coverage of the campaign reflects a constructedness normally identified with fictional programming. Even during live events at which an outcome is up in the air, as is pointed out in the analysis of the recount controversy (see sidebar), soap elements of emotion and a "real-time" orientation are used to keep viewers tuned in, with the sense that if they tune out, they may miss a dramatic moment. In this sense at least, journalism is no longer the first draft of history; it is more akin to play-by-play coverage of an athletic contest. The use of live reports to capture breaking news, the high emotion conveyed by protesters, and the use of surrogates and spokespeople both in studio and on the scene maintain a level of conflict that virtually overwhelms whatever actual information is being conveyed.

The underlying structure of the way politics is presented is a reflection of the soap opera paradigm. It does not treat viewers as citizens and participants in the democratic process but rather relegates them to the role of spectators whose role is to cheer on their favored participants. Those who accept and relish the current mode of reporting and enjoy the play element of this can be best thought of as political junkies, much akin to the soap opera fans who spend time online speculating with others about the next plot development. However, the remainder of the citizenry/audience may well be alienated by such an approach. Since they see governance not as a game but rather as a way of dealing with ongoing social problems and issues that affect their lives, such coverage leaves them empty. The low voter turnout in U.S. national elections, in contrast to the substantially higher turnouts in European elections, may be explained by the kind of coverage that television news, the source of news for most people, produces. The spike in ratings that apparently fosters such an approach does not reflect a preference by audiences for such soap opera–oriented news. CNN's daily ratings are in the low single digits, so even a threefold increase in audience means a small audience in the larger scheme of things. What the ratings may suggest is that the use of soap opera elements brings a marginally larger group of people into the news mix. Applying a junk food metaphor to this coverage, it is clear that such coverage may have an intriguing "taste," but the long-term nutritional implications of such a diet of news are murkier. That is, the news may be filling but of questionable nutritional value for one's needs as a citizen.

The way political decision making is treated as a contest of personalities rather than ideas serves to alienate the electorate. Voting against a

"MOMENT TO MOMENT": CNN'S SATURATION COVERAGE OF THE FLORIDA RECOUNT

The postelection 2000 controversy surrounding voting procedures and recounts in Florida provides an example of how an ongoing news story takes on soap opera characteristics. In what is becoming a familiar mode for twenty-four-hour cable news services, the Florida election recount controversy generated virtually nonstop coverage from November 8 through December 11. The round-the-clock coverage of this all-consuming story provides a window into how the structure and flow of the coverage appropriates soap opera storytelling.

The recount controversy sent CNN and other twenty-four-hour television news networks into crisis coverage from the day after the election until its resolution in mid-December. This commitment by the networks resulted in ignoring other major news during the periods, such as the strife between the Israelis and Palestinians and the California power crisis. Throughout the thirty-four-day crisis, there was ongoing placement of reporting teams and the dedication of satellite transmission times from the three counties where recounts were taking place or being negotiated in courts; the Florida capital Tallahassee; the Bush team headquarters in Austin, Texas, and Washington, D.C.; and outside Vice President Gore's residence. The provision of live television from these sites reflects the considerable investment in the story.

Coverage of this story essentially consisted of technological hops from one locale to another, where reporters gave updates with a backdrop of buildings and/or protesters signifying the "live" nature of the coverage. Regularly scheduled shows such as *Crossfire* and *Larry King Live* were unfailingly dedicated to the story as well, and live breakaways to the above sites during these studio shows presented a seamless coverage interrupted only by commercial breaks. This "wheel of coverage" had the effect of presenting a real-time soap opera in which reporters, spokespeople, and protesters provided the script and drama of the story.

A look at more than two hours of CNN on the evening of November 20, 2000, illustrates well how the structure of the broadcast served to build and hold an audience as the nation waited for a Florida Supreme Court decision regarding the Gore team's petition for hand recounts in three counties. With an announcement from Tallahassee imminent, Larry King continually reminded viewers to stay tuned and tried to engage with a panel of pundits and politicians. Comments such as the following from Bob Crawford of the Florida Election Canvassing

(continued)

Commission helped add to the drama even though there was little action: "[Y]ou can slice the tension in the air right now. It is getting pretty tense right here in Tallahassee" (*Larry King Live*, November 20, 2000).

Admitting that the speculation surrounding the Supreme Court was "a guessing game," most of the discussion centered on what the Republicans would do if the decision favored Gore. Republicans on the show (Senator Orrin Hatch and consultant Ed Rollins) maintained a militant stance, with Rollins explicitly stating that having lost the impeachment of President Clinton, Republicans felt cheated and would do anything to win this battle:

> ED ROLLINS: I think Republicans felt that Bill Clinton cheated them out of the impeachment and all the rest. . . . But they've had this long six year battle in which they think the Clinton-Gore team has always cut the edges and has taken advantage of them. I think in this particular case, where they basically thought they won this on election night, they thought they had won on the recount and now to basically have it taken away by dimples or whatever, I think today will make my party very, very angry. (*Larry King Live*, November 20, 2000)

The quote encapsulates the major thrust of the King show that evening: the growing animosity of Republicans toward Gore's challenges. Rollins puts this controversy in historical context, implying that having lost at their attempt to impeach Clinton in 1998 the Republicans will fight on if the imminent decision favors Gore.

After King cuts away to the announcement by the court mandating the recounts, he comes back to his guests for reaction and then cuts to CNN "legal analyst" Roger Cossack, who provides an overview of the decision while noting that he has not read the full forty-two-page document. King comes back to Cossack and reporter Bill Hemmer in Tallahassee for updates on their interpretation of the decision. The live coverage of course forces this approach—viewers are kept in real time as the journalists, legal experts, and two opposing sides make sense of the court's decision. Thus, accuracy about the nature and implications of the decision evolves throughout the evening, providing evidence that networks prioritize immediacy over accuracy.

After the King show signs off, Judy Woodruff and Jeff Greenfield serve as anchors for CNN's "special coverage" and begin what has become a familiar trail of jumping to live reports from Hemmer in Tallahassee, Candy Crowley in Austin, John King outside the Gore residence, and then back to Greenfield, who provides more details of the decision. Before each commercial break throughout this coverage,

Woodruff uses brief teasers to keep viewers tuned in, such as, "When we come back we're going to talk to our correspondents in those three south Florida counties where the hand count continues. We'll be right back."

The wait for the Gore statement is filled by reports from Tallahassee and from the recount counties, where inquiries about the logistics of the recount and the ability to meet the deadline are answered by local officials. The quote from reporter Bill Hemmer below shows the kind of minutiae saturation coverage generates:

> I can tell you, Judy, about 5:00 local time, which is now about 5½ hours ago, the rumors really started to swirl about town here in Tallahassee. We thought it could come down about 5:30, 6:00, but it again was delayed for several hours today. As to why, we really can't say. At one point, they said some of the copy machines were jammed. But it's quite a scene here. (CNN, November 20, 2000)

Numerous other live cutaways for interviews and updates are made until the Gore announcement. Reaction to the Gore announcement fills the time until lawyers from both sides make remarks. The late evening's action ends with an appearance by Bush spokesperson James Baker.

The content of the discussion throughout focuses on the "ratcheting up of tension" between the two sides, whether Republicans will be seen as sore losers if they continue to fight the recount, Gore's praise of the public officials who will conduct the recounts while the Republicans speculate about mischief during the process, whether Gore and Bush will meet as suggested by Gore in his remarks, and the lack of standards in the court decision regarding what counts as a vote in these recounts.

What is clear from this example of how CNN approached its coverage of the crisis is the ongoing effort to keep people tuned in. An emphasis on the emotion surrounding the story, the elevation of conflict between the Democrats and Republicans through the use of surrogates and spokespeople both in the studio and at the many live locales, and the staggered manner in which the full decision was reported are clearly designed to keep audiences tuned in by conveying the ongoing immediacy of the story. The audience clearly is put in an omniscient position by virtue of the technological hops throughout the country, creating a fly-on-the-wall sense for them.

But such an approach means getting a complete and coherent account of the story takes a back seat to the emphasis on emotion and

(continued)

immediacy. The frequent return to Hemmer in Tallahassee and the use of legal pundit Greta Van Susteren as she read through the decision exemplifies this as they make sense of the document for viewers over an hour and a half of postdecision coverage. Coming forty-five minutes after the announcement of the decision, the segment below identifies the importance of a thorough reading of court documents. The discussion is about a footnote in the decision noting that the justices asked both sides whether they wanted a statewide hand recount:

> GREENFIELD: And what that means, I think, is they were in effect inviting the Bush campaign to say, OK, if you are worried that these are three Democratic counties and you ask for a statewide hand recount, we'll give it to you. That could have been advantageous to the Bush campaign. I would surmise—and you're the legal expert—that the Bush campaign didn't want to concede that ground. You know, didn't want to admit that any kind of hand counts are appropriate and they may end up regretting that decision, yes?
> VAN SUSTEREN: And that's right. That's your grounds. That the political decision may have been an unwise decision, but anyway it appears in a footnote in the legal decision but they didn't take the bait.
> GREENFIELD: Well, sometimes footnotes contain mountains of legal stuff. (CNN, November 20, 2000)

CNN's ratings are known to spike quite high during events like this. Fully aware that a story is hot, CNN strives to maintain the fever pitch that is rather momentary with each twist and turn of the story. As the recount controversy proceeded (only to be stopped by the U.S. Supreme Court), CNN anchor Lou Waters (on December 1, 2000) cued viewers to their opportunity to witness the next mini-plot in this story. Noting that CNN would be covering a court hearing regarding recounts on Saturday, December 2, at 9 A.M., he told viewers to make sure they tune in, saying, "It will give you something to do tomorrow."

And of course the decision giving the presidency to George W. Bush on December 11, 2000, merely started speculation about the next phase of the story—whether Bush's presidency would be wounded by the election controversy. This is the way in which the news of politics and governance ultimately can be seen as a soap opera. The closure or resolution of one fight merely presages what it will mean for the next one.

candidate, rather than for someone one believes in, becomes the tactical choice of those who do bother to turn out. Elections don't produce winners, just survivors. Is it any small wonder that people expect so little from what they are told is democracy?

NOTE

1. The data presented in this section were originally published in *Media, Profit and Politics: Competing Priorities in an Open Society* (Kent, OH: Kent State University Press, 2003), 91–108. They are presented here with permission of Kent State University Press.

III

SOAP OPERA: THE GODZILLA GENRE

The utility of the soap opera paradigm in developing loyal audiences has meant a shift in storytelling during prime time evening programming. While daytime soaps were a staple of television from its inception, the development of prime time programming toward story lines that carry over several episodes of a program and other soap opera storytelling techniques is more recent. Chapter 8 presents an analysis of hourlong prime time dramas as they have come to look more and more like daytime soap operas. Prime time soaps have become pervasive in network schedules.

Chapter 9 looks in detail at the most recent genre, "reality television." While many of the programs in this genre have obvious links to soaps through their focus on intimate relationships, the reality show *Boot Camp* is examined precisely because the focus of the game—enduring the rigors of military boot camp—seems very *un*-soap-like. The structure of these programs and the kind of story lines created from the way the game proceeds clearly draw on the elements of the soap opera paradigm designed to hook viewers for a ten-week melodrama involving "real" people.

Sports are a major part of television these days, with several twenty-four-hour sports cable networks and regional sports channels promoting the fortunes and perils of local, college, and professional sports. Changes in the ways games/matches are presented to viewers and myriad forms of nongame programming aimed at sports lovers are examined in Chapter 10 to show how sports broadcasting uses soap opera narrative strategies as a way to expand its audience. The natural drama of live sports is a constant in live broadcasts of games, but how the games are described and presented has changed dramatically. Behind-the-scenes aspects of sports create a lot of fodder for sports gossip. Sports buffs gain a greater sense of knowledge and intimacy about what goes on behind the scenes with their favorite athletes and teams. The impression left by this cross-game analysis reveals the extent to which the frame of soap opera story-telling manifests itself, both obviously and more subtly.

8

Prime Time Storytelling

All cultures are reflected in and shaped by the stories they tell; the enduring lessons of life, delineations of right and wrong, and what constitutes the "good life" are all contained in the dominant themes of the stories we tell. Media scholar George Gerbner started analyzing stories as a folklorist in his native Austria. Gerbner went on to spend his career looking at the stories of television (Budd, Craig, and Steinman 1999). Television in many ways serves the same function as the oral tradition of telling stories at clan and community gatherings. As the "electronic hearth," television can tell a lot about our contemporary culture's value system. By looking at the kind of stories being told in prime time television, one can get a sense of what matters most—what our society celebrates, what it fears, what it aspires to.

While sitting around the television to watch the stories of contemporary culture is somewhat analogous to sitting around a fire and hearing elders tell stories that impart lessons of life, there are vast differences in who tells those stories, how those stories are made, and the motivation behind their telling. The oral tradition of passing on culture has long since receded. Reading to children is now often replaced by placing them in front of the television to watch videos or children's-oriented channels such as Nickelodeon. Television has become a dominant source of the stories of our culture. This chapter looks at prime time storytelling and what kind of culture it projects.

THE MASTER NARRATIVE OF CONTEMPORARY CULTURE?

Because culture is generally regarded as the glue of society—the well-spring of its values, the expression of its highest aspirations, and the harbinger of its deepest fears—the degree to which any one source of stories comes to dominate a culture must be examined critically to uncover whether that source expresses the authentic meaning of the culture or instead serves the self-interests of powerful elements within society. Chapter 1 shows how the television industry has evolved to reflect almost exclusively the "bottom line" interests of the parent companies that own it. The examination of news media shows how soap opera storytelling has come to dominate the way events are described to news viewers, to the detriment of meeting viewers' needs as citizens. When storytelling is put primarily in the hands of an industry, that industry's priorities and values will affect the kind of stories told.

Robert Fulford speaks of the "master narratives" of a society, which present a set of common themes and values that capture the aspirations of the people in that society. A master narrative provides lessons of history, provides guides for individual behavior, and generally serves to enlighten and mold a society (Fulford 2000). Master narratives represent highly idealized versions of culture—overlooking contradictions and flaws within a society's ideology and providing overgeneralized truths. Fulford argues that master narratives may be less powerful in explaining the vast changes that took place in the second half of the twentieth century, but nonetheless he points out that the choosing and assembling of any story involve a number of value-based choices engaged by story producers. He argues that the dominant value/mythology of a society will serve as the source of stories until that narrative has exhausted itself against reality.

Fulford cites the publication of the novel *Ivanhoe* as the beginning of mass storytelling in the United States; it also put romantic storytelling on the map. Even though the novel is set in a distant land, Fulford argues that it captured the imagination of the post–Civil War American South, with its highly romantic images of chivalry and the role of the reluctant hero serving to set forth a master narrative for that region. D. W. Griffith's film *Birth of a Nation* further reflects this idea as it tries to revive the South's myth about itself. The film is a depiction of a past that tries to counter the narrative of the victorious North, a last hurrah for the old order.

Film, and later television, turned away from folk culture and focused on the development of "industrialized" or mass storytelling whose primary goal is not necessarily the sustenance of a society's values or its mythology. Rather its focus is on making money for the "producer," whose interests are not necessarily those of the "author." As discussed in chapter 2, the assembly line method of producing soap opera episodes stands in stark contrast to the author's control over the story contained within a novel. This chapter explores whether there is a "master narrative" within the stories told during prime time television. Has the idea of master narrative taken on a new form in television? Perhaps in an age of market orthodoxy, the master narrative is one of consumption as the overriding activity in American society. How do elements of soap opera storytelling shape the stories that are told and the lessons that are imparted? Maybe the goals of industrialized narrative lie not in telling stories to inspire and enlighten but rather in conveying stories that serve to entice an audience being continually groomed to consume through the increasing amount of advertising aired during program breaks. If contemporary use of soap opera storytelling can be considered a commodified form of storytelling, one can appreciate that the product television really creates is not the program but the audience. The shows, the stories they tell are meant only to encourage loyalty or addiction to shows for exposure to commercials.

This chapter argues that the master narrative of the late twentieth and early twenty-first centuries is as much about the way the story is told as the content of the story itself. The soap opera paradigm is the framework for prime time storytelling, which celebrates consumption and accumulation as embodying the highest aspirations of society and provides viewers with stories and imagery that encourage them to define themselves through what they consume. Television's storytelling structure has the goal of maintaining audience interest to stay through program breaks. The stories themselves can reflect a number of life situations and social sectors, depending on the demographic group advertisers and producers are targeting. To better understand the meaning of today's "electronic" hearth, this chapter examines how prime time soap opera storytelling has become pervasive on network television. It also looks at trends in who the targets of these programs are.

FROM ANTHOLOGIES TO SERIES TO SERIALS

The focus here is on the history of the one-hour drama. While situation comedies and other genres have played important roles throughout the history of evening television programming, this discussion emphasizes the changes in the one-hour drama. To be sure, over the last decade or so, situation comedies have also taken on characteristics of soaps—continuing story lines and relationship histories, to name just two. But the modern cousin of the radio soap opera really is the dramatic series airing in one-hour blocks during the prime time hours. To illustrate this, this discussion looks at how one-hour programs have evolved since the 1950s and then analyzes the growth of prime time soap operas since 1960. What will become clear is that the one-hour drama has become colonized by serial storytelling, thus illustrating that television came to borrow heavily from its highly successful and profitable use of soap operas as daytime programming. The trend of the last few years in television, "reality" programming, might intuitively be seen as a new genre, but chapter 9 illustrates how this latest craze also is based on soap opera storytelling techniques.

A look at the schedules of the networks in the late 1940s and early 1950s finds that early prime time television was composed of many half-hour and even some fifteen-minute shows (Brooks and Marsh 2003). About the only programming that went beyond the half-hour limit was sporting contests: boxing, wrestling, and basketball. The type of hour-long show that found success in prime time was the "variety" show. A carryover from touring vaudeville shows, the variety format was so named because it could include just about anything—stand-up and/or sketch comedy, singing, and dancing. *Cavalcade of Stars, Arthur Godfrey and His Friends,* and *The Milton Berle Show* exemplified the variety format. Usually hosted by or starring a celebrity who got his or her start in radio, these shows offered a little bit for everyone—something that worked then because there were no multiple-set households so that each family member could retreat to a different program. Ed Sullivan, Ed Wynn, Jimmy Durante, Sid Caesar, and Jackie Gleason all became cultural icons in the 1950s and early 1960s as they hosted these kinds of shows.

The early prototype for the hour-long drama was the anthology. Anthologies offered different stories and casts each week. At this point, the center for television production was New York—not until the filmed drama came about did program production shift to Hollywood. Thus much of "serious" television was an extension of stage acting and "live" shows. Many of those who made or would ultimately make their name in movies appeared on these anthology shows—stars such as Peter Lawford, William Bendix, Bette Davis, E. G. Marshall, James Dean, Paul Newman, Jack Lemmon, and Joanne Woodward, to name a few. And many of the scripts for these shows came from short stories and adaptations of classic novels. *Kraft Television Theatre, General Electric Theatre, TV Playhouse, Studio One,* and *Fireside Theatre* were just a few of the numerous versions of these shows, which endured through the early 1960s.

Dramatic television series began to emerge in the late 1950s and really came into their own as program production shifted to Hollywood. The subject matter and settings for these shows changed over the years to respond to shifts in tastes and, more important, as advertisers began to de-

sire shows aimed at specific segments of American society. An early popular series setting was the Western. In 1955 the first of many Westerns was
aired on CBS. *Gunsmoke* became a blockbuster hit and aired for the next
twenty years. It was followed by shows such as *Bonanza; Cheyenne; Have
Gun, Will Travel; Wagon Train; Tales of Wells Fargo;* and *The Rifleman.* These
"adult" Westerns bore little resemblance to the earlier versions of Westerns made for kids. They had more complex plots (sometimes serving as
metaphors for modern-day problems) and featured a great deal of violence, much to the chagrin of political and religious leaders. By 1958–1959,
seven of the top ten rated shows were Westerns, and the total number of
Westerns aired during prime time had reached its peak at thirty-one
(Brooks and Marsh 2003).

As mentioned in chapter 1, ABC was the first network to air substantial
violence on the small screen. Its early relationship with United Paramount
Theaters meant it was an early innovator of filmed series, and the shifting
of program production to Hollywood helped to create a more modern
version of cowboys and Indians: the private detective and police dramas
that would take hold in the 1960s. The prototype for the detective show
77 Sunset Strip premiered on ABC in 1958 and spawned such efforts as
Hawaiian Eye, Peter Gunn, and *Burke's Law.*

Early Western and detective/cop series moved beyond the anthology
format of unique stories and casts each week. Each episode was a self-
contained story using a regular cast. Having regular casts meant that
"stars" would emerge on these shows, thus helping to generate loyal audiences who identified either with the characters in the show or the stars
who played them. Jim Arness, Michael Landon, James Garner, Efrem
Zimbalist Jr., Gene Barry, and Doug McClure became stars on these
shows. Some actors were typecast for the rest of their acting careers, while
others moved on to star in a variety of other series. But the idea that
celebrities could bring people to shows week after week and serve as
icons for the shows themselves helped producers ameliorate the uncer-
tainty and risk in creating programs. If a producer could procure the services of a "known commodity," the show could be counted on to draw an
audience, at least initially. The quality of the production would determine
whether audiences would stay with the show.

While there were some evening soaps in the early days of network television, most were carried over from radio and were a half hour in length.
Faraway Hill, The Goldbergs, and *One Man's Family* were sprinkled
throughout the evening schedule in the 1950s but didn't seem to generate the response that daytime soaps on television garnered. In the early
1960s the first hour-long soaps were aired during prime time, and legal
and medical dramas took their place alongside cop, Western, and detective dramas.

The grand dame of the hour-long evening soap was *Peyton Place*, which came on the air in 1964 and had a four-year run. Other, shorter-run soap operas from that era were *Long Hot Summer* and *Our Private World*. Two medical programs that came to embody continuing story lines and character histories were *Ben Casey* and *Dr. Kildare*. The medical program became a television staple; as a workplace staffed with men and women (most workplaces then were overwhelmingly male), medical shows offered the opportunity to develop intimate relationships and interpersonal conflicts and controversies. Shows centering on the law profession also began to emerge; *Perry Mason* and *The Defenders*/created drama using courtroom surprises and tearful confessions to generate emotion and suspense. Medical and legal shows were staples of network television for decades/ How these shows were structured changed as ensemble casts and continuing story lines permitted more complexity. Eventually, use of cliffhangers at the end of episodes furthered the commercial goals of generating audience loyalty and engendering the addictive nature of a soap opera.

As the situation comedy took hold in the late 1950s and early 1960s, television producers had discovered a few standard program formats that seemed to work well in attracting large audiences. But nothing remains static, and as advertisers began to crave particular kinds of audiences (affluent and youth oriented), producers began to shake things up a bit in the mid- to late 1960s. This turn toward youth and relevance was the result of advertisers' desire to focus on the baby boom generation, some of whom were becoming young adults. Sitcoms, from the campy *Batman* to the cornpone *Green Acres, Petticoat Junction, Mayberry RFD,* and *Gomer Pyle,* to the suburban *Ozzie and Harriet* and *Donna Reed,* were responses to the sheer numbers of youthful viewers. But at the same time older teens and young adults were searching for relevance in socially discordant times through drama programs.

Programs such as *Mod Squad* and *The Storefront Lawyers* were attempts to bottle the "rebellion genie" or find a way to safely channel the rebelliousness of the times. The turn toward relevance in the late 1960s and early 1970s provided a break from the often candy-coated world television had projected to audiences in the 1950s and early 1960s. The willingness to find stories in the headlines of the day provided opportunities to create characters that were not merely caricatures of heroes and villains. Writers could now create characters who had nuances, faults, and sometimes fatal flaws. This development was the antecedent for the ensemble cast shows that emerged in the mid- to late 1970s. The ensemble cast shows fed character and relationship development in programs that provided the basis for the evening soap operas that emerged from the late 1970s onward. Doctors were no longer always portrayed as healing gods, and cops were shown to have faults and shaky personal lives. The series, which emerged as the programming staple in the 1960s, transitioned to the serial/Serial storytelling became the prime tool around which shows have been organized and written to the present day. /

These changes, driven by multiple factors—a suburban, baby boom–driven culture, the evolution of the television industry under the larger umbrella of conglomeration, and the consequent need to lessen the risk inherent in any new television undertaking—helped propel the industry to increasingly adopt the characteristics of soap opera storytelling in prime time television programs. The next section makes the case for the increase in prime time soaps, most evident in 1970s and 1980s programs like *Dallas* and *Knots Landing*, but only slightly veiled in the "reality" genre.

THE GROWTH OF PRIME TIME SOAP OPERAS

Figures 8.1 and 8.2 illustrate the rise of prime time soap operas on television.[1] Figure 8.1 graphs the number of soap operas during prime time from the years 1960 to 2002. (As mentioned previously, there were some soap operas in the early days of network television, but these were only thirty minutes long and of limited duration in prime time. In their transition from radio to television, soap operas were always more successful as daytime efforts. Thus, the years charted in both figures start in 1960 to incorporate the serial elements in shows such as *Dr. Kildare* and *Ben Casey*.) Figure 8.1 shows that the progressive increase in soap opera storytelling began in the late 1970s and early 1980s. There was a rather substantial increase in the mid-1980s, from an average of about five to seven programs in 1980 to twelve to thirteen in the mid-1980s. After a slight drop, the number of soap operas in prime time increased dramatically in the mid-1990s. This trend mirrors the two phases of mergers in the television industry: The networks were bought out by larger media interests in the 1980s, and in the 1990s television was increasingly consolidated as ABC and CBS were sold to even larger parent companies. This explanation, however, could be seen as deceptive, because there was also an increase in the number of broadcast networks (FOX in the 1980s, WB and UPN in the 1990s), and thus one would find a natural growth in the number of hour-long dramas being aired. Figure 8.2 is an attempt to account for this increase in hours of prime time programming. It charts the increase in network soap operas over the same time span as a percentage of all prime time, hour-long dramas. The result obtained is not much different from the shape of the first graph. Soap operas as a percentage of all one-hour dramas on any of the networks increased rather consistently over time,

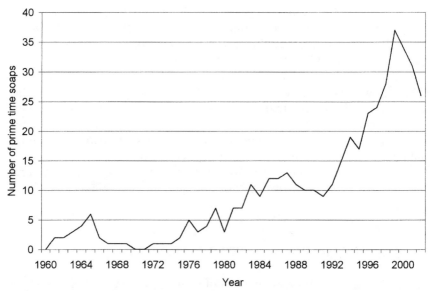

Figure 8.1.   Growth of Prime Time Soap Operas

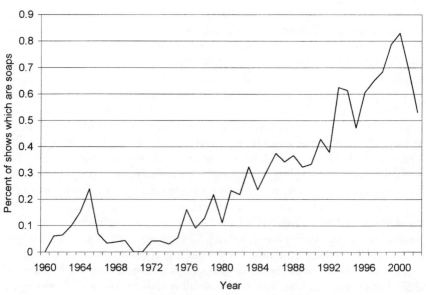

Figure 8.2.   Prime Time Soaps as Percent of Hour-Long Dramas

from 20 percent in the early 1980s to 35 percent by the mid- to late 1980s. By the time the mergers of the 1990s took hold, 50 to 60 percent of hour-long dramas were soap operas. In the late 1990s this rose to over 80 percent. The drop seen in the early 2000s can be attributed at least partially to the rise in the reality programming craze, which emerged in prime time form in the last years of the twentieth century. Although a strong case is made in chapter 9 that the reality craze also reflects elements of serial, soap opera storytelling, those programs were not included here so that the focus could be only on filmed and pre-scripted stories. While Figures 8.1 and 8.2 are overviews that provide ample evidence for the numerical growth of prime time soap operas, it is also necessary to look at how soaps in prime time have changed over the years, so the following section analyzes these shows from 1960 to 2002.

PRIME TIME SOAP OPERAS FROM 1960 TO 2002

Although *Dallas* is often the program cited as sparking the networks' attraction toward prime time soap operas, evening soaps did appear in the early 1960s. As mentioned previously, *Peyton Place* is regarded as the mother of prime time soaps. As an imitation of daytime soaps, this is certainly true—its domestic setting and projection of an upper-middle-class lifestyle bear a close resemblance to daytime television soaps. But there were a few other programs in the early 1960s that meet our criteria. *Ben Casey* and *Dr. Kildare* premiered three years earlier than *Peyton Place* and meet the criteria of continuing story lines and relationship histories. Three other programs from 1960 to 1969 were one-year shows that tried to draw upon the success of *Peyton Place: Long Hot Summer, Our Private World* (each aired in 1965) and *The Survivors* (aired in 1969). Another show that also emerged in the 1960s reflected a less conventional soap opera storytelling orientation. *The Fugitive*, loosely based on the real-life story of Dr. Sam Shepherd, aired from 1963 to 1967. The ongoing pursuit of Richard Kimble by Lt. Gerard provided the weekly grist for the continuing plot. The wrinkle in the story was that Kimble was chasing the person he really thought committed the murder of his wife, for which Gerard was trying to arrest Kimble. The continuity of the story and the heavily watched final episode were emblematic of many evening soap operas to come.

Television schedules of the early 1970s had few programs that contained soap opera story characteristics; the saga of *The Waltons* and the short-lived *Beacon Hill* on CBS were the only soap-oriented shows before 1976. The floodgates soon opened as *Executive Suite* and *Family* came on the air in 1976. These programs were transitions to more full-blown soap operas, using hooks and bait such as cliffhangers. When *Dallas* hit the small screen in 1978, its success unleashed several other shows, two of them conventional soaps: *The Chisolms* and *Knot's Landing*. A show called *Cliffhangers*, which tried to extend the soap format by having three separate stories per hour aired each week, premiered in 1979. An attempt to play off the idea of movie serials aimed at young people, these stories used the suspended story technique to keep viewers coming back, but the mid-season replacement failed to catch on. *Family* was a domestic soap featuring all the triumphs and tribulations of contemporary suburban American families. The show managed to break ground in terms of relevance through a story line involving the son's friend coming out as a homosexual. Other short-lived series included serials developed from novels such as *From Here to Eternity* and *Rich Man, Poor Man*. Another series, *Husbands, Wives, and Lovers*, tried to combine a sitcom and an hour-long soap involving the lives of five couples. The experiment did not last beyond a mid-season replacement stint.

It was *Dallas*, however, that set the stage for 1980s television. Coinciding with Nancy Reagan's glamorous White House years, the decade saw an explosion of the soap opera genre, many shows drawing on the opulence of *Dallas*. *Dynasty, Falcon Crest, The Yellow Rose, Paper Dolls, Bare Essence,* and *For Love and Honor* all came on the air between 1981 and 1985 (Feuer 1995). Two other programs took evening soaps into traditional television territory—the cop show (*Hill Street Blues*) and the medical/hospital drama (*St. Elsewhere*). Premiering in 1981 and 1982 respectively, the continuing story lines, cliffhangers to close weekly episodes, and the interpersonal relationships that were part of the lives of the ensemble casts provided the prototype for the modern evening soap opera. This formula was used in many future prime time shows, some with success, while others would not seize the popular imagination. These shows ran about five years—not a long run, but long enough to become attractive syndication properties. The glamour soaps *Dallas, Knots Landing, The Yellow Rose,* and *Dynasty* completed their longer runs on network television in the late 1980s and early 1990s.

Soaps emerging in the late 1980s moved away from the glamour of the Reagan 1980s and veered into a number of different settings. *LA Law* and *Thirtysomething* were aimed specifically at the baby boomers known as "young urban professionals," or more derisively, "yuppies." Such labeling and targeting of audiences for shows is indicative of the increasing priority advertisers brought to networks to find programming that would attract affluent segments of the population. The segmented targeting could be broken down further; *Thirtysomething* tried to capture the psychology and lifestyle of both singles and married couples. These shows and others—*A Year in the Life* and *Berenger's,* for example—reflected a movement in prime time programming toward a consistent projection of an upper-middle-class lifestyle downscale from the glamour of *Dallas* and *Dynasty* but sufficiently prosperous to reach the segment of the baby boom generation that made it during the Reagan years. Nonserial shows also responded to the growing prosperity of a segment of the baby boom population and served to project ideas on how yuppies, dinks (dual income, no kids), and two-profession households with children could spend their wealth. As much as the stories themselves, the upper-middle-class nature of these shows projected a consumption ethic or at least defined what was to be considered the "good life" and how to gauge when one had "made it."

Police soaps continued to prosper, as *Cagney and Lacey*, *Brooklyn South*, *Crime Story*, and *In the Heat of the Night* followed on the success of *Hill Street Blues*, integrating cop shop life and the personal lives of police. Quirky shows embodying soap elements included *Quantum Leap*, *Beauty and the Beast*, and *American Gothic*, indicating that soap-style storytelling could be integrated into just about any setting.

The next big transition in the evolution of prime time soap operas was the role they played for the new networks that came on the scene in the late 1980s (FOX) and 1995 (WB, UPN). These new broadcast networks each tried to reach segments of the population that were perceived as underserved. FOX started very much in the mode of trying to attract a youth audience and provided programming aimed at minority youth. WB and UPN took this a bit further; WB tried to focus on young people while UPN tried to lure minority viewers.

As mentioned in chapter 2, characteristically each mass medium in its formative stages has employed serial storytelling to attract audiences and to keep them coming back for more. It should not be surprising that the three networks born in the 1980s and 1990s invented soaps aimed at their audience slices. From 1990 to 1995 FOX premiered eight evening soaps, with *Beverly Hills 90210*, *Melrose Place*, *Ally McBeal*, and *Party of Five* as four of the more successful ventures. From 1996 to 1999, WB premiered ten soap operas, from the faith-based *Seventh Heaven*, to the youth-oriented *Dawson's Creek* and *Felicity*, to the supernatural-themed *Buffy the Vampire Slayer* and *Charmed*. Supernatural-themed soaps took their inspiration to some degree from the successful 1960s and early 1970s daytime soap hit, *Dark Shadows*, an early "youth-oriented" daytime soap opera.

The new networks helped move soap storytelling into new environments. The now common settings for soaps—cop shops like *NYPD Blue* and the standard hospital dramas that came on in the 1990s like *ER* and *Chicago Hope*—were being eschewed by the new kids on the block. The new networks took soap storytelling into science fiction, and more fully into the world of youth themselves. These networks were trying to attract a youth audience to match the advertisers' desire to reach young consumers and inspire their taste for a whole host of fashions, accessories, cars, and toys that they would want once they entered upwardly mobile professions. UPN, a less secure broadcasting enterprise than the more immediately successful WB, has stayed largely in sitcom territory. In today's advertiser-sensitive programming environment, reaching minority audiences is achieved through cheaper advertising rates available on many niche cable channels. Thus the few programs on UPN that reflect a soap storytelling orientation are science fiction programs like *Enterprise* and *Seven Days*.

The impact of the new networks on television in the 1990s can be seen in an analysis of where evening soaps were appearing. From 1990 to 1995, the three established networks aired around ten soaps each. FOX weighed in with eight during the same period; WB had one. From 1996 to 1999 CBS and NBC ran ten and eleven soaps, respectively, while ABC ran five and FOX and WB ran ten each. In the early 2000s, ABC continued to move away from evening soaps, running just four in comparison to the other four fully programmed networks: CBS, sixteen; NBC, eleven; FOX, eleven; and WB, eight. ABC's retreat from soaps took place after its purchase by Disney in 1996. There seems to be no specific reason for this, though in the years after 2000 it was running multiple weekly episodes of *Who Wants to Be a Millionaire?*

Some soaps of the 1990s were critically acclaimed and big hits; many were not. Even on the new networks, there were a lot of flops—*Pacific Palisades, Time of Your Life, Get Real,* and *Models Inc.* on Fox and *Hyperion Bay* and *Savannah* on WB. The older networks similarly had hits and misses. ABC found a hit with *NYPD Blue* (a younger sibling to *Hill Street Blues)* but also had only one-year runs of *Dangerous Minds, My So-Called Life, Crossroads,* and *Byrds of Paradise.* NBC generated a blockbuster hit in *ER* and less successful ventures in *Malibu Shores, Sweet Justice, Against the Grain,* and a *Dark Shadows* revival. CBS went quirky in the early 1990s with the frontier-oriented *Dr. Quinn, Medicine Woman* and the more contemporary but offbeat *Northern Exposure* and *Picket Fences.* Its one solid hit was *ER* competitor *Chicago Hope.*

DISCUSSION

The rise of the prime time soap opera from the 1980s onward is another indicator of how the soap opera paradigm helps explain the changes in television programming in an era of media conglomeration. Furthermore, this chapter illustrates how the development of soaps reflected the interests of advertisers as they tried to reach particular (generally affluent or

THE SAD DEVOLUTION OF
THE NETWORK NEWS DOCUMENTARY

This analysis of prime time television would not be complete without at least a brief look at the prime time news shows that now populate broadcast network schedules. In the early days of television, hour-long documentaries provided citizens with in-depth explorations of the issues of the day. Reuven Frank's (1991) book on his years at NBC, *Out of Thin Air*, explains in great detail how the documentary evolved at the network and the kinds of efforts networks made to produce quality and informative prime time public affairs programs for the nation's citizens. CBS developed a reputation for substance in prime time news programs early on with the work of Edward R. Murrow and Fred Friendly. Its documentary teams of the 1960s turned out such groundbreaking and eye-opening pieces such as "Harvest of Shame" and "The Selling of the Pentagon."

But the last two decades have seen a long decline in prime time evening news programs. There are rare shows that involve one-hour treatments of a single issue, but for the most part, hour-long evening news programs are broken into four or more segments that are edited for pacing and vividness as opposed to in-depth explorations of how powerful institutions affect the lives of regular folks. Except for the venerable *60 Minutes*, most network news shows have devolved into a bizarre mixture of celebrity interviews, lurid exposés, and other fare and generally avoid challenging the government or powerful institutions and corporations. Occasionally they may do something gutsy and important for the nation's citizens to know, but more often shows such as *Dateline, 20/20,* and the various permutations of *48 Hours* serve up murder mysteries, mildly hysterical consumer segments, and other fare that generally serves to tell the stories of human frailty and failures. These "news" shows are found throughout the weekly prime time schedule, with a number of editions of *Dateline, 48 Hours,* and *60 Minutes* per week.

The July 27, 2003, edition of *Dateline* typifies this kind of news. A two-hour show, the bulk of the program is titled "Missing" and features three situations involving two kidnappings and a bizarre story of identity theft within a family. Additional, briefer segments focus on the special effects involved in shooting a car chase movie scene and an "update" of the Kobe Bryant case. There are about seventy-seven minutes of actual story time in the program; another ten minutes (including the show's lengthy introduction) are spent on teasers for upcoming

(continued)

stories or future editions of *Dateline*. This analysis focuses on how these segments are set up at the beginning of the program, the use of the reporter in the story as a narrator of the drama, and the manner in which advertising breaks are used to create a suspended story line.

An introductory segment lasting two minutes, forty-one seconds opens the show:

VOICE-OVER: Her child simply vanished. Her two children disappeared. He lost his past. Tonight, they go in search of the missing . . .

VO: She disappeared, like so many others, without a trace. Where did they go? Who would take them?

REPORTER: Did you find any sign at all of her?

VO: And where are they now?

REPORTER: She was alive and well?

VO: Edie Magnus with a mysterious story of spies and innocence, of loved ones lost and found or just maybe lost forever. . . . It was a mother's worst nightmare. Her children were gone.

MOTHER: I'm panicking and then I find out they were in Cairo. (crying)

VO: She says the kidnapper was their father, her ex-husband. And he didn't just want the children.

MOTHER: He wanted huge sums of money.

VO: Thus started an incredible odyssey, a search that would take her half way around the world till finally her best hope was the last person you'd ever imagine . . .

MOTHER: For me, he was a hero.

VO: Hoda Kotb, with one mother's mission to save her children. . . . Imagine discovering that most of your life is a lie.

REPORTER: Chip, what's your birthday?

MAN: August 1, 1975.

REPORTER: Are you sure?

MAN: No, I am not.

VO: You learn that your name isn't what you thought it was. That your mother is a criminal. That your father has a dark secret. And that you may have even been kidnapped as an infant.

MAN: Maybe I replaced the child he killed.

VO: Tonight this young man learns his past is missing, his identity stolen and the thieves were his own parents.

MAN: I found a birth certificate and you hold it up to the light and it's been typed over.

VO: Dennis Murphy with a stunning story of secrets and lies. Tonight the missing . . . . Plus, the latest in the Kobe Bryant case and a look at life in the NBA, where life off the court can be a wild ride.

WOMAN: As the night went on the dresses got shorter, the women became more aggressive.
VO: What does the future hold for this athlete of impossible talent and once perfect image?
REPORTER: No matter what happens to Kobe Bryant—guilty, not guilty—is he tarnished?
VO: Dawn Fratangelo on celebrity, sex and scandal.

The introduction to the show serves as a teaser for viewers to remain at that channel by conveying the essence of very personal tragedies suffered by regular people. The Kobe Bryant story, the titillating celebrity piece for this edition of *Dateline,* is plugged throughout the program and closes it. But the bulk of the show is organized around and graphically identified with a "Missing" title, and each of the three stories is a heart-tugging and sometimes shocking tale of people searching for loved ones or trying to find out who they really are.

The first story is the story of a Japanese couple whose young daughter was kidnapped by North Korean agents and taken to the secretive country. While the reporter is occasionally seen asking questions of those involved in the story, she also serves as the narrator and uses transitions in the story to pump up the emotion:

REPORTER: What happened to Migumi is so unusual, so extraordinary; it is hard to believe it really happened and even harder to understand why. And so *Dateline* traveled half way around the world to investigate a story of love and loss, espionage and international intrigue. As parents, many of us fear our children being ripped away from us, from our homes and everything they know and love. For the Okotas and the other families, that dark and primal nightmare came true.

This transition is striking for the way in which the reporter helps the audience relate to the tragedy the now elderly couple has dealt with for over twenty years. Personalizing the story with "as parents, many of us fear our children . . . " helps involve the audience emotionally in the story. But the broad brushstrokes of the transition also help convey the story's multiple angles—if "love and loss" don't move you, maybe the "espionage and international intrigue" will keep your attention. Viewers also hear the phrase "halfway around the world" several times throughout the broadcast as a reminder that *Dateline* is in the business of tracking down these stories at considerable expense. The geopolitical connections of this story, a genuine news value, are actually under-

(*continued*)

played as the focus remains on the specific personalities involved in this particular case—the story is not set up to delve into the nature of the North Korean regime. This is a "micro" oriented story, and emotion, not global understanding, is the focus of its telling. This is clear in the tease offered before an ad break, which also includes one of the numerous plugs for the Kobe Bryant story:

> VO: Coming up, he's the spy who came in from the cold with a tale of espionage and astonishing ruthlessness.
> REPORTER: Was there no hesitation about taking ordinary citizens and just grabbing them and kidnapping them?
> VO: Does he know what happened to that little girl? . . . And later, inside the rarified world of the professional sports star . . .
> REPORTER: If a star NBA player wanted to have sex with a gorgeous woman every single night . . .
> WOMAN: A different one?
> REPORTER: Yeah, could he?
> WOMAN: Sure.
> REPORTER: No problem?
> WOMAN: No problem, no problem at all.
> VO: The temptations of fame and the case of Kobe Bryant.

The tease regarding the kidnap sets up the next segment, which focuses on a North Korean defector who had knowledge of the fate of the little girl. It seems the ease with which the North Koreans kidnapped Japanese children is paralleled by the ease with which NBA players can pick up women. The portion of the teaser devoted to the Kobe Bryant story is typical for each one broadcast that evening. But it appears the issue has transitioned from one of rape to a more titillating take on sex and sports celebrities. When it comes on at the end of the program, the segment itself seems to be a thinly veiled attempt to rationalize Kobe's behavior as he faces his own rape trial. After a brief update of what the case is doing to the small Colorado community where it is being tried, the guiding value shaping the construction of the piece is the glamorous life of an NBA star and how it can get you into trouble. The fact that so many women pursue these stars seems to serve as a rationalization of Kobe's behavior.

These teasers serve to demonstrate the soap opera storytelling that guides these "news" shows. The three "Missing" stories all use reporter transitions and ad breaks very effectively, as in these related to the second kidnapping tale:

Reporter transition:

VO: Hers is an odyssey so unbelievable it sounds like a detective novel. The plotline? An international kidnapping, millions of dollars, a handful of world leaders, a hunt across two continents.
And it all began simply enough with a man, a woman, and a marriage.

Teaser:
VO: Her search was about to take her half way around the world again to plead with a leader who was none too friendly to America.
WOMAN: He was very angry.
VO: Could she convince him to help her get back her children? When "Missing" continues.

This story relates the tale of a mother whose estranged husband kidnaps their children and takes them to Egypt and then to Cuba. The twist in this story is that Fidel Castro helped to arrange the mother's recovery of them. The line "he was very angry" in the teaser is a bit deceptive—she is referring to Castro, but the lack of context makes it seem as if the yet unnamed "foreign leader" would not be helpful to her cause. These teasers often serve to deceive viewers into thinking a story will progress in one way only to see it go in another direction. This is classic soap opera storytelling: Create a few plausible scenarios and have viewers try to tease out the truth. That's why they're called teasers, and they bring the viewers in as participants in the programs; viewers are playing along at home in deconstructing this mystery story. In the show's opening, the mother proclaims (about Castro), "he's a hero to me," and she later says he reminded her of her father. Again with this story, geopolitics takes a back seat, and this particular insight into Castro is neither developed nor critiqued in any way.

The third story, a bizarre tale of a son who was deceived by his parents until he was a young adult, has no larger political connection and is a lurid tale of criminal parents who used their stolen/adopted son's name to procure student loans and run up a bad credit rating. In the case of each of these stories, there are clear antagonists and sympathetic characters; right and wrong are not ambiguous.

While not serials in the strictest sense of the word, these shows still employ a lot of the tried-and-true techniques of audience baiting and loyalty building. Perhaps seen by audiences as more interesting for their "reality" angle than fictional material, these news shows nonetheless use the success of fictional serialized stories to weave their tales and tell the primary lesson of news: It's a scary world out there.

youthful) audience segments. As new broadcast networks hit the airwaves in the late 1980s and 1990s, they used prime time soaps to attract
the audiences advertisers find desirable.

The way soap stories are presented in an hour-long format can be seen
as working largely to prevent use of remote controls during advertising
breaks. But the content of the stories themselves also helps serve commercial interests by projecting the "good life" of largely affluent characters. There aren't a lot of soaps set in working-class environments, much
less stories focused on making ends meet. There's a consumption ethic to
sell, after all. The setting for these shows and the audiences they are targeted at suggest that the "master narrative" of contemporary American
society focuses on material prosperity as a core value around which
prime time television programs are organized. Absent any sense of the
common good, stories that focus on the travails of individuals seen
mostly in prosperous settings show people how to define their lives in
terms of individual material accomplishments. Contemporary versions
of an elusive master narrative have little to say to the American people
as a collective; almost all of television's lessons are individual, almost
egotistical in nature.

Given the hit-and-miss nature of evening soaps, it is not unreasonable
to ask whether the bubble has burst on serial storytelling. All of the broadcast networks began to take notice that cable channel offerings were taking a bigger bite of the ratings apple in the mid- to late 1990s. And this
continued into the 2000s—the recently renamed "Spike TV" (formerly
TNN, which was The Nashville Network and later The National Network) has seen its Monday night show WWE RAW overtake ABC's Monday Night Football among young male viewers.

In some ways, the filmed shows of the late 1990s and early 2000s have
taken a turn toward crime investigation—not necessarily by cop on the
street type characters but by a new set of "science trained" professionals
in no-nonsense shows such as CSI and Profiler. Meanwhile "relationship"-
focused shows have taken root in the most recent trend of so-called reality programs. These shows are essentially mini-serials, anywhere from a
half dozen to ten or more episodes in which people are brought together
to try to get along, win competitions, be tempted to stray from their current relationship, or find a presumable life partner. Thus the substance of
the conventional evening soap has been transferred, using "real people"
instead of actors reading scripted material.

Reality television has often proved successful because it is cheap to produce. Fictional programs, often called "scripted shows," involve things
like stars and writers, which are often some of the highest program expenses. Reality shows are not exactly "unscripted" shows, though for promotional reasons they might be projected as such. The next chapter ex-

amines a reality show and how it generates "buzz" among its viewers in venues such as the Internet. It illustrates that these shows are far from un-scripted, and that their construction as short duration serials makes them the latest adaptation of soap opera storytelling.

NOTE

1. A brief explanation of how shows were designated as soaps is warranted, as the difference between series and serials is increasingly fluid. Morris (1997) and Brooks and Marsh (2003) served as guides for what to designate as a prime time soap opera. The main criteria for inclusion were episode-to-episode story line "arcs" or continuity, relationship "histories" that play a role in the progress of the overall narrative, and the use of cliffhangers between episodes and seasons. A show was included as an evening soap if it met two of the three criteria. Where personal knowledge of a show was lacking, Brooks and Marsh (2003) was very helpful in deciding about shows that were on the borderline. Its detailed histories of programs for each show usually gave clear clues as to whether a show met any of the criteria.

Mini-series were included if they ran over several weeks (as opposed to con-secutive nights) and had seven or more episodes. As Brooks and Marsh (2003) pro-vides an encyclopedic treatment of prime time television, a second guideline was developed to eliminate shows that had such brief runs that they didn't really be-come part of the regular schedule. For hour-long dramas, the airing of ten episodes was required to be designated as a prime time soap opera.

Finally, though chapter 9 demonstrates that the most recent popular genre, re-ality shows, embodies many characteristics of soaps, reality shows were not in-cluded in the prime time soap opera database that comprises figures 8.1 and 8.2.

9

Reality TV: "This Is Just Like a Soap"

The emergence in the last few years of what has come to be called "reality" television has become an object of curiosity for television critics and news pundits. The wide publicity such programs receive through parodies, copycatting by local media outlets, and placement after audience blockbusters such as the Super Bowl has turned them into a larger cultural trend or fad that has infected virtually all media.

Depending on how one defines reality TV, it has been around since the emergence of *Cops* or MTV's *Real World*, two programs that are more widely known and discussed beyond their fan base. Others cite prime time versions of reality programs such as *Survivor* and *Big Brother* as the emergence of a distinctly different television genre. Like soaps, the reality genre is pleasing to network producers if for no other reason than that the shows are cheap to produce, costing as little as one-fifth as much as a drama or sitcom (Shales 2003). It is this latter form of reality TV that this chapter examines.

As the latest fad to hit television, reality shows generate a lot of interest in the broader culture because they have emerged in the Internet age. The numerous show-related websites provide a means to evaluate how audiences respond to what are basically mini-serials. Beyond describing how these shows use structural elements common to soap operas, this chapter tracks fan commentary on a number of Internet bulletin boards organized around television programs.

What can be gleaned from participants in these shows, from the premiere of MTV's *Real World* onward, is that the "realness" these shows project is indeed a construct of what the producers intend as they focus on capturing and maintaining an audience. Indeed, these shows are "post-scripted" along story lines producers choose to highlight (Farhi 1999). Interpersonal conflict is at the center of these programs: Shifting alliances of players, consciously assembling different personality and lifestyle types to encourage conflict, and rules designed to enhance and promote lying and backstabbing are common to each of these programs. (See sidebar on the "worldview" of reality shows.)

The typical approach to producing these shows starts with an eye for bringing together people who will inevitably clash in the course of living together. Played as experiments in human living, the shows are scripted in a post hoc way that allows producers to take the raw footage and craft a story that may or may not reflect the actual participants' experiences. The production values focus on the voyeurism or "fly on the wall" positioning of the audience. The seeming intimacy of these shows is a primary drawing card, and the fact that the participants are not celebrities beforehand serves to enhance its projection of realness.

Boot Camp, which aired from March through May 2001 on the FOX network, was selected for analysis by virtue of its uniqueness among the stable of shows regarded as part of the reality genre. This program was selected from the many different reality shows because the setting of the show—a military-like boot camp in which contestants have to both compete and cooperate with each other—is seemingly far removed from the world of soap operas, something far less true of reality shows such as *Survivor*, *Big Brother*, and *Temptation Island*. A program that presumably focuses on physical demands and accomplishments as "recruits" become shaped into soldiers should be the farthest removed from what is typically identified as soap opera storytelling. Thus, the degree to which the show employs the soap opera storytelling elements is a measure of the utility and breadth of the soap opera paradigm in explaining the changes in network television programming. The implementation of military discipline would seemingly mitigate against the kind of infighting and backstabbing found in reality shows such as *Survivor* and *Big Brother*. Further, the emphasis on military machismo and toughness would in theory dampen the degree of emotion felt and expressed by recruits as they execute a series of "missions," led by a squad leader, for which they are rewarded or punished based on the achievement of the mission's goals. However, these "military" characteristics proved not to matter much, as the game element of the show actually encouraged infighting and backstabbing and generated significant emotion. In the course of one of the episodes, an exasperated "recruit" looked directly at the camera and proclaimed, "This is just like a soap."

The show ran for nine episodes in the spring of 2001. Each episode was recorded and viewed multiple times. The task in analyzing the show is to

COOPERATION AND SOLIDARITY? CAN'T HAVE THAT!

The reality show *Big Brother* reemerged for its fourth edition in summer 2003, and unlike other multiple edition reality shows, the way the fourth edition is structured bears little resemblance to the first edition.

The evolution of *Big Brother* tells a tale about the kind of human behavior producers feel they need to make compelling television and what kinds of individual and group behaviors must be dampened and squelched within the "reality" setting. As the producers of *Big Brother* discovered, the rules of the game can result in different strategies by the participants involved in the show.

The experience of the initial *Big Brother* resulted in a rather drastic reworking of the rules so that the cooperation and solidarity that emerged in the first edition would be virtually impossible in later ones. In essence, the producers were determined to eliminate examples of getting along to foster more dishonesty and backstabbing among the participants. *Big Brother* was similar in some respects to the more Darwinian *Survivor*, in that various competitions were built into the game to foster divisions and alliances. For example, the first *Big Brother* group faced collective challenges that determined the quality of the food they were to get for a week.

But the primary factor in making the first *Big Brother* different was the involvement of the audience. While each house member nominated two of their own to leave, the audience then chose one of the two nominees for elimination by voting via telephone. Each week television viewers got a clearer picture of the honesty of some of the relationships in the house through the airing of each member's nominations for removal from the game. These comments were given in the "diary room," a place where house members could speak without the others hearing their comments. Thus, viewers had a better way to assess who was trustworthy and who was not.

Audience involvement in eliminating house members resulted in the first two eliminated from the game being those who clearly tried to stir things up among the others. An argumentative male and an exotic-dancing young woman clearly developed resentment among the others. Audience sympathies were clearly oriented toward the "nicer" members of the house.

Once these two were eliminated, there was a fair degree of harmony in the house, with the exception of some antics by a young woman who clearly tried to make her mark by being different. In response to this, the producers tried to bring more conflict and interpersonal disputes to the show. About midway through the program, the producers
(continued)

tried to bribe someone to leave the house, with an escalating offer of cash starting at $10,000, which was increased when no one took the initial offer. During the episode in which the group discusses what they see as the producers' motives in making such an offer, the television audience is introduced to the young woman who would replace the departed house member. In a brief three-minute piece, it is quite clear that the replacement would stir up a group that had grown to like each other for the most part. The attempt to pump up the conflict failed, as no house member elected to take the money.

Audience involvement in *Big Brother 1* didn't stop there, however. The location of the *Big Brother* house, at a CBS facility somewhere in Los Angeles, prompted a rather elaborate and somewhat expensive means of communication from friends and relatives of several contestants in the form of airplane-towed banners, which flew in the vicinity of the house. The fact that the game was influenced by outside communication resulted in different behaviors and strategies by those within the house that the producers did not anticipate.

The steady diet of flyovers of the house by airplanes towing banners that made comments about house members was resented by the group. At a cost of $300 per hour, friends and relatives of remaining house members tried to communicate information about who in the house was or was not trustworthy and who was "winning" the game.

While this created divisions among the house members, it also created a bit of a siege mentality within the house as members spent a fair amount of time speculating how they were being portrayed to the viewing public. A sense of solidarity emerged among the group, especially by the time it had been reduced to five individuals. At one point (after the attempt to insert a rabble-rouser into the house) a serious discussion emerged about walking out of the house collectively, sharing the prize money equally, and generally trying to outwit *Big Brother*. The producers as "big brother" intervened to thwart the group from carrying out its nascent plans by not allowing them to conspire and share the prize money or otherwise engage in acts of social solidarity.

This sentiment wasn't fully "united we stand, divided we fall," as some members of the house had self-interested motives. Several were open about how their appearance on *Big Brother* might lead to career opportunities. Britney, the resident with multicolored hair, also openly courted post–*Big Brother* opportunities and signed with an agent almost immediately after being voted out. Most blatant was Jamie, the beauty queen who was the only female to stay to the group of five. Her desire to pursue acting and modeling was made clear when she won an opportunity to have a brief reunion with a friend or relative or a brief meeting with an acting/modeling agent. She met with the agent.

The reactions by the participants to some of the developments in the show, while also in their own way making for interesting television, were seen as problematic for the producers. The degree of conflict and strife in the house was lessened immensely after the two most problematic members were voted out. The solidarity that developed within the group and the attempted rebellion presented CBS with a dilemma: Was this the cause of a fall-off in ratings, or were the producers not selecting intriguing enough material to maintain the audience?

While not abandoning the *Big Brother* concept, the show's producers substantially changed the rules for subsequent editions of the show. For starters, the audience role in eliminating one of the house members was eliminated. Hierarchy was introduced into the show via the Head of Household (HOH)—a position achieved by winning a competition. The privileges associated with this were one's own bedroom for a week and the ability to nominate two other members for eviction. Another competition gave another member the chance to veto one of the two nominations. Remaining members of the house then voted on who was evicted. A final rule change concerned the weekly food provisions. Instead of a group competition, which resulted in the entire house eating well or merely subsisting, the house members were divided into two groups, and one group won substantial bounty while the other ate peanut butter sandwiches for a week.

Needless to say, these rule changes made subsequent editions of the show more replete with resentment, lying, backstabbing, and conflict, which the producers apparently felt was important to achieve acceptable ratings. But even that wasn't enough; by the time *Big Brother 4* premiered in summer 2003, a new twist had been added. Although eight house members were introduced early in the first episode, the producers tweaked things by bringing in five additional players, all of whom were ex-boyfriends or ex-girlfriends of five of the initial eight introduced. *Big Brother 4's* subtitle was, "The X Factor."

This had the effect of creating mixed motivations among the former couples and adding another element to the show. In the second episode, current boyfriends and girlfriends of those in the house were interviewed and expressed their fears and jealousies about having their sweeties living with "exes" for an extended length of time. *Big Brother 4* was quite successful in generating the conflict and dishonesty that producers feel is an important part of reality television's appeal. And the winners of *Big Brother 4* were two of the more scheming and duplicitous players of the whole group.

(continued)

/Celebrations of competition, acquisitiveness, and greed and the identification of self with personal triumph can be found in nearly all the reality shows conceived so far. Reality TV? Certainly it is a kind of reality, a reality shaped by the larger system of capitalism under which American television operates. Television's primary function in promoting a consumer society and definitions of self through the things one acquires is plainly on exhibit in what is called reality television. Greed, cunning, and conflicts of interest are the hallmarks of American capitalism, and increasingly they are the same values in which television invests its ability to promote and sustain a consumer-oriented society.

While solidarity and cooperation are values taught and celebrated in the real world, in the world of reality TV, they have no place. There's money to be made in creating conflict and emotion. Are the values of reality TV the values most people live by? Let's hope not./

examine the extent to which the five elements of soap operas are evident in *Boot Camp*. To accomplish this, this chapter describes the structure of a typical episode and how that structure reflects and facilitates soap opera storytelling. It then takes a look at the stories of *Boot Camp*: the strategizing, duplicity, and episodes of conspiracy among the "recruits" as they work together yet compete for the $500,000 top prize (with the second finalist garnering $100,000).

Interspersed are audience reaction, discussion, and analysis of the show drawn from several websites and bulletin boards dedicated to the show. This helps provide a sense of the effectiveness of the soap opera paradigm in attracting and maintaining audiences. As the structure and story of *Boot Camp* unfold, viewers' comments and analyses of the show are used to illustrate how the soap storytelling techniques are reflected in what viewers choose to talk about in chat room and bulletin board sections of websites dedicated to the show. The viewer segments quoted below come from a number of websites dedicated to *Boot Camp*, including the forum from the official program website, www.lmnotv.com/new/shows/bc/. Other fan websites or dedicated television show sites were also monitored. There were no perceptible differences in the kinds of things discussed at each of these sites, although each had a rather regular set of participants in the bulletin boards:

forums.realitytvfans.com/dcforum/
bootcamp.50megs.com
www.televisionwithoutpity.com/ijsbb/forum.cgi

Because much of the bulletin board discussion has been taken down from these websites since the show completed its run, individual portions quoted below do not have Web addresses.

STRUCTURAL ELEMENTS OF *BOOT CAMP* AND THE SOAP OPERA PARADIGM

The first task in understanding how this reality show takes on the characteristics of soap operas is to describe a typical episode. "Typical" means the characteristics of recurring segments on the show meant to encapsulate the days as the recruits spend them. The last two episodes ("The Gauntlet"), in which the remaining two recruits compete head-on for the $500,000 first prize, reflect a different episode structure from the first seven and are addressed separately. Analyzing the structure of episodes peels away the veneer of reality to show that the program is indeed a *constructed* reality. In essence, an episode is not merely a play-by-play account of the flow of the game but rather a reconstruction of the real behavior of the participants. While seemingly contradictory in terms of the "reality"-based nature of the show, this understanding is crucial to seeing how producers process the events that transpire into a story for an audience and bring soap opera techniques and values to this kind of programming.

Each episode embodies a variety of views of the recruits in their day-to-day lives in the camp. The show projects the idea that the cameras were trained on the recruits constantly. The level and intensity of each episode are paced through a variety of activities and locations. Action sequences consist of training exercises that project rigor and military discipline as the recruits are trained by three "DIs" or drill instructors. Usually accompanied by sound and music, these segments employ a rapid editing style to enhance the sense of rigor felt by the participants. A second kind of action sequence is found in the "mission" given to the squad, which will earn rewards or punishments depending on the mission's success. The skills and training received prior to each mission are linked to the tasks of each mission. While these action segments are meant to help the squad determine their individual and collective strengths and weaknesses, they also reveal the personalities of individuals and the fissures within the squad. It is this level of personalization and intimacy that drives the soap story elements of the show in these activities.

Those elements of training and mission then serve as the subject matter for conversations among the squad, which bring the audience into the group by demonstrating how alliances are formed and the backstabbing of other participants evolves. These interaction segments typically take place in the barracks, in the mess hall, or around the evening "fire pit" and consist of dyads or triads of the squad, which allows for information sharing and speculation. Other downtimes involve the whole squad, allowing viewers the opportunity to see lies told or true accusations denied. Much of the interaction eventually concerns the assessment of others' performance in training and mission sessions and inevitably leads to speculation about who will be dismissed by the squad and who the dismissed individual will choose to take with him or her. The separation of the recruits' living quarters by gender also allows the camera to capture the unease/mistrust that developed between the men and women.

Then there are interview segments. These segments represent the one instance in which the show veers from its realness to look more like a news show. The interviews—in which the recruit directly addresses an off-camera interviewer—allow recruits to be even more candid in their feelings about the other recruits and reveal whatever additional agendas they are pursuing individually, such as in deceiving those who may think of them as allies. They also bring the audience into a genuinely omniscient position of knowing all the inner thoughts (or at least those determined significant by the show's producers) of key squad members and thus help viewers determine which recruits are playing more honestly than the others and which are best setting themselves up to win. There are also interview segments with each of the drill instructors, which help the audience understand some of the positions and reactions by the drill instructors to the behavior and demeanor of the recruits.

Each show ends with a ritual on "Dismissal Hill," where the squad votes to eliminate one of the recruits. The dismissed recruit then chooses another squad member to be eliminated from the competition. If that episode's mission has been successful, the squad leader is given amnesty from being voted out or selected for elimination by the one being voted out.

Beyond the structure of the game, the show's structure also includes other elements that reflect soap opera storytelling. A set-up segment at the beginning describes the game, tells what has happened so far, and, in later episodes, teases the all-important "Gauntlet" at the end to determine the final winner. This weekly bait is intended to draw new viewers in or perhaps update someone who missed the last episode. Occasionally there are teasers before commercial breaks to entice the audience to stay tuned. Each show closes with a brief teaser about what transpires in the next episode.

These teasers were very effective in prompting speculation by the show's fans:

> I think that the previews for next week were actually trying to lead us in the right direction for a change. It seems obvious that the ladies are concerned

that they are losing ground and may be picked off one by one by the male contingent. I would not be too surprised to see all of the remaining women, Meyer, Thomson, and possibly Lauder all vote for one of the other males, most noticeably Wolf. Of course, any move like this will seal Meyer's fate since he would most likely be discharged afterwards. Because of this particular problem I will ignore the preview and go with strategy instead.

The ladies are nervous and Meyer is once again their ear. But instead of taking out one of his enemies and risking discharge he convinces them to instead turn their vote towards Lauder. In spite of Meyer's betrayal, Lauder takes Hutak with him.

In this example, the writer is making a comment about the show's strategy in using teasers and, in this case, ultimately decides not to take the producer's bait from the tease. This exemplifies the active engagement some viewers make with suspended story lines. As they speculate about the future story lines, viewers are drawn to make sure they watch the next episode to see their suspicions confirmed or refuted.

The tease for another episode drew on emotion to create speculation:

I saw the preview tonight and it looks as though Thomson suffers some sort of heart attack maybe?? Something serious enough that the girls were crying and even the men seemed visibly upset. So it's not just a twisted ankle.

The recruit's condition was an object of curiosity in the episode leading to this tease. When the next episode is viewed, the show of emotion by the women is not related to the man's condition. The emotion has to do with a woman remembering a recently deceased sister. The teasers are often not sequential in terms of what transpires in the following episode. Perhaps beyond the obvious attempt to steer people one way and then veer quickly to an alternative, this is also a mechanism for hyping an episode that otherwise lacks sufficient melodrama. This certainly is the case when a teaser for another episode leads one to believe a recruit's revelation that she is a lesbian will be a big deal but the following episode reveals the reaction by recruits is relatively mild.

The final example of how viewers use material promoting future episodes demonstrates the extent to which some viewers try to deconstruct the meaning of a tease. In this case, this comment is posted after episode 6 and anticipates the result of episode 7, when the final two recruits for "The Gauntlet" will be selected:

If you caught the beginning of this episode, you probably noticed that it was expanded to give us a better picture of what happens in the final episode. I mentioned above where the currently dismissed and discharged recruits are in regards to this final 48-hour exercise. However, the clip also hinted at who I believe the final two are, Moretty and Moretti. Moretty is easy to pick out when you get that quick shot of her doing what looks like sit-ups. Moretti doing push-ups was a little harder to identify. However, learning this trick from *Survivor* analysts, I loaded the clip onto my computer and examined it frame by frame to be sure. Since he does not look at the camera, he is a little harder to pick out (even though his skin color seemed to match Moretti). Finally, I found one shot that showed some of the letters on the back of his sweater (where his last name is printed). I could not read any of the letters but there were two [sic] many letters on his sweater to spell "Wolf." Therefore, he is Moretti. So now comes the most important question. Can we trust this clip? I will leave that answer up to you.

What's notable here is the technological extent to which this viewer goes to try to outwit the producers. Other segments also demonstrate that this is a favorite activity of fans of these shows—a need to demonstrate their own sense of suspended belief about the nature of "reality" television. However, this viewer's "research" ultimately leads him or her astray, as the final two selected are the ones he or she thinks will be eliminated.

Also notable is that the viewer cites similar activity surrounding the more famous reality show *Survivor*. The frame-by-frame analysis of the videotapes, almost Zapruder-like in its intensity, illustrates the addictive nature of the serial format. The exchanges of information and the debate (described later) they lead to are somewhat time-consuming activities. But this investment is exactly what is sought by producers. Though the ratings for *Boot Camp* proved disappointing, the general sense of the age demographics (eighteen to thirty-five) one gets in the chat rooms and bulletin boards is the one desired by advertisers.

Thus the episode structure of *Boot Camp* can be seen to promote a soap opera orientation to the story of *Boot Camp*. The opening and closing of the show emphasize the serial nature of the program—that what happened last week has consequences for what will go on during the current episode, and that the results from this week's episode will have implications for next week's episode. The sense of intimacy and being there is achieved through the action sequences and the interview segments throughout the episode. Being able to witness at least some of the conversations among a subgroup of the squad and the additional perspectives gained through the interview segments puts the audience in a position of omniscience—they can see who is cheating, who is honest, and how some of the squad truly feel about their counterparts. The show is also careful to keep viewers in the real-time sequence the show projects by graphically flashing which day ("Day 7") it is. Occasionally the show engages in flashbacks, such as the controversy over the loss of harnesses ("d-rings") during a mission.

The ritual of Dismissal Hill becomes the closer of each episode. The suspense is built by having the DIs approach potential dismissees to openly speculate about whether they are worthy to stay in camp. This is where the speculation offered during interaction and interview segments is confirmed or refuted. The program producers were very adept at using the interaction and interview segments to set up at least a couple of scenarios for the dismissal ritual. The scenarios are often contradictory yet equally plausible and become fodder for debate among the viewers. For example, the revelation by one of the female recruits that she is a lesbian leads to speculation as to whether that will be a factor in who gets dismissed. While seemingly titillating and pushed in the tease for the next episode and in the summary segment at the beginning of the next episode, the woman's orientation proves largely to be a nonfactor for the squad.

With the structure of the show defined, it is now appropriate to review storytelling elements in *Boot Camp* that helped foster a soap-like atmosphere for the show. In doing so, the reactions of fans to story developments are presented by summarizing controversies and presenting further fan commentary from Internet bulletin boards and show-related websites.

THE STORY OF *BOOT CAMP*

Developments during the first episode present dilemmas for the producers when one of the female recruits drops out during the episode, which means the individual voted out does not get to select someone to leave with him or her. Two story elements—the faking of his own abilities and a false display of emotion by recruit Meyer—are seen by viewers and suspected by other members of the squad. The first mission is led by the youngest and, in many ways, most aggressive recruit (Wolf). Gender resentments are evident when the women complain about how they are treated by the men. The one perceived as most aggressive in his sexism (Park) is voted out by the women acting as a bloc. The tease at the end of the episode strongly hints at a revelation that one of the women is a lesbian.

The duplicity and fake emotion from Meyer singles him out as the first recruit who has a hidden agenda. Feigning injury spares him some of the harshness of the training sequences and, early on, resentment from the other recruits toward him builds. (Resentment of those who, for mostly injury reasons, do not participate in all the training exercises is a common feature for the life of the show.)

His fellow recruits suspect his duplicity or think him just plain weird after he sobs as he apologizes to his fellow recruits for his slacking. This generates considerable comment on bulletin boards, and the exchange below is representative of this discussion:

> Well in my opinion it seems that recruit Meyers is nothing but a snibbling little boy that should not have showed up to play the game in the first place. Hopefully the D.I.'s will dog him so hard that he will start to cry and beg to leave the game. Him crying was so fake it looked like a little kid trying to get out of trouble from his parents. . . . The women seem to think that they are the target to be the first ones to be voted out of the game, but I think it will be the cry baby Meyers. But that is just my opinion, what do you think?

Responding to this comment, another fan writes:

> But the women bought it, and that's all he needed. And remember it wasn't him that came up with the idea, it was the big guy. He even convinced them that Park was a sexist so that they would all vote for him. Yeah he's a dink, but it's a game and he's playing it. He wouldn't last 10 seconds doing that crap in a "real" military boot camp setting. He's manipulative, something that I think people need to be in these game shows.

The comment about players "in these game shows" needing to be manipulative shows that the second writer is more aware of the game aspects of the show, while the first writer sees Meyer's behavior as a reflection of his personality and disdainful attitude toward military discipline. The second writer, in acknowledging motives and behavior as flowing from the rules of the game, is enjoying the show at two levels, while the first writer seems focused on the melodrama, seeing the behavior as less contrived and game oriented and more a product of Meyer's personality.

Two other fans' comments get even more into the gamesmanship and strategy in Meyer's behavior. Their admiration is not for the tactics he is using but rather for his being a fairly savvy player of the game. The second of these comments even addresses the fact that Meyer's story line helps make the show worth watching. Anticipating that his strategy will ultimately do him in, the viewer recognizes the elements of "comic relief and surprise" as crucial to the creating of an interesting, if melodramatic, game:

> MEYERS: He has definitely got the right idea. They are there for a game. Some are there for the personal experience of it too, but I think all of them admitted to being there for the money. He certainly has the brains to pull

this off. The crying thing was just sweet lol. It is kind of a mockery to our armed forces, but this is more of a game than anything.

* * * *

Meyer knows what he's doing. He's aligned himself perfectly between the men and women telling each that he is "with them." One by one he'll get them voted off, but he needs to not piss off anyone enough to have them take him with them. That's what I mean by Meyer staying in the game. Without him we're not left with much in terms of comic relief and surprise. He really keeps us guessing with his plans.

The introduction to the second episode claims a "war of the sexes" has exploded among the squad. The men elect one of the women to be squad leader to ostensibly make up for their earlier sexist attitudes, but viewers learn during interaction segments that the men really think they are setting her up for failure. The "big" revelation that one of the women is a lesbian is only mildly controversial for the rest of the squad.

Meyer continues to mystify and anger both the recruits and the DIs when he actually starts working hard and being more cooperative. While the women begin to think him silly and untrustworthy, their attention shifts from the other men to threats about getting rid of recruits (in this week, both women) who cannot or will not cut it physically.

In episode three, a male recruit is medically discharged while Meyer, who has been faking it (and whose only friend is the medically discharged male) is voted out by the women. Fan opinion about this is mixed. Those for whom the show is more boot camp than game are glad to see him go. Viewers who are more interested in a compelling "story" are more reluctant to see Meyer's demise:

I like having Meyer around. But the problem is that there are at least 3 people who have already seen through his act and are aching to get rid of him. Fox most likely included the discharge rule for *Boot Camp* with people like Meyer in mind. You can still backstab and you can still play the game in an underhanded manner but you have to be less obvious about it.

The "gaming" aspect of the show—the duplicity and backstabbing among the squad—picks up substantially during this episode. Emotions run high as well when the rest of the squad learns about the medical discharge and especially when each recruit gets a personal item (e.g., photo of family) for achieving a successful mission. As the squad members remember or long for loved ones, tears are shed by both men and women. The tease at the end plugging episode four seemingly puts the show on a different tack—a dangerous mission and explosion are featured in the brief tease.

The mission of episode four proves to be crucial for the outcome, and the producers place an emphasis on an incident—viewers are given a video review of the controversy—that leads to a different conclusion of who is at fault than what most of the squad comes to believe. The controversy surrounds which one of them left behind a piece of rappelling equipment (d-ring) during the mission. This results in the entire squad being punished, which breeds resentment toward the male (Wolf) thought to be responsible. The battle of the sexes continues, with the women resenting Wolf for his ego and bossiness. The tease for episode five focuses on the DIs' behavior in directing anger toward the recruits and a recruit yelling back at them.

The final three episodes before "The Gauntlet," a decathlon-like playoff between the two remaining recruits, feature in interaction and interview segments more of the two recruits who would end up as the finalists. Each is seen in some way resenting the other. A split among the women occurs when the one who outed herself admits she has been manipulating her fellow female recruits. One of the male members (Jackson), who is resented for his treatment and attitudes toward the women, is voted out. A tease for the next episode makes the claim that the "backstabbing is out of control." In episode seven, the rivalry between the final two recruits, Whitlow (the female) and Wolf, intensifies as he claims he saved her from elimination by ensuring that the mission she led was successful, thus giving her amnesty and advancement to the final Gauntlet.

At this point, viewers are somewhat encouraged by the teasers and other clues to believe Wolf will be the ultimate victor. Wolf's reputation among the others as a bossy egotist is also noted, however, as viewers learn that dismissed recruits will play a role in determining the winner, and they don't particularly like Wolf.

At this point the audience is fully into predictions and the game element of the show. Viewers, like those in the comment below, seem to admire and enjoy the reality constructed by the show's producers:

> This is turning out to be a great reality show. It combines the drama and backstabbing from *Survivor* with the interesting missions of the *Mole*. The DI's are very entertaining and the editing has given us a chance to see into nearly everyone's personality. Let's hope the show stays on this course and we will all continue to be entertained like we were tonight.

On the other hand, the authenticity of *Boot Camp* as a military experience is questioned by some, especially those who identify themselves as ex-military or retired Marines:

I have been watching the show, and I must say I am displeased. As an Active Duty United States Army Soldier, I am disgusted by the attitude and behavior displayed by the recruits. Boot Camp is essentially the foundation where teamwork is built, not betrayal and deceit. Even though the show is a competition. Teamwork is essential in completion of the missions. The DI's have not done a good job of teaching the value of TEAMWORK to the recruits. The next time FOX or any other broadcasting station wants to do a reality show about anything having to do with soldiering, the company should recruit some of this country's finest soldiers and put them into a competition for a cash prize. Then all of you civilians can really see what an outstanding fighting force is protecting our way of life.

This kind of comment is frequently met with responses such as those below, which remind others that this is a show and not to be taken as authentically military:

You do realize that this is a reality game show, right? I don't know anyone that is assuming that this is the exact same type of rigorous training that all military recruits have to endure. It only "borrows" ideas from actual Boot Camp. Boot Camp is probably half of the show. The other half is the plotting, planning, friendships, and emotional interactions that occur between the contestants. This is the game show half.

I'll take it one step further. I never thought that Gomer Pyle and Sergeant Carter were true indicators of military life, either. How about the crew from McHale's Navy?

* * * *

Well, they need the emotional interactions to bring in a wider audience. I enjoyed watching the DIs give the recruits a lesson in discipline, too. But a large part of the reality television viewing audience is going to want a little drama. In other words, they can't save all the drama for their mama's.

Those disappointed in the lack of military authenticity and discipline were the same who cried foul at the outcome. The producers were very adept at providing clues about the final two squad members while also occasionally laying down an alternative or two so as to generate doubt about each plausible scenario projected. The final two episodes focus on the forty-eight-hour marathon of competition between Whitlow and Wolf. Most of these two episodes concern the physically and mentally demanding tasks the two must perform to win "dog tags," which will lead them to victory. These competitions are interspersed with comments from the recruits voted out earlier, who will also cast votes in determining the winner.

The audience typically sees one or both contestants speculating about how one of the eliminated squad members will vote and then an at least tentative comment from the person who will cast a vote. Some of those interviewed declare they won't decide until the last minute. All this is done to extend the suspense in the last two episodes, which is especially important because Wolf wins most of the competitions—he had six of the seven dog tags from them and needed only one of the seven votes from those dismissed. The one competition won by the female—Whitlow—was a source of controversy because the recruits in essence competed against themselves rather than their adversary. The recruits ran the same course twice, and the winner was determined by how much each contestant bettered his or her previous day's run. One fan of the show comments:

> [A]s you can see, there was no official checkpoint, such as a building or any such immovable object. It was a DI. Clearly, the DI could have just walked up about 100+ feet, giving Whitlow less of a distance to travel by. I am very mad that Wolf did not win.

Perhaps arising from the resentment and suspicion with which the men and women regarded each other, many fans (especially males who had served in the military) regarded the game as fixed in favor of Whitlow. A sense that the producers of the show desired this was also prevalent in bulletin board and chat room discussions. Other fans were upset with the criteria used by the dismissed recruits in their votes for the winner.

The audience is placed in a position of omnipotence in the last two episodes because the winners of each competition are not immediately obvious to the participants. The audience, however, is fully aware that Whitlow needs all the votes of the squad to overcome Wolf's six out of seven victories in the Gauntlet competitions. The harness dispute becomes a key element in the decisions of some of the squad to vote for Whitlow, who believed Wolf was largely responsible for leaving one of the harnesses. Some bulletin board members questioned why the squad was not corrected by the DIs on the matter of Wolf and the d-rings. Others were angry about his unwillingness to admit his role in the matter, regardless of whose fault it was:

> Why didn't they tell them about the d-ring incident? The same reason they didn't tell them what people were saying about them off camera. They were each to judge each other on their own perceptions, not what they were told by the DIs or anyone else. The show was not rigged. Wolf lost because of his attitude and nothing more. The game is not solely based on the one with the most physical strength, but instead is based more on how you treat those that get dismissed. And although Whitlow had her shortcomings in

this department as well, she never displayed arrogance to the others and unfortunately for Wolf that is what the others remembered most about him.

* * * *

Wolf just rubbed everyone the wrong way. Any reality show that allows other contestants to vote against each other will boil down to politics only. That's just reality in life as well, if you think about it. I know it is at work. . . . Politics, Politics, Politics . . . geesh.

* * * *

Wolf had to win! Whitlow didn't deserve it at all! That voting thing was pure bull sh*t it should have been the "one with the most dog tags wins"! The other recruits didn't pay attention on who worked the hardest but they didn't let go of that one mistake he made, all they wanted was revenge, which is not fair cuz that's not at all what the game was about!!!

Again, a major fissure in the fan perspectives expressed in these forums seems to be whether the fans treated the boot camp situation as real, as emblematic of military training or whether the fans regarded it more as a game show that bore little resemblance to the rigors of military training. Whether Wolf was treated fairly or not depended on whether the fan felt merit gained through the competitions during the Gauntlet should be the deciding criterion for who ultimately wins.

The outcome of the game generated considerable controversy among fans. Those who were heavily vested in picking a winner tended to treat *Boot Camp* as more of a military setting than it actually was. Others resented the fact that the most able recruit, Wolf, lost due to the pettiness of other squad members. The debate about the "realness" of *Boot Camp* and whether it captures the reality of a marine boot camp again surfaced in light of the outcome:

If it comes down to a popularity contest, it is pretty much guaranteed that the best boot camp recruit is not going to be the most popular. Competitive people rarely are, and the ones that go in to these shows to make friends usually don't win. . . . In this respect, *Boot Camp* is a lot like *Survivor*. It's not just who is the best at playing the game, but who can do it while still maintaining respect of the ones they vote out.

Personally I don't care if these shows are rigged or not (well, maybe a little). I still love watching them and will continue to watch. Of course if I was a contestant I definitely would care . . . LOL. It's tv folks . . . entertainment.

It amazes me how heated one gets over people they've never met on a show that most likely is manipulated by the producers.

It is quite clear that this program managed to motivate many of its viewers to participate in the debates over the show—and that itself is a measure of the success of using soap opera storytelling techniques. Although it would be wrong to generalize about the entire viewing audience from the relatively small number of participants in a variety of chat rooms and bulletin boards, the amount of "work" that goes into participating in these forums is substantial and indicative of the dedication of the fans to the show. It is now appropriate to assess the degree to which the producers of *Boot Camp* successfully incorporated the soap opera paradigm into their programming decisions.

DISCUSSION AND ANALYSIS

It is interesting to note that the ratings for *Boot Camp* do not exactly provide encouraging news for the soap opera paradigm. The highest-rated episode was the first week, with a 10.8 rating and 16 share. Each succeeding episode (with the exception of week four) lost audience, so that by the time the last episode aired, it garnered a 5.1 rating and an 8 share. This suggests that the soap opera elements evident in *Boot Camp* failed to accomplish the desired result: creating a faithful viewing audience and word of mouth buzz to increase the size of the audience over its nine-week run. The experience of *Boot Camp* stands in contrast to most other reality shows, for which the audience built over time, leading up to the climactic finale (James 2003). However, the review of the show presented here provides much evidence that it wasn't for lack of trying. A brief review of how the five soap opera elements were employed in this show reveals that considerable effort went into using techniques identified with audience attraction and maintenance.

The serial nature of the program used the traditional suspended story line to lure viewers to the next episode. We saw how these teasers were, in some cases, meticulously deconstructed in chat rooms and used as fodder for discussion and debate on the Internet between episodes. The producers were very good at constructing teasers ambiguous enough to allow for multiple interpretations. The varying nature of these interpretations by different fans generated a reason to come back to the chat room or bulletin board to respond to feedback to their musings.

The pacing of each episode and the "insider perspective" generated through the way the program was shot and edited leant toward a real-time orientation. Viewers were shown rather full days; a graphic to mark a new day and events clearly taking place at night were meant to give viewers the sense that they were seeing a full rendering of the boot camp story. The rapid pacing and sequencing helped the story advance in the context of a one-hour episode. The fact that the story moved along left a lot of questions unanswered, thus contributing to the ambiguity that inspired multiple readings by different audience segments.

The camera work and seeming constant recording of boot camp life by the cameras definitely contributed to a sense of being a fly on the wall at the camp and general intimacy for the viewers. The frequent display of emotion and other "low" moments for recruits further gave viewers the sense that they were in on something. The behind-the-scenes interviews with recruits also gave the viewers a sense of having greater knowledge about the state of the game and the prospects of each of the recruits than the participants themselves. By synthesizing all the tidbits of conspiracy and backstabbing, viewers could play the game of guessing who would be voted out and who would survive to the Gauntlet.

The manner in which the story unfolded also proved to be a significant factor in how *Boot Camp* came to reflect soap opera storytelling. Action sequences, combined with more intimate looks at some of the strategizing among subgroups within the squad, placed the audience in a state of omniscience. Because the audience possessed more knowledge of the state of the game than the squad, this introduced even more opportunity for critique of some of the players. As shown in the segments from bulletin boards and fan websites, fans enjoyed thinking about the "show" elements of the game and moving beyond the game itself to think about the motives of producers in projecting a story line or "fixing" the outcome. The fact that the audience could view and enjoy the show at several levels was another reason for them to come back. As they speculated about episode or final story outcomes, viewers became more involved with the show, thus creating the likelihood that they would not allow themselves to miss an episode.

The importance of story exposition in soap opera storytelling cannot be overstated after this analysis of *Boot Camp*. The structural elements of the show, which allowed for the revelation of duplicitous and conspiratorial behavior by some of the participants, put the audience in a position of being the moral authority to best judge who was most the deserving of removal and later, most deserving to win.

Three story characteristics—conflict and chaos, good versus evil, and middle-class-lifestyle and concerns—were identified as typical elements of soap opera stories. In *Boot Camp* one can see the first two as the primary elements around which the story of the game was built. Conflict was rife throughout the nine-week run of the show. The game aspect of the show raised the level of conflict to fever pitch both on individual and "alliance"

levels. This conflict was not always manifest but ran through the interview and interaction segments, in which squad members revealed true
feelings or deceived others by feigning honesty with them. Conflict was
also the inevitable theme of the relationship between the drill instructors
and individual recruits and the squad as a whole. Many recruits came to
deeply resent the drill instructors, while others admitted that they understood the role of the drill instructors in the game/show. The final two
episodes—"The Gauntlet"—were a head-on competition between the final two recruits over forty-eight hours. The structure of these final
episodes—competition interspersed with commentary by the two finalists and speculation by dismissed members who would be casting their
votes for winner—was all about stretching out the conflict involved in
who would prevail in the game. Especially when Wolf won most of the
competitions, the latent resentment toward him was built throughout the
show to indicate that there was still reason for suspense.

The element of good versus evil was also present, though perhaps not
always in such stark terms. Goats on the show were identified by the comments of other squad members and evaluative comments by the drill instructors. The more heroic behaviors were situation specific. More virtu-
ous behavior by some recruits was followed by less than honorable
behavior in many cases. Much as in soap operas, where characters make
good or bad turns and go through redemptive processes, the story construction around *Boot Camp* focused on creating enough ambiguity to encourage multiple and contradictory readings. Keeping the audience
guessing and debating about who was the most deserving to make it to
the final two and then who was most deserving to win was the prime feature of the show's structure and storytelling techniques.

In summary, it is clear that this most "unsoap"-like situation—a game
built around military training camp—was quite fitfully fashioned into a
soap opera for a national television audience. A scan of other reality show
situations reveals that they are more explicitly designed to simulate soap
opera storytelling. As this book fully defines the presence of the soap
opera paradigm in a variety of television genres, it is evident that *Boot
Camp*, as part of the "reality TV" craze, was structured by producers who
were focused on creating a story that viewers would be willing to invest
nine weeks in watching before the story was completely resolved.

Much as the world of advertising focuses on developing and maintaining
brand loyalty, this newest of television genres has defined itself in ways
quite similar to soap operas by developing a story designed to keep people
coming back. Along with other examples of how the soap opera paradigm
functions across all kinds of different programming, this new television
"trend" is largely a product of a continuing shift away from artistic values
toward television as a vehicle for generating profits for corporate parents.

10

A Little Soap
with Your Sports?

Sports journalism has always existed somewhere between entertainment and the traditional boundaries of journalism. Sports teams as business enterprises have relied on local media to help stir passion for local teams, and local media have found that consumers' desire for news about the sporting world can be a boost to sales of newspapers and ratings for local television stations. This symbiosis between media and professional and collegiate sports has only increased as sports have become big businesses whose teams are now owned by larger media and/or entertainment companies. This arrangement has generated the vertical integration of ownership of both content (the sport contests) and distribution (the television channels that air the contests). Furthermore, the scheduling of games and changes in game rules are made with an eye toward enhancing the consumption of sports via television (Boyle and Haynes 2000).

Long adored as "heroes" by children and young teens, professional athletes have become part of the celebrity-driven media culture that occupies so much of television programming. The process of incorporating sports into the media/entertainment nexus has many parallels to the changes that have been underway in the television industry. The creation of twenty-four-hour sports networks, the cable casting, and subscription services that make available almost all major league sporting contests to television are a fairly recent development. This means television has picked up the role once played by newspapers; sports programs are a mix of hard news (recapping of games, showing the key moments in games via replay packages) and soft news (features about stars, biographical pieces providing a more intimate look at players, and the gossip that inevitably emerges throughout a season) (Boyle and Haynes 2000).

This chapter looks at how the soap opera paradigm functions within sports programming. It examines how play-by-play broadcasting has evolved to incorporate increasing insiderism and analysis, a lot more discussion of interpersonal rivalries among teams, and the conscious development of "story lines" in the broadcast. It also looks at some of the new programming that has been invented to fill the twenty-four-hour channels. The fierce competition between a national cable service like ESPN and local regional channels (the bulk of which are owned by FOX) has resulted in a series of new styles of delivering both sports news and play-by-play. Enhancing the drama and the staging of sports-centered spectacles is seen as a way to expand the audience for sports. An increased focus on individual athletes and personalities allows fans to feel as if they "know" these stars (Gruneau 1989). Most fans now access sports primarily through television; far fewer fans actually go to the games than watch them on TV, and sports leagues have now become dependent on the television revenue to feed the skyrocketing salaries of even mediocre players. Sut Jhally argues that this has shaped television production of sports in four ways:

Hierarchization: Some contests matter more than others. Television prioritizes the contests that matter.

Personalization: Events are conveyed from the perspective of the individuals involved.

Contextualization: Frames of reference are created, both by reminding audiences of the past histories between two teams or rivals and by identifying the implications of the outcome of a contest for the future.

Narration: Events are now told in story formats. (Jhally 1989)

This last aspect has great relevance to the concerns of this chapter. Play-by-play broadcasters are clearly situated as storytellers and not reporters. There are a number of ways that this has evolved over the years. The early days of baseball broadcasting more or less demanded that broadcasters "enhance" their descriptions of the games. "Away" games were conveyed via telegraph, because radio stations did not go to the expense of having their broadcasters travel with the team. Since only the basic facts were telegraphed from the game site, the announcer on the other end had to fill air time with sound effects and other obviously fictional elements and events in the game to maintain audience interest. Former president Ronald Reagan got his start in the entertainment world by serving as one of these telegraph-dependent announcers (McChesney 1989). This early kind of melodrama has grown over the years as the key medium for sports shifted from radio to television. A commentator's role is to place the fans in the middle of the drama of the event even if they are not at the event. The addition of the "color commentator" in the last two decades, a role often filled by ex-players of the game, provides a sense of insiderism and can enhance the speculative aspects of the game as well as convey any juicy gossip that may further inform events taking place in the game (Boyle and Haynes 2000).

Analysts of sports broadcasting have identified the elements of media presentation that lend themselves to melodramatic treatment in sports broadcasting (Rose and Friedman 1997; Daddario 1997; O'Connor and Boyle 1993). Rose and Friedman argue that sports are an "open text," much like a soap opera, and as such have a natural tendency to lend themselves to melodramatic treatment; the human angle, personal drama, and mental element of athleticism are enabling factors in conveying sporting contests as mini-dramas set within a larger time frame of stories. Sports highlight individual struggles, moral conflicts, and high emotion as two competitors—either individuals or teams—engage in a contest of wills and skills (Rose and Friedman 1997).

Gina Daddario's analysis of the Olympics as a feminine narrative form argues that enhancing the presentation of the Olympics by using soap opera storytelling characteristics is meant to make them attractive to female viewers. The Olympics are presented through an entertainment and storytelling lens rather than as a "live" contest. The profiles of athletes—full of the Horatio Alger kind of stories of struggling against adversity—before their appearances in competition add a level of personalization and intimacy. The lack of closure, the construction of multiple characters and plotlines, the emphasis on getting into the heads of competitors, and portraying female athletes as empowered women are all ways in which the presentation of the Olympics is designed to expand the Olympic audience from the sure-bet male segments to women who may need reasons beyond the athletic appeal of the games (Daddario 1997).

O'Connor and Boyle argue that the presentation of sports in a soap opera storytelling context also makes sports broadcasts more attractive to men. Televised sports are a "constructed drama" that provides a different experience from viewing sports on the scene. In many ways, those watching at home know more about the game than viewers in the stands—technological factors such as cameras that can bring close-up images to viewers allow them to see or guess the state of mind of a player. The added details from the play-by-play caller and the ex-jock color "expert" convey a greater sense of command over what's going on in this contest. O'Connor and Boyle point out that sports are one arena in which emotion from men is permitted, and that sports have a serial feel because one game merely provides the background for another game (O'Connor and Boyle 1993).

These perspectives are kept in mind as the chapter explores televised sports programming. The long history of televised baseball provides a feel for how the presentation of postseason play has changed over the last few decades. Furthermore, the growth of channels and networks presenting sports programming has resulted in using the twenty-four-hour sports format to create new shows—some based on fact, others fictional—that further capitalize on soap storytelling to attract audiences.

PLAY-BY-PLAY AS STORYTELLING

As a sport that has transcended the development of mass media in the twentieth century, baseball makes for an interesting case study in how play-by-play announcing has evolved over the many decades it has been part of the popular consciousness in the United States. The ascendancy of radio in the early part of the century was the first opportunity to move beyond the sports pages of newspapers and present games live. But much like the relationship between radio and Hollywood described in chapter 1, baseball owners were uneasy about the broadcasting of games. They thought making the game available in the comfort of one's home would reduce the number of paying spectators at the stadium. It instead had the opposite effect—creating "buzz" and greater interest in local teams. When games started to be broadcast on television, there was a brief drop in attendance that didn't last long. (And in fact the greatest historical attendance drop in baseball is attributable to baseball's self-inflicted wound—a strike that canceled the 1994 World Series.)

Gary Gumpert and Susan J. Drucker conducted in-depth interviews with two noteworthy broadcasters—Bob Wolff and Bob Costas—for their book *Take Me Out to the Ballgame* (Gumpert and Drucker 2002). Those men's remarks about their work provide a great deal of insight about how play-by-play broadcasters ply their trade. Costas notes a key difference between play-by-play commentary for local teams versus those who voice nationally broadcast games. "Homerism" is accepted by the local fans; they expect those calling the game to favor the home team. At the national level, much more "journalistic detachment" is expected by both fans and the media companies broadcasters work for. (Despite this requirement, Costas maintains that sports fans constantly accuse them of bias one way or the other.) Interestingly, Costas says games broadcast nationally require play-by-play callers to make the game interesting in other ways: "[Y]ou want drama, you want excitement, you want a good storyline but beyond that you do not care about the outcome" (Gumpert and Drucker 2002, 8). Local broadcasters, on the other hand, develop deeper connections with their teams and have a connection with their audience that makes trying to be more exciting less important.

The addition of a color commentator in the 1970s brought a different kind of announcing to the game call. Now there were ex-players in the booth who could convey inside information and a "what it feels like to be there" perspective to the play-by-play description. This kind of intimacy brings the audience even more into the action and intrigue. The emphasis in game calling is increasingly on the need to entertain, not just inform audiences about what is happening. Bob Wolff puts it this way: "I am an entertainer and there is a lot of acting that goes into it as well. . . . I look for storylines. . . . All I want is to call an entertaining game. I am a sports entertainer" (Gumpert and Drucker 2002, 10; ellipsis in original). Agreeing with Wolff, Bob Costas is even more explicit about what he feels matters most when calling a baseball game: "You have to engage the audience's interest, you have to be able to tell a story, you have to have a good eye on what to emphasize in order to highlight the drama. So, to that extent, if that is being an entertainer . . . then that is what they are" (Gumpert and Drucker 2002, 10; ellipsis in original).

What Wolff and Costas so beautifully articulate is the challenge of creating a stimulating story out of an event whose conclusion is not known. Pregame shows serve a function of providing preliminary story lines, such as rival pitchers going up against each other, managers with bitter relationships, or team dissension influencing the play on the field. Is it not inevitable that sports commentary ends up sounding like a soap opera script? With the task of play-by-play commentary so explicitly defined, one should fully expect the presentation of baseball contests to reflect characteristics of soap opera storytelling.

A BRIEF LOOK AT PLAYOFF BASEBALL

The proliferation of sports channels since the 1980s has helped to provide a historical perspective on how baseball broadcasting has evolved over the last three decades. The programming of ESPN's Classic Sports Channel shows the outlines of the changes in how postseason games have been called since the 1970s. This examination is textual because the way games are replayed on the Classic Sports Channel makes statistical analysis problematic. Because these classic contests are edited for presentation in a two-hour (with ads) format, complete game broadcasts, a requirement for acceptable statistical analysis, are unavailable. It is assumed that the innings skipped in these classic sports presentations are inconsequential (three up and three down innings, for example) for the outcome and that the moments of high drama in the game are presented. The selection of games by ESPN for these condensed presentations is probably based on their historical import, the closeness of the games, and the teams involved. This analysis compares some of the ways in which the play-by-play of baseball has evolved in the last three decades. As a way to highlight these differences, 1972, 1984, and 2003 postseason games were analyzed for how they create story lines within a game and use soap opera storytelling techniques to enhance the drama.

Two of the three games were chosen by monitoring *ESPN Classic Sports'* broadcasts of classic postseason games. Game four of the 1972 World Series between Oakland and Cincinnati and game five (the final game) of the 1984 World Series between Detroit and San Diego were separated by twelve years but shown in one week of World Series replays. A postseason but non-World Series game was selected in the fall of 2003 for analysis—the second game of the division playoffs between New York and Minnesota. The World Series was specifically excluded in this case because of the way championship games/series are showcased by networks these days. By using a playoff game, the analysis can determine whether soap opera storytelling is a feature of network broadcasts that are not final championship games.

Table 10.1 presents a summary of how play-by-play can turn a game into a melodrama. Soap opera storytelling techniques used reflect the same elements employed in other forms of broadcasting discussed throughout this book. Contextual elements provide the serial qualities of the broadcast: what happened in the last game, who's hot, who's not. The playing up of emotional elements of the game helps fans relate to players' trials and tribulations. Intimacy in the way that broadcasters project the mental state of a player and details about a player's off-field life provide a way for fans to feel that they know the player. Insiderism is a reflection of both intimacy elements and the multiple perspective insights of those who have been there before. The evolution of television technology can be seen as an enabler of some of the ways to spin a game as a soap opera. More cameras, more replays, tighter close-ups, and use of interview segments help contribute to a sense of liveness, intimacy, and broader story exposition.

The way the 1972 World Series game between Oakland and Cincinnati was presented seems to embody many of the same characteristics of televised baseball evident in the 1960s. It is clear the game is presented much more from a perspective similar to fans watching it at the ballpark. Most of the views of the game are wide shots; there is not much focus on individual players. The presentation of the first game being analyzed here is drastically different from the way games are presented today.

Table 10.1. Soap Opera Elements in Baseball Broadcasts

Soap Elements of Game Call	1972	1984	2003
Context: Off-field developments/history	Both pitchers good college athletes/Tolan's comeback from injury/ Managers have history with each other/Trade for pitcher one of Finley's biggest	Managers renew rivalry Pattern to series games- Padres try to play catch-up Father/son combos in series	Giambi is struggling, Yanks making mental errors Twins win first game, not intimidated by Yankee Stadium
Pump up the emotion	"tight game," "low scoring, but good action"	"Could be the break they are looking for"	"Giambi comes through!" "Another chance gone for the Yankees." (crowd booing)
Speculation as implication	"Error could prove costly"	"A better right fielder catches that ball" "Imagine if Kennedy's ball gets by Whitaker"	Broken bats indicate good pitching Yanks need to tie series; Twins 'invincible' at home
Intimacy—getting into players' heads/ personal lives	Johnny Bench dates daughter of Oakland's owner	"Suffering pain and anguish of other pitchers" Tigers "did a job on Gibson," working on his game	Manager's interview segment about players' slump You Didn't Ask graphics— details about players' lives
Insiderism: how the game is played	Umpires give permission for pitcher to blow on hands (cold) Positioning of defense leads to out	Much more detail about pitches thrown Pitcher talks manager out of intentional walk, results in homer	Location, types of pitches are keys to success
Technological factors	Mostly wide shots Fewer replays	Dugout shots Split-screen shots Review controversial plays	Lots of full-head shots Split-screen replays Interview segments/graphics

Yet the play-by-play description from the beginning is geared toward trying to generate excitement. When Cincinnati gets an early break on an error, Curt Gowdy remarks, "the action has started early in this game tonight." When the game becomes a pitching duel (a "boring" game for casual fans of baseball), Gowdy remarks that though it is a "low scoring game we've really had some action." A fair amount of background on a player's season is provided—it is pointed out one player is just coming back from an injury and that the Cincinnati pitcher recovered from hepatitis in the off-season.

Analyses of pitching performances become considerably more complex over the three games examined. In 1972, the commentators' remarks are focused on how each pitcher does against right- or left-handed batters. The fact that both pitchers were star athletes in several college sports is noted. But these analyses pale in comparison to those of later years.

There is not much discussion of the players' off-field lives, though the oddity of a Cincinnati catcher dating the daughter of Oakland owner Charley Finley is played for a good ironic chuckle:

> You know, Johnny Bench is leading off. Last night he took an owner's daughter out only it was the wrong boss. It was Charley Finley's daughter. He called her up, took her to the basketball game. She's a beauty, too—former homecoming queen at the University of Colorado. I was kidding Charley about that. Charley has a big family.

At one point each of the owners' boxes behind their respective dugouts is shown and several of those sitting there are identified. But there are no shots of players' wives and kids or celebrities attending the game. Similarly, the two managers are identified as "going back a long way," with little elaboration (this series is referenced as a "past history" for the two managers, who face each other in the 1984 World Series managing different teams).

Speculative remarks about the implications of a play (usually an error) are not prevalent in the play-by-play of this game. An early error by Oakland is cast as perhaps "proving costly," but the next player hits into a double play. A hard slide by a Cincinnati player does not generate speculation about whether the shortstop will try to exact revenge, although it is noted that the player really doesn't go down to slide but rather semi-tackles the shortstop.

The expertise of former player Tony Kubek comes into play throughout the game as he adds his comments about how players react to various game situations. He notes how the positioning of the Cincinnati defense led to an out. Later when the third baseman misses a grounder between third and second, Kubek points out that he was hugging the foul line to prevent a double and that an infield single is a reasonable price to pay. From a historical perspective, the most interesting discussion is about how relief specialists "now come in for an inning or two." Considering today's world of eighth-inning "set-up" pitchers and ninth-inning "closers," it is quite clear that the game over the last thirty years has come to be played with more specialized roles and strategies.

What's also noteworthy about this 1972 World Series game is the lack of seriality in the way the games of the series are linked by the commentators. It isn't until the game is over that viewers are informed that Oakland has taken a three to one lead in the series and that they can win the series with a win the next day. Gowdy also notes that each game has been won by one run, indicating a tough, tight series. These are the elements of drama that make for a great World Series, yet it is quite evident that network sports broadcasts in the 1970s lacked the hype that is so common in today's playoff sports. The contextual factors presented to fans are generally minor or "filler" comments that are not elaborated upon or redundantly repeated throughout the game. This is quite a contrast to the coverage of the 2003 playoff game.

The 1984 World Series game analyzed here proved to be the final game, as Detroit won it in five games. The differences between this game and the 1972 series lie in the more intense discussion of pitching strategies, a more conscious development of a "story line" for the game, and increased speculation about "what might have been" had the ball bounced a little differently. This is evident early on as the lineups and pitching match-ups are reviewed. Each pitcher's most effective pitches are reviewed and revisited in detail. Whether a pitcher has "run out of gas" or should have walked a dangerous batter are comments exemplary of how important the pitchers are perceived to be in this contest. When Detroit scores early, as it often had in the series, Vin Scully remarks that, "Mark Thurmond is suffering all the pain and anguish of the other San Diego pitchers" and that "San Diego is on the rack already." Remarks like these reflect a conscious effort to identify the "story line" for the series as continuing into the current game. The frustration San Diego is experiencing is a common theme throughout the game; a few errors in the later innings undo what had been a tight game. In the first inning the commentators, perhaps not relishing the ratings consequences of a series between two smaller-market teams, try to build an early story line around a San Diego comeback; an errant throw by the Detroit catcher to catch a runner stealing second prompted one broadcaster to say, "that could be the break they are looking for." Very quickly this is undone after a San Diego player is thrown out at home: "The Padres suffer a severe setback right at the outset."

Coverage of this game has more "what ifs" than that of the 1972 game. When Tony Gwynn loses a fly ball, leading to a hit, Vin Scully notes "I would think a better right fielder catches that ball." But a closer replay analysis shows that Gwynn loses the ball in the lights. Scully also carefully reminds viewers of the series history that seems to be repeating itself in this game—the Tigers score early, the Padres' starting pitcher leaves the game early, the Padres try to play catch-up. This plays into a series of miscues by the Padres in the late innings that take them out of a game they had tied. This mental aspect of the game gets lots of attention as the commentators try to get into the heads of those making the boneheaded plays. "He can't believe he did this to himself," remarks Scully after one such play. It is quite clear throughout this broadcast that the emotional element of sports is played up by the broadcast team. From Gibson's first home run ("I'm certain Gibson was excited about that home run") to a score from third on a routine pop-up to shallow center field ("it's the kind of a play an outfielder takes charge. We'll have to see what he says—did he lose it?"), there are a number of instances in which commentators try to project what a player is thinking or feeling.

There are more moments of intimacy as well. A home run by Kirk Gibson brings this remark about a player who in his early years was prone to bad streaks and emotional outbursts: "They did a job on him as far as I am concerned. He is really a determined young man, working on all the facets of baseball." Gibson is also the center of the game- and series-clinching play in the eighth inning. With two men on base and first base open, Padres reliever Goose Gossage convinces the manager to allow him to pitch to Gibson (who has already hit one home run in the game) instead of intentionally walking him. Gibson hits a three-run homer on the first pitch. The bedlam that follows is accompanied by silence from the broadcast team as they let the emotion of the moment tell the story. Since Gibson had struck out in his previous at bat and was shown angry with the umpire's called strike, Scully remarks, "Just to show you how things can change, does this look like the man who was so angry in the seventh inning?"

This game may have had more emotion to it because it ended up being the final game of the series, but there remain substantive differences between this game and the 1972 game examined above. In this game, the broadcast team is much more conscious about building the drama of the game—bringing in relevant aspects of prior games between the two teams, projecting and emphasizing the emotions of the players in the game, and placing a greater emphasis on shifts in momentum and strategy in how the game plays out. Despite these differences, the 1972 and 1984 series broadcasts have much more in common than they do with a more contemporary game, a 2003 playoff game between the Minnesota Twins and the New York Yankees.

The story line set-up for just the second game of the divisional series between the Twins and the Yankees takes place in the introductory segment of the broadcast. In capsule form, it is the upstart, young Twins against the veteran, if slightly slumping, Yankees. One subplot, the slump that Yankees slugger Jason Giambi had been experiencing as the designated hitter, is part of a team slump with sloppy defensive play. Replays of earlier Yankee gaffes in the field become prophetic, as several plays in the infield generate boos from Yankee partisans. The second subplot focuses on the intense pitching match-up between the Twins' Brad Radke and Yankee ace Andy Pettitte.

Giambi breaks out of his slump and drives in the winning runs. But that is not evident from the beginning. He flies out early on. This prompts use of an interview segment featuring Yankee manager Joe Torre before his second at bat:

> You try a little bit too hard, try to do too much and it takes its toll on you. And I sense that first off, Jason is a very proud individual and he's here to help this ballclub. He sits in the middle of our batting order and I think he's just pressing a little bit. The only thing I can do for him is go talk to him, pat him on the rear end and write his name in the line up which is gonna happen.

This segment embodies much of what makes contemporary sports so soap-like. This is an insider's look at the mental state of a manager and one of his stars. Understanding that perhaps only a manager can get inside the head of one of his players, these segments are recorded well in advance of the game. The producers are planning on a particular story line being emphasized throughout the game. When Giambi flies out to end the inning with men on base in the bottom of the fifth inning, broadcaster Joe Buck concludes, "another chance gone for the Yankees."

Anticipating what will matter in a game yet to be played is a tricky proposition to say the least, but these kinds of production values pump up the sense of intimacy viewers can feel with their favorite players or teams. In this case, the producers hit the nail on the head; Giambi gains some redemption ("Giambi comes through!") with a two-run hit in the seventh inning to put the Yankees ahead for good. The drama of that moment is enhanced by Minnesota's decision to pitch to the "slumping" Giambi even though first base is open for an intentional walk. That moment is also somewhat redemptive for the whole Yankee team, because their sloppy play cost them dearly in the early innings, and their play is generating speculation in the booth that the charm of several championship seasons is beginning to wear out for New York.

Minnesota is portrayed as a possible thorn in the side of the Yankees. A video interview segment with Twins manager Ron Gardenhire addresses why the Twins didn't get much respect as they went up against the Yankees in New York. The fact that the Twins have "surprised" the Yankees by taking the first playoff game on their turf provides fodder for speculation about what might happen if Minnesota could get two wins in New York: "[T]he Twins have rolled into town and not been intimidated one bit." Further commenting on the Yankees' dilemma, one broadcaster notes, "the Yankees are trying to tie it (the series) up before it goes back to the Metrodome, where the Twins are invincible." A graphic is then put on the screen highlighting the "David versus Goliath" scenario with which the network is framing the series. The next shot focuses on a second deck facing at Yankee Stadium honoring "26 World Championships."

There are even more production values geared toward these mini-dramas called playoff games. The cameras follow players into the dugout in a way not seen in the earlier games analyzed. Extremely tight head shots of both batters and pitchers are common. The close-ups of the pitchers are the cause of much commentary; the broadcast team speculates whether the pitcher is reaching the end of his effectiveness. The comments and analysis of the pitching in the game are also much more detailed because slow motion cameras can reveal whether the pitches are hitting the outside edges of the plate where each pitcher needs to place them in order to be effective. What type of pitch is thrown, the number of total pitches, total balls, and total strikes are highlighted in the later innings as possible indicators of whether the pitcher is losing some steam.

Another attempt to put fans in touch with the players is the use of a graphic segment called "You didn't ask, but," slices of information about various players' personalities. One about Twins player Matthew LeCroy indicates that he uses the word "foot" as a substitute for cursing, as in, "Aw foot, man, catch the ball!" Another, about Torii Hunter, talks about his music preferences. Another way to generate an intimate connection with the game is the practice of putting a microphone on a player and tuning in at various points to see what the player is saying. This is not done more than twice in this game; the Twins' first baseman is heard talking to his counterpart after he reaches first base safely. This tactic is handled very carefully—the comments are recorded and played shortly after they are made. It does not seem to be used live.

There is substantial use of dugout shots to gauge the moods of both teams. A particular facial expression on a pitcher, for example, may generate a comment that he looks tired or overwrought about his pitching performance. Use of split-screen replays helps to determine whether umpires have made the right call on close plays as well as helping to point out the actions of each player in a particular sequence of run scoring.

This adds up to a substantially spiced-up game description and presentation by, in this case, FOX network. Sophisticated introductions set the stage for the game. Preplanned interview segments are inserted at opportune moments to give viewers a sense of being insiders to the action. Game themes repeated throughout the innings keep the story line foremost in viewers' minds. The natural drama of playoff sports, in which teams can be eliminated or win by virtue of quirky plays or failures by the normally reliable, plays a part in hyping and pumping up the emotion of a sports broadcast. As an "open text," sports present particular challenges for television producers, and sometimes the best planning can end up not being accurate or useful once the play begins.

Whether all this activity by networks serves to expand the audience for the playoffs to marginal sports fans or merely makes for a more pleasurable experience for hard-core fans can be debated. This case study of three games illustrates that the storytelling aspects of presenting sports contests on television have been evolving for at least two decades. The reportorial approach to presenting sports is no longer viable in today's multi–sports channel environment. There are too many sports, too many games available for viewing to count on audiences staying for any length of time unless coverage is accompanied by the enhanced drama generated by networks very conscious of the bottom line.

DISCUSSION

Some of the previous research on sports broadcasting examined the soap opera elements of sports news and live play-by-play. Changes in how the Olympics are presented as an attempt to expand the audience have definitive ties to soap opera storytelling.

The analysis of game calling in the case study of baseball playoff games found that networks and commentators drive home the idea that they are presenting stories and that insider comments, story line development, and highlighting emotional elements of the game are emphasized by contemporary sports broadcast teams. There is no reason to assume that such techniques are restricted to slower-paced sports like baseball. But there are probably some variations in how sports contests are presented on TV across a wide variety of sports now covered.

The growth of twenty-four-hour cable sports channels has resulted in a saturation of sports programming and has led to the development of nongame sports programs to fill in the time. With the recent foray into fictional programming, channels like ESPN fully understand that viewers have a number of choices to view. Not content with just the predictable young male demographic that makes up a sports channel's natural constituency, sports productions are trying to reach new audience segments in their never-ending quest to build audiences for sports. Showbiz and soap opera drama in sports are apparently here to stay.

AFTER THE GAME IS OVER . . .

The twenty-four-hour cable sports channels offer a lot of programming in addition to carrying games live. Both the regional Fox Sports Net channels and ESPN produce highlight shows and sports journalist talk shows meant to be sports equivalents to CNN's *The Capital Gang*. But both sports networks have also in recent years turned to more melo-dramatic presentations: Fox Sports Net's *Beyond the Glory* and ESPN's *Playmakers*.

Beyond the Glory takes an hour-long look at an individual star ath-lete's career. The pattern of these shows is to tell the story of an athlete's rise to fame and glory. Then, inevitably, a life crisis emerged and the hero was faced with some kind of adversity. Typically by the end of the hour, the athlete had survived the test or gained redemption from overcoming personal flaws. These mini-serials are punctuated with cliffhangers before ad breaks and occasionally run in two-part segments, such as the summer 2003 airing of a *Beyond the Glory* episode about controversial boxer/convicted rapist/opponent biter Mike Tyson. Typically the show involves a series of interviews with the ath-lete, members of his or her family, and current and/or former team-mates. The structure of this show is also encapsulated within the numerous and often lengthy promotional segments for upcoming edi-tions. The transcription of one reproduced below mixes and matches future editions of the show but focuses primarily on an upcoming show about football player Corey Dillon. The two and one-half minute piece begins by interspersing highlights of an athlete in action with a voice-over describing the athlete's legacy:

"Sosa tags one to left center."
  VO: He's the modern day Babe Ruth.
  "Reggie White's gonna take over this game."
  VO: He's the Moses of Football.
  "Look at Holyfield, what a warrior."
  UNIDENTIFIED: You talk about heart, there's nobody that has more heart.
  "Brought down by Lawrence Taylor."
  UNIDENTIFIED: He makes the cliché and says here's how you really play . . . .
  VO: He's a record breaking running back toiling in obscurity.
  AL MICHAELS: When I think of Corey Dillon, I think very much of the beginning of Walter Payton's career when the Chicago Bears weren't very good and Walter was very good.

VO: Once wayward teen with a talent for finding trouble.

COREY DILLON: Being held behind your back and have a police officer question you and pressing you to say this and tell that, it's really tough.

VO: His youthful indiscretions threatened to derail his professional career.

UNIDENTIFIED: He started bringing up the past, they started dragging his name through the mud.

DILLON: It just got to the point where after the first round, I just turned off the TV, it was like, whatever.

VO: Determined to prove his worth, he unleashed his anger on the field.

UNIDENTIFIED: He wanted to show all the teams that passed on him that he was the best running back there was.

BOOMER ESIASON: He definitely had a chip on his shoulder. There's no question about it. I think that he was an angry young man for a lot of different reasons and I'm sure some of them had to do with football and a lot of them probably didn't.

VO: Until a religious epiphany calmed the raging turmoil that boiled inside him.

UNIDENTIFIED: It shocked me, it was totally unexpected.

DILLON: It was somebody speaking to me like, "It's your time."

VO: And helped catapult him into the stratosphere of football elite.

ESIASON: He broke Jim Brown's rushing record, now he also broke Walter Payton's single game record and he just seems to have these unbelievable games.

DILLON: The way it was written up, I had no chance at all.

VO: This is Corey Dillon, beyond the glory.

DILLON: That's real that's what I do.

(Graphical flourish, transition to general promo)

SAMMY SOSA: It was hard on me everyday. It was terrifying, man.

LAWRENCE TAYLOR: There's people who make things happen, people who watch things happen and people who don't know what the hell is happening. Well, I'm the kind of person who's going to make something happen.

VO: Beyond the Glory, Sundays 8:00 p.m. on Fox Sports Net.

While this promo looks rather confusing on paper, the opening and closing segments are meant to establish the tone for what *Beyond the Glory* is all about. By using brief segments about well-known athletes, it sets the stage for the longer middle segment, which focuses on the

(continued)

less famous Corey Dillon. The bulk of this piece is a mini-version of the show itself. It is implied that Dillon lived a tough life as a youth and that his run-ins with the law threatened any success on the playing field. His "anger" is alluded to as a way of moving on to the more redemptive aspects of his life. His closing comment, "That's real, that's what I do" strikes a somewhat defiant tone. There are enough unanswered questions raised in this tease to pique the interest of even more casual football fans. Those with more intimate knowledge of Dillon's career will probably tune in to see whether they get it right.

The larger point of the show is to demonstrate the human frailties of today's professional athletes. Breaking through cartoonish images of athletes as heroes, *Beyond the Glory* presents the careers of athletes from a more intimate perspective than most sports features. But its formula of "promise met with failure or adversity followed by redemption/transformation" embodies much of the substance of soaps.

* * *

Playmakers, on the other hand, is cable sports' first fictional soap opera set in professional football. Premiering in August 2003, ESPN's first serial is an attempt by the network to "draw more casual sports fans to the network, even some women for a change. One thing we don't have to worry about is the rabid fan. With all of our live games and sports news and information, he's already with us," Ron Semaio, senior vice president of programming for ESPN Original Entertainment, was quoted as saying in *Variety* (Dempsey 2003).

The show quickly became both controversial and financially successful for ESPN. The network was very pleased with the 1.9 average rating (anything on cable getting higher than a 1 rating is judged successful) for the season run (August to November), and the show was particularly popular with the key eighteen-to-thirty-four-year-old male demographic. But the league and the players' union were critical before the show aired, fearing that it would show players in a poor light, and to some degree they were right. The episodes showed numerous instances of recreational drug abuse (during the game!), use of performance-enhancing drugs, a coming out of the closet, wife beating, marital infidelity, and a quarterback who used team staff to ensure the termination of a pregnancy he helped create. And this does not exhaust the numerous story lines. The show displayed good production values, and the writing was somewhat ingenious—one episode took place entirely during halftime of a game.

But the controversy and resentment toward the show from the league and players led to the show becoming its own soap opera. Players complained about their portrayal, only to see the season of the Jacksonville Jaguars look an awful lot like the stories on *Playmakers*. Jags quarterback Mark Brunell and tight end Kyle Brady were forced to swallow their criticisms after teammates were suspended for substance abuse, called before a grand jury in a drug case, and arrested for felony assault with a gun, and a punter injured his leg swinging an ax (Hubbuch 2003).

Despite the show's ratings success, its future was the object of much speculation in the press given the league's disdain. The fact that the contracts between the NFL and the various networks that air their games are up for renegotiation in 2005 has caused many to guess that ESPN will not pick up the show for a second season, even though it did much better in its time slot than the sports news programming that it replaced. Given ESPN's relationship with ABC (which airs *Monday Night Football*) under the Disney umbrella, there is a lot at stake should the NFL decide to exact retribution for ESPN's running of the series (Romano 2003; Dempsey 2003).

Another complication for ESPN with this experiment in sports soap opera lies in its commitment to future efforts in original programming. A series produced by Spike Lee, based on his successful move *He Got Game* and set in the world of high school sports, has generated speculation about how the NCAA and NBA might react to story lines involving zealous recruiters and agents (Romano 2003; Dempsey 2003).

Oddly enough, it's not its coverage of real sports that has brought on a rift between ESPN and the leagues it covers. The equivalent in government and politics would be a spat with NBC about the content of *The West Wing* instead of coverage of the real president in its news shows. Perhaps there will be new soap opera drawing upon this real-world experience about the uneasy relationship between athletes and the journalists who cover them. Oh, right, that already *was* a story line in *Playmakers*.

Conclusion

This book carved out a substantial task at the outset: to examine the effects of media conglomeratization on the kinds of programs and the kinds of stories told on television. Historical analyses of several kinds of television programming have been helpful in showing that much of the change in the way television shows are presented to audiences finds its roots in soap opera storytelling. Other analyses have brought an understanding of how audiences use soap opera storytelling to enhance their enjoyment of the programs they watch.

The examination of news found substantial support for increases in the use of the soap opera paradigm over time, especially in the aftermath of the mergers and takeovers of the 1980s and 1990s. Serial elements in news stories were present from 1970 onward with a sharp jump in 2000. Intimacy, story exposition, conflict, and affluence elements in news stories showed a consistent pattern of increased use from 1988 onward. The look at combinations of three or more soap elements in news stories demonstrates a clear pattern that seems to correspond to the changes in network ownership after 1988. The use of three or more elements in a news story in 10 to 20 percent of all news stories in these years helps make a case for the soap opera paradigm's effect on the way news is conveyed to television news consumers.

The textual analysis of news coverage of natural disasters yielded further evidence that news takes a more intimate, emotional approach to covering floods in more recent years. Victims were more prominent in stories and official perspectives less so when two flood stories from 1982 and 1997 were compared. Coverage of presidential visits to disasters was also seen to change dramatically from 1982 to 1997. News organizations' approach to covering official visits, as shaped by White House PR strategists, provided a narrative of the visit that cast the president as the great "comforter" of those affected in 1997. The emotionalism of coverage of presidential visits to disaster areas also provides evidence that soap opera storytelling occurs regularly in the news, regardless of the news story.

The examination of coverage of political campaigns reinforced this notion. The soap opera paradigm nicely encompasses many of the trends media campaign analysts have been decrying for some time: horse race coverage driven by polls and fund-raising and the framing of campaigns as highly personal battles, with issue debates clearly taking a back seat to high levels of minutiae about the "insider" political strategies of campaigns. These trends were apparent in abundance in the exploration of the early 2000 campaign season and the saturation coverage of the 2000 Florida recount story on a twenty-four-hour cable news outlet. While perhaps making for interesting television, the implications for helping citizens arrive at their preferences knowledgeably are problematic at best. Framing politics as a soap opera is not the news media's finest moment in their role as facilitators of democratic decision making.

Fictional programming on television, the more traditional home for the soap opera, has seen a big jump in soap opera storytelling in prime time. The increase in serially structured programs began in the 1980s and jumped further in the 1990s when new networks and new segments of desirable audiences were identified by advertisers.

The look at reality programming demonstrated the effectiveness of this most recent craze in generating buzz on Internet bulletin boards and chat rooms. Intense discussion about the meaning behind a program teaser and speculation about whether producers fixed the outcome illustrated that the soap opera paradigm in many cases achieved its goal of engendering loyal audiences. Cheaper to produce than filmed, "scripted" series, reality shows share with the traditional soap opera cost-effectiveness. While they sell themselves as "unscripted," an awful lot of production values and techniques are used to structure a soap-like version of what can accurately be called a constructed reality, however oxymoronic that might sound.

The examination of the growth of sports on television found that soap opera programming and the use of soap opera storytelling in the narration of live contests have found their way into sports cable channels and network sports broadcasts. This development is thought to have two purposes: to expand the audience beyond the traditional demographic of males eighteen to thirty-four years old and to enhance the experience of sports for sports buffs. Some of the approaches to describing games seem targeted at females, who may feel a greater need to know some of the people under the helmets and caps. But soap opera storytelling also allows for greater detail about the behind-the-scenes aspects of games, players, and leagues sought by sports junkies.

When these analyses are looked at as a whole, perhaps the most significant commonality between these many types of television programming is that in several cases—news, prime time television, and to a lesser degree sports—the transition to adapting soap opera storytelling techniques grew as the networks became subsumed under a larger parent conglomerate. These mergers clearly triggered a commercial orientation to storytelling. This suggests that there is nothing random about the way television has evolved over the last twenty years and that the linkage between the content of television and its transformation into an arm of conglomerate capitalism helps to understand why television is the way it is. Soap opera storytelling is "industrial strength" storytelling, designed to please advertisers by attracting affluent and desirable segments of the population.

Thus, looking across the various forms of television programming, it is evident that the soap opera paradigm is a powerful tool for explaining the changes television has undergone in the era of conglomeration. This is perhaps no more obvious than when considering the reality television craze that has become the seeming answer to the continually shrinking market share garnered by the traditional broadcast networks. Cheap to produce and formatted in soap opera storytelling techniques, reality shows are a quick fix for networks looking at the bottom line. And their proliferation has resulted in a certain sameness across the programs, such that audiences have begun to define them as passé. This may play out for some time, and producers are no doubt scrambling for the next gimmick or program format that will drive audiences to watch in droves. In the meantime, producers are tweaking the presentation of television shows in other ways which are consistent with the soap opera paradigm. Each of the recent "innovations" in the presentation of programming and advertising described below clearly incorporates some aspect of the commercial value system inherent in soap opera storytelling:

- Prime time soaps continue to see growth in network schedules. At least six new series premiered in fall 2003 that can easily be classified as soap operas (Levin 2003). The reality show genre has gone in a distinctly "relationship" direction, with shows such as *The Bachelor, The Bachelorette, Joe Millionaire,* and *Meet the Parents* getting prominent attention from media critics and audiences (Stanley 2003).
- The WB network started providing brief recaps of hour-long shows during the advertising break at the half hour in fall 2002. The stated purpose is to catch viewers from half-hour sitcoms who may be

channel surfing for something to watch for the rest of the hour. *Gilmore Girls, Everwood,* and *Smallville* have used this technique to increase audiences during the second half of the show, though those with a sharp eye for trends in television ratings say there is "natural" audience growth as the drama within an episode builds (Vogt 2002).

- The fall 2003 premier episode of the spy-soap *24* was presented without commercial interruption. But that didn't mean there were no commercials. Instead, the Ford Motor Company opened and closed the show with a six-minute "film-ercial" that also referenced *24* star Kiefer Sutherland's character Jack Bauer. Developed by the JWT advertising agency, the six-minute thriller "stars" the redesigned Ford F-150 pickup truck and is part of a $100 million advertising campaign for the vehicle. The first segment ran three and one-half minutes and featured car chases and an arrest of a man thought to be Jack Bauer. Viewers learn in the second part after the regular episode of *24* that the arrest of the man is a case of mistaken identity based on the fact that Bauer is also supposedly at the wheel of an F-150. This convergence of commercials and programming is thought to be the first of its kind. ABC is taking a similar approach, stringing out "mini-movies" over the course of an evening of programming to encourage audience loyalty for at least one night. "It's all about keeping viewers tuned to shows," FOX network executive Jean Rossi is quoted as saying (McCarthy 2003).

- Similarly, NBC is planning to run a series of mini-movies between a series of ads as a way of keeping viewers in front of the set during commercial breaks. The one-minute movies will be broken into two thirty-second segments, with a cliffhanger closing the first segment. The network also hopes to keep viewers watching the network the whole evening to see the conclusion of the movies. Some of these will be built around suspense plots, while others may have a comic conclusion. As media executive Tim Spengler puts it, "Retention throughout entire programs, start to finish is definitely a challenge for the networks . . . any ploy or strategy that holds the audience throughout a whole program would be of great interest to advertisers" (Carter 2003).

We have come quite a ways since the infamous Taster's Choice serial advertisements, which had viewers guessing whether two unnamed neighbors would find love over a cup of coffee. According to Robin Andersen, the ads became a cult hit, and television critics defined the ads as another form of fiction (Andersen 1995). The point of this book has been to show that regardless of how much audiences like or dislike soap opera storytelling, it is a genre that has long served the needs of advertisers.

And as corporate conglomerates have become media owners, the use of soap opera techniques has soared. Some of the results of the increase in the serialization of everything on television have been benign; others can be cast as decidedly negative, such as the trivialization of issues in political campaigns when news reports focus on personalities and catfighting among the candidates. But the concerns of television executives no longer have to do with public service values, if they ever authentically did. No, the changes wrought in television over the last two decades have been for the benefit of advertisers. The challenges of remote control instruments, and more recently, digital video recorders, have made the prospect of viewers staying to watch commercials a far less certain outcome. So program producers have tried to invent new tactics to keep viewers tuned in to their networks. And the long history of the soap opera in broadcasting has resulted in the resurrection of techniques first seen in radio soap operas.

Media scholar Raymond Williams's seminal concept of flow (Williams 1975) is worth revisiting in this respect. The idea of flow in television programming is an understanding that the presentation of programs in a commercial television environment must be seen by audiences as almost a natural phenomenon. Other media and entertainment vehicles contain "interruptions," which audiences see as necessary to the medium or event. Plays contain acts, which allow for audience relief and changing of sets onstage. Novels contain chapters as a way for audiences to pick up later what they cannot finish in one sitting and as a way of transitioning the story over time or space. Though programs may define television in discrete terms, audiences often refer to their viewing as not watching a specific program but rather merely "watching television." Thus program breaks are seen by audiences as a natural phenomenon in the world of television, and the "flow" in television is part of the natural daily course of viewing—a complex of advertising, programming, news breaks, and public service advisories.

But as Williams points out, the construction of television's natural feel was in large part a product of its commercial orientation. Media technologies do not evolve in a vacuum, and as shown in chapter 1, television broadcasting in the United States has taken a specific path toward a commercial orientation and value system since early in the twentieth century. Television's character, its core values, were built, at least in the United States, around the need to further the cause of a consumer society. Television's purpose in its emergence after World War II was to sell things, to encourage the values of a consumer society. The construction of programming had to prioritize the time advertisers, the source of television's profitability, were paying for. Initially audiences were told commercials were necessary to make television "free" to viewers. Stories were built around advertising breaks—even nonserial series had moments of suspense that inevitably led to advertisements.

Thus, according to Williams, television in the United States has a commercial character evident at several levels: making programs guided by the profit motive, serving as a channel for a powerful new form of advertising, and as a cultural/political project in selling a commercial, material-oriented "way of life." The upswing in consumer goods production after a war in which almost all production was geared to the war effort required a means to create perceived needs and sell mass-produced goods to fulfill those needs. In other words, while watching a night's worth of TV may result in perceiving this flow as natural, there is a great deal of intention behind the mix and presentation of program elements and advertising.

Another way to understand this is to consider how the soap opera has evolved in other cultures. Chapter 2 noted that British soaps are traditionally more community oriented and set in working-class environments. The *telenovelas* of Brazil and Latin America in general have historically served an educational as well as an entertainment function by raising awareness of a social issue. Elsewhere serial, melodramatic stories have served similar functions (Allen 1995). But the increasing advancement of commercial values on the U.S. media industry has meant soap opera storytelling techniques here are at the service of profit.

Media scholars drawing from Williams's seminal work have elaborated on its meaning for a commercially grounded system such as it exists in American society. Sut Jhally calls television a "colonizer of time" (Jhally 1987). He sees the consumption of TV as an activity that goes beyond preference for certain programs; as TV programs are geared to lure audiences just for the exposure to advertising, inevitably the flow of programming on any one channel is carefully constructed and monitored for its effectiveness. Advertising, Jhally says, shows us how to consume and to draw our ideas for consumption from the myriad advertising we are exposed to throughout daily life. He defines advertising as indispensable to the stability of capitalism.

A micro-analysis of flow is found in a study of the stories and ads run during an episode of *Fantasy Island* (Budd, Craig, and Steinman 1983). This study illustrates that stories in a program are often linked to the problem/solution orientation of advertising. Linking the "myths of entertainment" with the "myths of commercials," for example, can be seen in a plotline in the program about a mother's concern for her child, which is then followed by commercial featuring a mother healing a child's itching with a salve. Another subplot in the program tells of a mother reuniting her family; this is followed by an AT&T telephone ad about reuniting with loved ones via long distance. As the authors put it, "as the narrative moves from problem to solution, from disequilibrium to equilibrium, from search to discovery, the product is there at every step, showing the way, providing therapy for what ails the characters in the commercials and, less obviously, in the program as well" (Budd, Craig, and Steinman 1983, 75). The same authors studied the interplay between programming and advertisement using the critically acclaimed *Northern Exposure* as a vehicle. Linking the show's star to commercials via his role as a voice-over during one of the show's commercial breaks, the use of doctors as authority figures in ad breaks during a show whose lead character plays a doctor, ads with environmental values ("80 percent less trash" by using a refillable laundry soap container), and "rustic" graphics in other ads seem to play off the values of a show set in the wilds of Alaska (Budd, Craig, and Steinman 1999, 138–52).

The soap opera paradigm is an attempt to expand on this work and make sense of television in a fully corporate conglomerate environment. By using a number of methodologies in an examination of how soap opera storytelling has come to permeate the many disparate subjects television programs take on, the soap opera paradigm can be seen to extend the concept of flow and show how entertainment and commercialism are being continually joined and geared toward encouraging television audiences to consume as if there is no tomorrow.

"Flow," in the sense conveyed by bringing a soap opera lens to the examination of many forms of television, can be defined as those tactics that have been invented and evolved to keep an audience's attention. The pace of stories and the use of teasers and cliffhangers have been shown to proliferate in news programs, prime time dramas, reality shows, and sports programming. Emotion and intimacy in these same programs manifest themselves differently in each format. Tragedy in the news, competitiveness in reality shows, relationship-oriented prime time soap operas, and close-up camera work filling the screens with the faces of athletes "on the spot" are all evident in abundance on an average television viewing night.

This increasing concentration of power by a few dominant media companies gives the impression that the kinds of storytelling described in these pages will remain with us. Until a media system geared toward noncommercial values is sought societally, there is no reason to think television will change from its present course. But the possibility of reinventing television (and all media for that matter) to serve the values of citizenship, community, and global solidarity exists as long as the public is willing to reassert public control of the airwaves. The concept of public ownership of the airwaves has withered on the vine with a succession of decidedly market-oriented FCC chairpersons. But in 2003, citizen fears of a media system beholden to a few corporate interests resulted in an unusually heavy public reaction to rules changes that would allow even greater concentration of mass media in the hands of a few. If the 2003 public response is sustained in the future, it is possible the public interest could once again be a guiding principle in what values the media system serves.

News programming must be at the top of the list of any change in the way television presents the world to audiences. The soap opera paradigm's role in trivializing the concept of citizen via the way news is presented is a particularly problematic aspect of the growing influence of soap opera storytelling. The "infotainment" that currently passes for news must be eschewed, and news formats that respect the needs of citizens in a democracy must be a priority for a system genuinely geared to serve the public interest.

In the meantime, the issues put forth here can serve as an organizing tool for further research into the soap opera phenomenon as it continues to evolve in television programming. Further audience studies can expand on the idea that soap opera storytelling techniques are particularly effective in generating audience loyalty. Situation comedies, a staple of prime time television, have shown signs of taking on serial elements and will probably become more serial in nature as time goes on. Plots of prime time soaps can be further explored for their celebration of the consumption ethic. And studies of sports audiences can help to determine whether "nontraditional" sports audiences can be cultivated using soap opera storytelling techniques. Some argue that soaps are a particularly feminine form of storytelling. The data and analyses presented here suggest that a larger project is being undertaken by television producers, who understand the political economy of their industry. If television's purpose remains to encourage consumption and celebration of material life in the United States, the use of soap opera techniques in presenting news, culture, sports, and other fare will no doubt grow and take on new forms. Television programming as an art form has reached a creative cul-de-sac; the commercialization of the form may not be complete, but the beat goes on. Will a citizens' movement responding to these developments take hold and create the change needed to realize television's educational and artistic potential? Only time will tell.

References

Abercrombie, N. 1996. *Television & society*. Cambridge, England: Roeing Press.

Alger, D. 1998. *Megamedia: How giant corporations dominate mass media, distort competition*. Lanham, MD: Rowman & Littlefield.

Allen, R. 1985. *Speaking of soap operas*. London: University of North Carolina Press.

———. 1995. *to be continued: Soap operas around the world*. New York: Routledge.

Andersen, R. 1995. *Consumer culture and tv programming*. Boulder, CO: Westview.

Ang, I. 1985. *Watching Dallas*. New York: Methuen.

Ball, M. 1990 *Professional wrestling as ritual drama in American popular culture*. Lewiston, NY: Edwin Mellen Press.

Barbatsis, G., and Y. Guy. 1991. Analyzing meaning in form: soap opera's compositional construction or "realness." *Journal of Broadcasting and Electronic Media*, 35, 59–74.

Barringer, F. 1999. CBS news may face cuts. *New York Times*, September 9, 8.

Bauder, D. 2001. Networks seek new fans for slipping soaps. *Buffalo News*, August 8, D-6.

Baym, N. K. 1998. Talking about soaps: Communicative practices in computer mediated fan culture. In *Theorizing fandom: Fans, subculture and identity*, edited by Cheryl Harris and Alison Alexander. Cresskill, NJ: Hampton Press.

Bennett, L. 1988.. *News: The politics of illusion*. New York: Longman.

Bercovici, Jeff. 2002. Meet the band of media angels. *Medialifemagazine.com*, March 25, at www.medialifemagazine.com/news2002/mar02/mar25/2_tues/news3tuesday.html (accessed March 26, 2002).

Borg, E. 1999. Daytime drama fosters addiction. *The California Aggie*, February 19, at www.californiaaggie.com/archive/99/02/19/soaps.html (accessed February 15, 2001).

Boyle, P. 1988. *Who killed CBS? The undoing of the number one news network*. New York: Random House.

Boyle, R., and R. Haynes. 2000. *Power play: Sport, the media and popular culture.* Essex: Pearson Education Ltd.

Brooks, T., and E. Marsh. 2003. *The complete directory to prime time network and cable TV shows, 1946–present.* 8th ed. New York: Ballantine.

Brown, M. E. 1990. Motley moments: soap operas, carnival, gossip and the power of utterance. In *Television & women's culture: The politics & the popular.* Beverly Hills, CA: Sage.

Budd, M., S. Craig, and C. Steinman. 1983. Fantasy island: Marketplace of desire. *Journal of Communication* (Winter): 67–77.

———. 1999. *Consuming environments: Television and commercial culture.* New Brunswick, NJ: Rutgers University Press.

Cantor, M., and S. Pingree. 1983. *The soap opera.* Beverly Hills, CA: Sage.

Carter, B. 2003. NBC hopes short movies will keep viewers from flipping. *New York Times,* August 4, C-1.

Carveth, R., and A. Alexander 1985. Soap opera viewing motivations and the cultivation process. *Journal of Broadcasting and Electronic Media* 29:259–73.

Cassata, M. 1985. Plus ca change, plus c'est la meme chose: An analysis of soap opera from radio to television. *Journal of American Culture* 6:50–58.

Cavazos, N. 2001. Friends on the move? *Buffalo News—TV Topics,* September 2, 3.

Chad-Olmstead, S., and K. Yungswook. 2001. Perceptions of branding among television stations managers: An exploratory analysis. *Journal of Broadcasting and Electronic Media* 1:75–91.

Czistrom, D. 1982. *Media and the American mind.* Chapel Hill: University of North Carolina Press.

Daddario, G. 1997. Gendered sports programming: 1992 summer olympic coverage and the feminine narrative form. *Sociology of Sport Journal* 14:103–20.

Dempsey, J. 2003. Will ESPN play hardball? *Variety,* November 10, 22.

Dorschner, J. 2000. WWF builds empire on brains as much as brawn. *Buffalo News,* December 10, B-1.

Eco, U. 1985. Innovation and repetition: Between modern and post-modern aesthetics. *Daedelas* (Fall): 161–84.

Farhi, P. 1999. It's not such a "real world" after all. *Buffalo News,* November 8, B-9.

Ferguson, M., and P. Golding. 1997. Cultural studies and changing times: An introduction. In *Cultural studies in question,* edited by Marjorie Ferguson and Peter Golding. London: Sage.

Feuer, J. 1987. Genre study of television. In *Television and contemporary criticism,* edited by Robert C. Allen. Chapel Hill: University of North Carolina Press.

———. 1991. Melodrama, serial form and television today. In *Television criticism: approaches & applications,* edited by Leah VandeBerg and Lawrence Wenner. White Plains, NY: Longman.

———. 1995. *Seeing through the eighties: Television and reaganism.* Durham, NC: Duke University Press.

Frank, R. 1991. *Out of thin air: The brief wonderful life of network news.* New York: Simon & Schuster.

Fulford, R. 2000. *The triumph of narrative: Storytelling in the age of mass culture.* New York: Broadway Books.

Garnham, N. 1997. Political economy and the practice of cultural studies. In *Cultural studies in question*, edited by Marjorie Ferguson and Peter Golding. London: Sage.

Gitlin, T. 1986. *Watching television: A pantheon guide to popular culture*. New York: Pantheon.

Greenberg, B., and R. Busselle. 1996. Soap operas and sexual activity: A decade later. *Journal of Communication* 46:153–60.

Gruneau, R. 1989. Making spectacle: A case study in television sports production. In *Media, sports and society*, edited by Lawrence Wenner. Newbury Park, CA: Sage.

Gumpert, G., and S. Drucker. 2002. *Take me out to the ballgame: Communicating baseball*. Cresskill, NJ: Hampton Press.

Gunther, M. 1994. *The house that Roone built: The inside story of ABC news*. Boston: Little, Brown.

Hagedorn, R. 1995. Doubtless to be continued: A brief history of social narrative. In *To be continued . . . soap operas around the world*, edited by Robert Allen. London: Routledge.

Hall, J. 1996. Cap Cities/ABC delays plan for all-news cable channel: firm cites high start-up costs. *The Los Angeles Times*, May 24, D-1.

Hayward, J. 1997. *Consuming pleasures: Active audiences and serial fictions from Dickens to soap opera*. Lexington: University Press of Kentucky.

Healey, J. 2003. Soaps online may appeal to young but not restless. *Los Angeles Times*, February 26, C-1.

Hertsgaard, Mark. 1988. *On bended knee: The press and the Reagan presidency*. New York: Farrar, Straus & Giroux.

Hightower gets Mickey Mouse treatment. 1995. *Extra! Update*, December, at www.fair.org/extra/9512/hightower.html (accessed November 29, 2003).

Hilmes, M. 1990. *Hollywood and broadcasting from radio to cable*. Chicago: University of Illinois Press.

Himmelstein, H. 1994. *Television myth and the American mind*. Westport, CT: Praeger.

Hobson, D. 2003. *Soap opera*. Marsden, MA: Polity, Blackwell.

Hubbuch, B. 2003. Jags learn the hard way—"Playmakers" not so outrageous. *Florida Times-Union*, November 2, D-16.

James, M. 2003. Networks to offer bigger dose of "reality." *Los Angeles Times*, April 15, F12.

Jensen, E. 2002. Networks shopping their news. *Los Angeles Times*, March 22, F-29.

Jhally, S. 1987. *The codes of advertising*. London: Routledge.

———. 1989. Cultural studies and the sports/media complex. In *Media, sports and society*, edited by Lawrence Wenner. Newbury Park, CA: Sage.

Kaufman, L. 2000. The sock puppet that roared: Internet synergy or a conflict of interest? *New York Times*, March 27, C-1.

Keith, S. 2001. *The buzz on professional wrestling*. New York: Lebhar-Friedman Books.

Kellner, D. 1990. *Television and the crisis of democracy*. Boulder, CO: Westview.

———. 1997. Overcoming the divide: Cultural studies and political economy. In *Cultural studies in question*, edited by Marjorie Ferguson and Peter Golding. London: Sage.

Krajicek, D. 1998. *Scooped: Media misread story on crime while chasing sex, sleaze, and celebrities.* New York: Columbia University Press.

Kreit, A. 1998. Professional wrestling and its fans: A sociological stuffy of the sport of pro-wrestling. Unpublished manuscript, Jump City productions.

Lavin, M. 1995. Creating consumers in the 1930s: Irna Phillips and the radio soap opera. *Journal of Consumer Research* 22:75–89.

Levin, G. 2003. Prime time soaps slip into schedule. *USA Today,* August 1, E-7.

Lieberman, D. 1995. A Roone's-eye view of ABC news and Disney. *USA Today,* December 6, 3–D.

———. 1996. Disney, CAP Cities shareholders ok $19 billion deal. *USA Today,* January 5, B-12.

Liebes, T., and S. Livingstone. 1994. The structure of family and romantic ties in the soap opera: an ethnographic approach. *Communication Research* 21:717–41.

Livingstone, S. 1994. Watching the talk: Gender and engagement in the viewing of audience discussion programmes. *Media, Culture & Society* 16:429–47.

Lowry, B., and E. Jensen. 2002. Letterman bid reflects ABC's shift from news; network moves toward entertainment replaces "20/20" with a Disney-produced drams. *Los Angeles Times,* March 2, A-1.

Lozano, E. 1992. The force of myth on popular narratives: The case of melodramatic serials. *Communication Theory* 2:207–20.

Mazzocco, D. 1994. *Network of power: Corporate tv's threat to democracy.* Boston: South End Press.

McCabe, P. 1987. *Bad news at black rock: The sell-out of CBC news.* New York: Arbor House.

McCarthy, M. 2003. Turn on "24" and you'll also catch a 6–min. film-ercial. *USA Today,* October 27, B-4.

McChesney, R. W. 1989. Media made sport: a history of sports coverage in the United States. In *Media, sport and society,* edited by Lawrence Wenner. Newbury Park, CA.: Sage.

———. 1993. *Telecommunications, mass media and democracy.* New York: Oxford University Press.

———. 1999. *Rich media, poor democracy: Communications in dubious times.* Urbana: University of Illinois Press.

McDonald, J. F. 1990. *One nation under television: The rise of network TV.* New York: Pantheon.

McManus, J. 1994. *Market-driven journalism: Let the citizen beware.* Thousand Oaks, CA: Sage.

Meyers, C. 1997. Frank and Anne Hummert's soap opera empire "reason why" advertising strategies in early radio. *Quarterly Review of Film and Video* 16:113–33.

Modleski, T. 1982. *Loving with a vengeance: Mass produced fantasies for women.* Hamden, CT: Shoestring Press.

Morris, B. B. 1997. *Prime time network serials: Episode guides, casts and credits for 37 continuing dramas, 1964–1993.* Jefferson, NC: McFarland.

Mosco, V. 1979. *Broadcasting in the United States.* Norwood, NJ: Ablex.

Mumford, L. 1994. How things end: The problem of closure on daytime soap operas. *Quarterly Review of Film & Video* 15 (2):57–74.

Nicols, John, and R. W. McChesney. 2003. FCC: Public be damned. *The Nation,* June 2, 5–6.

O'Connor, B., and R. Boyle. 1993. Dallas with balls: Televised sport, soap opera and male and female pleasures. *Leisure Studies* 12:107–19.

O'Guinn, T., and L. J. Shrum. 1997. The role of television in the construction of consumer reality. *Journal of Consumer Research* 23:278–94.

Palacios, C. 1998. Vince McMahon's foresight. Unpublished manuscript, at www.Wrestlingclassics.com/fe/fe-vince.html (accessed May 13, 2000).

Parney, L., and M. S. Mason. 2000. Selling soaps. *Christian Science Monitor,* July 7, 13.

Perse, E., and R. Rubin. 1989. Attribution in social and parasocial relationships. *Communication Research* 16:59–77.

Piscia, J. 2002. WWE working to regain its viewers. *The State Journal-Register,* October 3, 16.

Pitts, L. 1999. The new journalism: No offense intended. *Times-Picayune,* October 7, B-7.

Pope, K. 2001. *The encyclopedia of professional wrestling: 100 years of the good, the bad and the unforgettable.* Iola, WI: Krause.

Potter, D. 1977. Soap time: Thought on a commodity art form." In *Television: The critical view,* 3d ed., edited by H. Newcombe. New York: Oxford Press.

Revlon pays for story line on ABC soap. 2002. *Buffalo News,* March 20, D-6.

Riegel, H. 1996. Soap operas & gossip. *Journal of Popular Culture* 4:201–10.

Rogers, D. 1995. Daze of our lives: The soap opera as feminine text. In *Gender, race, and class in media: a text reader,* edited by Gale Dines and Jean M. Humey. Thousand Oaks, CA: Sage.

Romano, A. 2003. Is "Playmakers" off to the showers? *Broadcasting and Cable,* November 24, 30.

Rose, A., and J. Friedman. 1997. Television sports as mas(s)culine cult of distraction. In *Out of bounds: Sports, media and the politics of identity,* edited by Aaron Baker and Todd Boyd. Bloomington: Indiana University Press.

Rose, C. 2001. Blood, sweat and cheers; when world wrestling federation comes to town, the arena is full, the rock n' roll is loud and you definitely be ready to rumble. *Times-Picayune,* January 23, D-1.

Rosenberg, H. 1997. Not-so-far-fetched villain? *Los Angeles Times,* December 26, F-1.

———. 2001. The day the world shattered: A junket that will live in infamy. *Los Angeles Times,* May 25, F-1.

Rutenberg, J. 2000. Viacom units bridging the generations. *New York Times,* November 20, C-15.

———. 2001. 85 take buyouts at ABC news as Disney pares expenses. *New York Times,* May 26, C-4.

Shales, T. 2003. All too real. *Washington Post,* January 13, C-1.

Silverman, F. 2002. Grappling to grow: Behind the often outrageous WWE, a no nonsense ceo maps rebound. *Hartford Courant,* December 22, D-1.

Slattery, K., M. Doremus, and L. Marcus. 2001. Shifts in public affairs on network news: A move toward the sensational. *Journal of Broadcasting and Electronic Media* 2:290–302.

Smillie, D. 1998. Television news that's fit to quit over. *Christian Science Monitor*, April 23, 13+.

Smulyan, S. 1994. *Selling radio: The commercialization of American broadcasting, 1920–1934*. Washington, DC: Smithsonian Institution Press.

Stanley, A. 2002. How to persuade the young to watch the news? Program it, news executives say. *New York Times*, January 15, C-6.

———. 2003. Blurring reality with soap suds. *New York Times*, February 22, B-9.

Stedman, R. 1971. *The serials: Suspense and drama by installment*. Norman: University of Oklahoma Press.

Sterling, C., and J. Kitross. 1990. *Stay tuned: A concise history of American broadcasting*. 2d ed. Belmont, CA: Wadsworth.

Stevens, E. 1998. Mouse-ke-fear. *Brill's Content* (December 1998/January 1999): 95–103.

Traynor-Williams, C. 1992. *"It's time for my story": Soap opera sources, structure, and response*. Westport, CT: Praeger.

Tuggle, C.A., and S. Huffman. 1999. Live news reporting: Professional judgement or technological pressure? *Journal of Broadcasting and Electronic Media* 4:335–44.

———. 2001. Live reporting in local news: Breaking news of black holes? *Journal of Broadcasting and Electronic Media* 2:335–44.

Underwood, Doug. 1993. *When MBAs rule the newsroom*. New York: Columbia University Press.

UPN, WWE pin down new "Smackdown" wrestling pact. 2003, March 12, at yahoo.com (accessed April 17, 2003).

Vogt, H. 2002. WB's nifty scheme to lure channel surfers, at www.media lifemagazine.com/news2002/nov02/nov11/4_thurs/news5thursday.htm (accessed November 14, 2002).

Wenner, L. 1989. *Media, sports and society*. Newbury Park, CA: Sage.

Westin, A 1982. *Newswatch: How TV decides the news*. New York: Simon & Schuster.

Williams, R. 1975 *Television: Technology and cultural form*. New York: Schocken Books.

World Wrestling Entertainment. 2003. WWE corpbiz, at corporate.wwe.com/media/r_facts.html (accessed March 7, 2003).

Index

About the Author

James H. Wittebols is professor of communication studies at Niagara University. He published *Watching M*A*S*H, Watching America: A Social History of the 1972–1983 Television Series* in 1998. He has published his research in *Communication Theory, Political Communication,* and the *Canadian Journal of Communication.* He lives in Buffalo, New York.